THE BEST OF COUNTRY COOKING

Forthcoming titles in series

The Best of Prue Leith
The Best of Cordon Bleu
The Best of Mediterranean Cooking

THE BEST OF

Country
Cooking

Mary Norwak

J M Dent & Sons Ltd

LONDON   MELBOURNE   TORONTO

First published 1979
© Mary Norwak 1979

All rights reserved. No part of this publication may be
reproduced, stored in a retrieval system, or transmitted,
in any form or by any means, electronic, mechanical,
photocopying, recording or otherwise, without the prior
permission of J. M. Dent & Sons Ltd.

Photoset by Northampton Phototypesetters Ltd
and Printed in Great Britain by Billings Ltd, Guildford
for J. M. Dent & Sons Ltd
Aldine House, Welbeck Street, London

This book is set in 11 on 11 Monophoto Baskerville

British Library Cataloguing in Publication Data

Norwak, Mary
    The best of country cooking.
    1. Cookery, British
    I. Title
    641.5'941   TX717

ISBN 0-460-04392-7

Contents

This book is for Barbara Hargreaves, Babs Honey, Suzanne Beedell, Sally Smith, Keith Mossman, Keith Huggett and Roger Turff, colleagues who have done so much to maintain the country way of life

Introduction

A generation ago, few people in Britain were more than a step re-moved from their country backgrounds. Certainly, during the Second World War, even the most diehard town dweller could count on having an aunt or cousin with a farm or cottage to retreat to, and children were still brought up to know that they could spend part of their school holidays enjoying country pleasures and country food. Places which are now part of Greater London or Greater Manchester were still villages, and the newly-affluent housing estates of the 30s were surrounded by fields and streams where sheep and cattle grazed, corn was stooked and peas were picked by hand. Men and women still only in their early middle-age remember these days with nostalgia, and the simple foods of their childhood stir particular memories.

What has happened to the gob-stoppers and humbugs, the crusty loaves and milk from the churn, the sweetly-sticky greengages, the rather runny jam and the Harvest Festival marrows? They are being swept away on a tide of standardization, of plastic packaging, of food hygiene and so-called convenience. But happily, there are still many people who care and I am lucky enough to meet them.

For the past fifteen years one of my favourite jobs has been writing on food for a farming magazine. Our readers are mainly, of course, serious working farmers, and the nature of their job makes them and their wives care deeply about the food on their table. An interesting section of our readership, however, lives in towns but regards the magazine as a link with the long-lost countryside. They read it because their fathers were farmers, or their small sons love pictures of tractors, or they long for a way of life which is vanishing fast. It has been my pleasure to sharpen all their appetites for many years and to exchange views with them, and I am very grateful that I am now able to share the fruit of my labours with an even wider audience. My particular thanks are due to Travis Legge, editor of *Farmers' Weekly*, for his permission to use material and recipes which first appeared in that magazine.

MARY NORWAK

Soup

Seasonable Soups

There's nothing like a comforting bowl of soup when the days are cold. Luncheon or supper can be a simple meal of nourishing soup, followed perhaps by bread and cheese or sandwiches, and some fruit. A formal party will get off to a good start with a light and appetizing soup, and evening guests will appreciate a cup of broth to see them home. The china manufacturers have made it easy for us to serve soup elegantly, reintroducing giant tureens to the new dinner services, and a variety of pottery bowls and mugs to replace the formal soup plates which cool the soup too quickly.

Beef is expensive for stock-making these days, but bones are not, and they provide excellent stock. Put the cracked bones into a large saucepan and cover with cold water, adding two tablespoons of vinegar to each quart of water, as this helps to extract calcium from the bones. Older animals and mature vegetables give the best flavour to stock, and the idea is to extract all this flavour from the raw materials instead of retaining it, as in most branches of cookery. Bring the stock very slowly to the boil, skimming frequently, then simmer very gently, partly covered, for up to twelve hours. Strain the stock, cool it uncovered, then store tightly covered in a refrigerator for no more than four days. Boil stock every day, and boil well before using.

Vegetables may be added to make the basic stock, but strongly flavoured ones like onion, carrot and turnip should be used sparingly. For the same reason, avoid adding strongly flavoured vegetable waters to the basic stock. Try not to use green vegetables and starchy items in stock, as they cause souring, and be careful of liquids in which cured hams or tongue have been cooked as these are so often very salty. Avoid fatty meats too, as greasy stock is unpleasant. Don't leave stock in a covered saucepan near a warm place, and don't leave vegetables in stock overnight.

When you have your basic stock you are ready to tackle any recipe, but do remember the importance of eye-appeal in cooking. Fresh green herbs always look good as a garnish, and a blob of cream makes a colour contrast on tomato or pea soup. Little cubes of toast or fried bread improve appearance and add bulk. A new loaf pulled into rough pieces which are then lightly crisped in the oven is another way of adding the necessary bulk, or try a herb or garlic loaf. Make this by slitting a French loaf diagonally at intervals and spreading the cuts with butter creamed with fresh herbs or garlic. Wrap the loaf in foil and pop it into a moderate oven for fifteen minutes. The smell is just wonderful, and the buttery bread is an appropriate accompaniment to a hearty soup. Fresh vegetables from the garden make good and cheap summer soups. They should not be heavy and cloying, so are better thickened with egg yolks or cream rather than with flour. During hot weather iced soup is light and nourishing, but it must be very cold and, as the flavour will lessen during chilling, this should be allowed for when the soup is prepared.

Creamy cheese soup

This is an unusual soup, and a particularly nice one to serve as a main luncheon or supper dish with plenty of crusty bread.

1 tablespoon minced
   onion
2 tablespoons butter
2 tablespoons plain flour
¾ pint (450 ml) chicken
   stock
8 oz (225 g) cooked carrots
¾ pint (450 ml) milk
4 oz (100 g) grated cheese
Salt, pepper, parsley

Cook the onion in butter until soft and golden. Work in the flour, then blend in stock and carrots which have been mashed to a purée. Cook gently, stirring in the milk, until the soup has thickened slightly. Add cheese and stir until melted without cooking. Season well with salt and pepper, and garnish with chopped parsley.

Serves 4

Mutton broth

A really good winter family soup. It is important to serve it very hot, and to avoid all traces of fat.

8 oz (225 g) lean middle
   neck of mutton
2 pints (1 l) cold water
Thyme, parsley, bay leaf
1 oz (25 g) pearl barley
Salt and pepper
1 stick celery
1 small leek
1 onion
1 carrot
1 turnip
Parsley

Remove all fat from meat, cover in cold water, and add herbs, barley, salt and pepper, and vegetables cut in small pieces. Simmer for 1½ hours. Remove meat and cut from the bones, trimming into neat pieces. Return meat to the broth, reheat and remove fat from surface of the soup with soft paper. Reheat, adjusting seasoning and serve sprinkled with chopped parsley.

Serves 4

Chicken soup with parsley balls

This is a very good soup for an informal supper party or a buffet and looks particularly nice in a large tureen, served into pottery bowls.

1 boiling chicken cut in pieces
4 pints (2.25 l) water
4 oz (100 g) sliced onions
6 sprigs parsley
1 carrot
1 celery stick
1 bay leaf
6 peppercorns
1 rasher bacon
1 tablespoon plain flour
1½ teaspoons salt
¼ teaspoon pepper

Parsley balls:
2 tablespoons butter
2 eggs
1 teaspoon chopped parsley
¼ teaspoon salt
3 oz (75 g) plain flour

Cover chicken with water, and add sliced onions, parsley, diced carrot and celery, bay leaf, peppercorns and diced bacon. Boil for thirty minutes, skim, then simmer for three hours. Cool, strain and take off fat. Cut chicken flesh in neat pieces and return to stock. Mix flour with a little water, salt and pepper, and add to stock. Bring to boil and simmer for ten minutes.

Make the parsley balls by softening the butter and adding the rest of the ingredients. Drop teaspoonsful into the simmering soup and cook for five minutes.

Serves 4

Artichoke soup

This is a soothing soup which makes a meal on its own with fresh crusty bread.

1 lb (450 g) Jerusalem artichokes
3 potatoes
1 leek or onion
Salt and pepper
½ pint (300 ml) stock
1 pint (600 ml) creamy milk

Serves 4

Scrape the artichokes and cut them up, together with the potatoes and the leek or onion. Just cover with water and add salt and pepper. Simmer for thirty minutes and put through a sieve. Add stock and milk and heat for fifteen minutes.

I like to add a spoonful of cream or a knob of butter at the end, and a good scattering of chopped parsley. Chicken stock is the nicest to use – and you can leave out the milk and just use plenty of stock if you have it.

Spiced tomato soup

A good soup to serve before a formal meal in traditional wide soup plates.

1 oz (25 g) butter
2 medium onions
1 teaspoon paprika
1 oz (25 g) plain flour
2 pints (1 l) chicken or
   vegetable stock
2 lb (1 kg) fresh tomatoes
   (or large can)
Thyme,
   parsley,
   bayleaf } tied in a muslin bag
   2 cloves
   1 blade mace
Salt and pepper
Pinch of sugar
Strip of lemon rind
Nutmeg
1 tablespoon sago
1 large wineglass port
   (optional)

Melt the butter and add sliced onions, cooking until soft and pale golden. Add paprika and flour and cook for a minute or two, then add stock, tomatoes, herbs and seasonings. Simmer for thirty minutes, then remove herbs and put soup through a sieve. Return soup to a clean pan, and add the sago. Simmer until clear, add the port if liked, and taste the seasoning, adjusting if necessary.

Serves 4

Oxtail soup

1 oxtail
Salt, pepper
Butter or bacon fat
3 pints (1.5 l) water
2 carrots
1 turnip
1 large onion
2 sticks celery
½ teaspoon salt
Pinch of pepper
1 teaspoon Worcestershire
   sauce
1 teaspoon lemon juice

Serves 4

Cut oxtail in pieces, sprinkle with a little salt and pepper, and dredge with flour. Fry in a little butter or bacon fat for ten minutes until golden. Add water and simmer for two to three hours until tender. Strain soup into a saucepan, remove meat from bones and add it to the soup. Add all the vegetables cut in small pieces and continue cooking until they are soft. Add salt, pepper, Worcestershire sauce and lemon juice and serve very hot. (More water may be added during cooking if the liquid becomes very reduced.)

King's onion soup

4 thinly sliced onions
½ pint (300 ml) water
3 pints (1.5 l) milk
½ teaspoon nutmeg
4 oz (100 g) butter
2 egg yolks
Chopped parsley
Diced toast

Serves 4

Stew onions in water until soft, add milk and continue simmering for thirty minutes with nutmeg and butter. Pour a little of the liquid on to the beaten egg yolks, and return this mixture to the saucepan. Heat but do not boil, add salt and pepper to taste, garnish with chopped parsley, and sprinkle each serving with a few pieces of diced toast.

Fish chowder

This may sound unusual, but it is a nourishing dish, and full of flavour. A few lemon slices can be floated in the tureen, and if you have access to some oysters, a few of these stirred in with their liquid at the last moment make a delicious addition.

2 lb (1 kg) fresh cod
    (with bones and skin)
2 rashers streaky bacon
1 large onion
1 lb (450 g) potatoes
1 pint (600 ml) milk
1 teaspoon salt
¼ teaspoon pepper
1½ oz (40 g) butter
8 cream cracker biscuits

Cut cod into cubes. Put bones and trimmings into a pint of water, heat to boiling point, then simmer for twenty minutes. Cut bacon into small pieces, put into a heavy pan, and cook slowly until it is crisp and the fat runs. Remove bacon pieces and set on one side, and cook sliced onion in the fat until soft. Peel and slice potatoes and cook for five minutes in boiling water, then drain. Put potatoes, bacon and onions together, pour on 1 pint (600 ml) boiling water and cook five minutes. Add fish stock and cod pieces, cover and simmer for ten minutes. Heat milk just to boiling point and add to soup, and season with salt, pepper and butter. Serve piping hot, garnished with broken cream crackers.

Serves 4

Fresh tomato soup

1 large onion
6 large tomatoes
1 oz (25 g) butter
Salt and pepper
1 tablespoon vermicelli

Serves 4

Mince the onion and cut the tomatoes in quarters. Toss in butter until the onion is lightly coloured. Add 1½ pints (900 ml) boiling water with salt and pepper to taste. Bring to the boil and simmer until the tomatoes are soft. Sieve, add vermicelli and cook gently until the vermicelli is soft. Serve in bowls with a blob of cream and a little chopped parsley or chives, accompanied by crisp toast.

Leek and potato soup

2 oz (50 g) butter
3 large leeks
1 onion
8 oz (225 g) potatoes
2 pints (1 l) chicken stock
Salt and pepper
2 teaspoons chopped
  parsley

Serves 4

Melt butter and cook sliced white part of leeks and chopped onion until soft but not brown. Add sliced potatoes and stock and seasoning, bring to the boil, and simmer for thirty minutes. Stir in chopped parsley and serve with crusty French bread.

For a party version of this soup omit parsley, sieve finished soup, then chill it. Stir in ¼ pint (150 ml) single cream and garnish with chopped chives before serving ice cold.

Watercress soup

2 oz (50 g) butter
1 onion
8 oz (225 g) potatoes
½ pint (300 ml) chicken
  stock or water
1½ pints (900 ml) milk
1 bunch watercress
Salt and pepper
Pinch of nutmeg
½ teaspoon cornflour
2 teaspoons water
2 tablespoons double
  cream

Serves 4

Melt butter and cook chopped onion until soft but not browned. Add peeled potatoes and stock or water, bring to boil and cook gently for fifteen minutes. Add milk and simmer for ten minutes. Reserve four small sprigs of watercress for garnish, and put remainder into soup. Cook with lid on for three minutes, then put soup through a sieve or into a liquidizer. Return soup to pan and season to taste, adding nutmeg and reserved watercress. Blend cornflour with water and stir into soup. Return to boil and cook for a minute. Remove from heat and stir in cream.

Bacon and pea soup

1 knuckle bacon
2 medium onions
8 oz (225 g) dried peas
  or lentils
Pepper
1 oz (25 g) butter
Top of milk

Serves 4

Put bacon to soak for an hour, then put into 2½ pints (1.5 l) cold water, bring to boil, add chopped onions, and simmer until bacon is tender. Meanwhile soak peas or lentils in cold water. When bacon is tender, remove from stock (use the meat on the bone for sandwiches or with salad). Put peas or lentils into stock and simmer until tender. Sieve or liquidize and return to pan, adding pepper to taste. Salt will not normally be needed. Add butter and the top of a bottle of milk, and reheat. Serve with tiny squares of fried bread as a garnish.

Lettuce soup

4 small firm lettuces
1 cucumber
2 tablespoons chervil
  leaves
1 oz (25 g) butter
Nutmeg, salt and pepper
1 tablespoon flour
3 pints (1.5 l) chicken
  stock
3 egg yolks
6 tablespoons top of milk

Wash lettuce very thoroughly and chop finely. Put into saucepan with peeled and chopped cucumber, chervil, butter, a pinch of nutmeg, salt and pepper. Cover and cook quickly for ten minutes. Stir in flour, add stock and stir over gentle heat until boiling. Reduce heat and simmer for thirty minutes. Beat egg yolks and milk, and stir gradually into the soup. Serve with squares of fried bread.

Serves 4

Pea soup

2 oz (50 g) butter
1 tablespoon finely
  chopped onion
1 lb (450 g) shelled peas
½ teaspoon salt
1 teaspoon sugar
½ pint (300 ml) creamy
  milk
Mace and pepper
Chopped parsley or chives

Melt butter and cook onion until soft and yellow. Add peas, salt, sugar and ¾ pint (450 ml) water and cook for twenty minutes. Sieve, add milk and heat gently. Season to taste with a pinch of mace and pepper and sprinkle with finely chopped parsley or chives.

Serves 4

Spinach soup

1 lb (450 g) spinach
1 large onion
3 oz (75 g) butter
1 tablespoon plain flour
2 tablespoons bread-
  crumbs
Salt and pepper
2 egg yolks
2 tablespoons creamy
  milk

Wash spinach thoroughly, drain well and chop finely. Put in a saucepan with chopped onion, butter and flour and simmer for ten minutes. Add 4 pints (2.5 l) boiling water, breadcrumbs, salt and pepper and simmer for an hour. Before serving, beat up egg yolks and milk in a tureen, and pour on spinach mixture, stirring gently.

Serves 4

Iced cucumber soup

2 cucumbers
¾ pint (450 ml) natural
  yogurt
1 teaspoon salt
4 tablespoons olive oil
Parsley

Peel cucumbers, slice thinly and take out seed. Thoroughly mix with other ingredients and serve cold, sprinkled with a little parsley.

Serves 4

Eggs

Eggs Galore

Eggs are marvellous. We can eat them at all times of the day, on their own or with other protein foods or vegetables, and they make nourishing sweet dishes too. Weight for weight, they compare more than favourably in both price and protein value with other favourite foods, but above all, eggs are so versatile, even when cooked in a simple way.

Poached eggs are great on buttered toast, or partnering bacon or sausages. Try them on smoked haddock or kipper fillets. If you have some frozen spinach or some of the perpetual variety, cook it and put it in a serving dish. Top with poached eggs and cover with cheese sauce, browning the top under the grill. Try a mixture of mashed potatoes and cooked chopped onions, well seasoned and topped with poached eggs, or use them to top a dish of buttered sweetcorn mixed with flaked smoked haddock.

Hard-boiled eggs are good in sandwiches or salads, but try them thickly sliced, seasoned, topped with a rich parsley sauce, dotted with grated cheese and breadcrumbs and browned under the grill. They're good too in onion sauce, again with a sprinkling of grated cheese. For a more filling meal, put both these egg variations into a bed of creamy mashed potatoes. Or try making Scotch eggs: wrap hard-boiled eggs in sausagemeat and deep-fry them. Alternatively, wrap them in a herb stuffing, or a bacon forcemeat, or even mashed potato if you prefer.

Scrambled eggs are nicest cooked very slowly until creamy, and served as soon as they are ready, with bacon or sausages, or plainly on toast. If you like, spread the toast with a little anchovy paste or yeast extract. You can stir in chopped bacon, lightly cooked chicken livers, chopped fresh herbs, grated cheese, or even small cubes of fried bread, just as you fancy.

Baked eggs are particularly easy if your oven is permanently on: they cook best in the lower oven of an Aga. You need some small individual ovenware dishes. Butter them well, drop in an egg, top with more butter and cook until the white is just set. You can put a little fried bacon, ham or chicken liver under the egg, and top with a spoonful of thick cream, some grated cheese or a little tomato sauce. Be sure the eggs are well seasoned. It makes a nice light supper for someone who needs a little nourishment. For something more conventional, put a couple of rashers into a small two-handled frying pan or ovenware dish. Let them cook in the oven for ten minutes, then break in a couple of eggs and return them to the oven until set.

Here are some of my favourite main courses made with eggs:

Egg and sausage tart

4 oz (100 g) shortcrust
 pastry (recipe p. 97)
8 oz (225 g) sausage meat
8 eggs
Salt and pepper
1½ oz (40 g) grated cheese

Serves 4

Roll out the pastry to line a tin about 7 in (17.5 cm) square (or you can use a sponge sandwich tin). Prick the base and bake at 400°F/200°C/Gas Mark 6 for fifteen minutes. Shape the sausage meat into rolls to form a border pressed firmly on to the pastry edges. Break eggs inside the sausage meat, and sprinkle with seasoning. Cover with cheese and bake at 400°F/200°C/Gas Mark 6 for thirty minutes. Serve hot with vegetables, or cold with salad.

Egg and mushroom rarebit

4 slices white bread
2 oz (50 g) butter
4 oz (100 g) mushrooms
Salt and pepper
8 eggs
1 tablespoon beer or cider
4 oz (100 g) grated cheese
½ teaspoon made mustard

Serves 4

Cut the bread into triangles to cover the base of an ovenware dish. Heat half the butter and fry the bread crisp and brown on one side only. Put the fried side down in the dish. Slice the mushrooms thinly and spread over the bread. Sprinkle with salt and pepper and break the eggs on top of the mushrooms. Melt the remaining butter, take off the heat, stir in the beer, cheese and mustard. Spoon this mixture over the eggs. Bake at 400°F/200°C/Gas Mark 6 for 25 minutes. Serve hot with vegetables or a side salad.

Coldstream eggs

8 oz (225 g) cooked
 smoked haddock
6 eggs
Salt and pepper
4 tablespoons double
 cream

Serves 4

Flake the haddock and mash to a purée. Put into six individual oven dishes. Break an egg into each one, season with salt and pepper and top with cream. Bake at 350°F/180°C/Gas Mark 4 for ten minutes.

Sunday omelette

This omelette doesn't fold easily, and is best cut in wedges.

1 chicken liver
2 bacon rashers
1 small onion
1 large boiled potato
2 tablespoons cooked peas
4 eggs
Salt and pepper
Butter

Serves 4

Cut the chicken liver and bacon into small pieces. Put in a thick-bottomed frying pan and cook gently until the fat runs from the bacon, and the liver is just coloured. Chop the onion finely and add to the pan with a little cooking oil if there is not much fat. Cook until the onion is just coloured, then add the potato chopped in small pieces. When all the ingredients are tender and golden, stir in the peas. Beat the eggs lightly with a fork, just enough to break them up. Add plenty of seasoning and some fresh chopped herbs if you like them. Add a large knob of butter to the frying pan, and as soon as it has melted, pour in the eggs. Move them lightly with a fork as the mixture sets, lifting the ingredients so the eggs run beneath and round them. When just set, turn on to a plate.

Egg and onion casserole

2 large onions
3 oz (75 g) butter
6 eggs
2 oz (50 g) plain flour
¾ pint (450 ml) milk
2 oz (50 g) grated
    Cheddar cheese

Serves 4

Cut the onions in slices and fry them slowly in 1 oz (25 g) butter. When soft and golden, put the onions in the bottom of a casserole. Hard boil the eggs, cut in slices, and put them on top of the onions. Melt the remaining butter, and work in the flour. Cook for two minutes and add the milk gradually while stirring. Simmer for five minutes, stirring at intervals. Remove from the heat and stir in most of the cheese. Season well with salt and pepper, and pour the sauce over the eggs. Sprinkle with the remaining cheese and brown under the grill or in a hot oven.

If liked, some chopped bacon may be fried with the onions: it is most important that the onions should be kept soft and golden, and not allowed to brown or the flavour of the dish is spoiled.

Stuffed eggs

4 hard-boiled eggs
5 tablespoons butter
10 anchovy fillets
Pepper and salt

Serves 4

Cut eggs in half crosswise or lengthwise. Remove yolks and pound with butter and anchovies. Season carefully (the anchovies may be rather salty). Refill egg whites and serve on a bed of lettuce with garnish of tomatoes and parsley.

Egg curry

6 oz (175 g) mixed
  vegetables
1 large onion
1 oz (25 g) butter
1 tablespoon curry
  powder
2 teaspoons plain flour
¾ pint (450 ml) stock or
  water
1 bay leaf
1 lemon
8 oz (225 g) long-grain
  rice
8 hard-boiled eggs

Serves 4

The vegetables may be frozen, fresh, or left over from a meal. A mixture of roots, with peas, beans and corn gives a variety of textures. Cook the vegetables and put on one side. Chop the onion finely and fry until soft in the butter. Add the curry powder and flour, and stir over heat for three minutes. Add the stock gradually, with the bay leaf, sliced lemon and a pinch of salt. Simmer for twenty minutes and then remove the bay leaf and lemon. Cook the rice in boiling salted water for twelve minutes. Drain and spread on a baking sheet in the oven until fluffy. Heat the vegetables in the curry sauce and add the hard-boiled eggs. Continue heating for 5 minutes, and then serve with rice and chutney. More curry powder may be used if a hot curry is liked.

Egg mousse

Delicious first course if topped at the last minute with prawns tossed in mayonnaise flavoured with tomato purée.

6 eggs
3 egg whites
¼ pint (150 ml) white
  sauce
½ pint (300 ml) double
  cream

Boil eggs for seven minutes and cool in running water. Shell and chop finely. Mix into white sauce and cool thoroughly. Whip cream until thick and add to egg mixture, seasoning well and adding a suspicion of garlic (a little garlic powder can be used). Whip egg whites until firm but not dry, and fold into mixture. Put in serving dish and chill for four hours.

Serves 4

Cheese baked eggs

An excellent high tea or supper dish to be followed by fruit.

2 oz (50 g) soft butter
3 oz (75 g) grated
  Cheddar cheese
4 eggs
4 tablespoons top of milk

Serves 4

Butter four small fireproof dishes. Using three-quarters of the cheese, sprinkle equal amounts into the base of each dish. Break eggs into dishes and sprinkle remaining cheese on top. Put a tablespoon of top of milk on each egg, and dot with remaining butter. Bake at 400°F/200°C/Gas Mark 6 for fifteen minutes, and serve at once.

Swiss eggs

Delicious with new bread and a green salad. Cheddar cheese an be used, but the result will not be so smooth.

2 oz (50 g) Gruyère cheese
Salt and pepper
Nutmeg
4 eggs
2 tablespoons double
    cream
1 oz (25 g) butter

Grease a shallow fireproof dish and line with thin slices of cheese. Season with salt, pepper and a pinch of nutmeg. Break in eggs, allowing yolks to mix with whites. Season lightly. Put cream on top and more thin slices of cheese. Dot with butter, and bake at 375°F/190°C/ Gas Mark 5 for thirty minutes.

Serves 4

The Perfect Omelette

What can be more delicious on a hot summer day than an omelette for lunch or supper, with a fresh green or tomato salad? Indeed this is the perfect meal combining lightness and delicious flavour with healthy nourishment.

Most people are a bit frightened of cooking omelettes, classing them with soufflés as dishes for the professional cook. Nothing could be further from the truth. The only requirements are good fresh eggs and a proper omelette pan, carefully maintained during and after use. The perfect omelette pan should be thick and flat, made of thick iron or aluminium (for small 2-3 egg omelettes, use 7 in (17.5 cm) pan; for 4 egg omelettes, use 8½–9 in (22 cm) pan. To 'season' a new pan, cover the bottom well with salad oil and leave for twelve hours, then heat the pan, pour off the oil and wipe it well with a dry cloth. After use, wipe the pan with kitchen paper, then with a damp cloth dipped in salt. Avoid washing the pan, as scouring will roughen the surface. For this reason, the pan is best kept for omelettes and pancakes and not for everyday frying which tends to leave bits of food which stick and are hard to remove.

Don't let an omelette wait for its filling; have the filling ready when the omelette is cooked, and also hot plates, and of course the people to eat it. The nicest omelettes are made one at a time and eaten at once; for larger families, you can make an eight-egg omelette using a 10 in (22.5 cm) pan, and divide into four for serving.

Most people know about the basic omelette, but a soufflé omelette is delicious, particularly with a sweet filling. Another version is the Swedish baked omelette, which is very useful if the top of the stove is crowded, or you prefer to use the oven heat of a solid fuel cooker.

Basic French omelette

Break 3 eggs into a basin, add salt and pepper, and mix eggs with a metal fork until they are lightly mixed (not beaten). Heat the pan containing $\frac{1}{2}$ oz (15 g) butter, and slowly get it hot so that the butter sizzles but does not brown. Pour eggs into the hot fat, and use the fork to keep drawing some of the mixture to the middle from the sides of the pan, and in $1\frac{1}{2}$ minutes the omelette will still be soft but not runny. Don't overcook; as the omelette is served it will still be setting firmly. Draw pan off heat and using fork, fold the omelette half over away from the handle. Tilt the pan over the hot plate and the omelette will slip forward on to the plate, neatly folded.

Some fillings, such as herbs and cheese can be added to the beaten eggs; others must be put on the omelette just before it is folded.

Baked omelette

Mix together four eggs and $\frac{1}{4}$ pint (150 ml) very creamy milk, and season with salt and pepper. Pour into well-buttered omelette pan or baking dish and bake at 350°F/180°C/Gas Mark 4 for fifteen minutes until golden brown. Add filling, fold over and serve immediately. This type of omelette is particularly good with a creamed filling such as creamed mushrooms, asparagus, shrimps, sweetbreads or kidneys; or chopped herbs, bacon or cheese may be added to the beaten eggs.

Fillings for three-egg omelette

Cheese: grate 2 oz (50 g) hard cheese finely and add to the eggs, saving a little for sprinkling on the finished omelette.

Herbs: chop finely one tablespoon parsley and a few chives, and add to the eggs before cooking.

Kidney: cut two lambs' kidneys into small pieces and toss in a little butter with a small chopped onion or shallot. Fill omelette with this mixture just before serving.

Mushroom: chop 2 oz (50 g) mushrooms and toss in a little butter until tender, filling omelette just before serving.

Shellfish: warm shrimps, prawns, lobster or crab in a little white sauce, and fill omelette just before serving.

Spanish omelette: cut 6 oz (175 g) raw potato in thin slices, also a medium onion and 2 oz (50 g) bacon or ham (a little chopped green pepper, mushroom or chicken liver are all good additions). Cook in olive oil until potato and onion are soft. Drain off oil, sprinkle mixture with salt and pepper, and pour in four beaten eggs. Cook until firmly set, and cut like a cake to serve. This is really filling and delicious to eat hot or cold.

Soufflé omelette

Separate yolks and whites, and add half an egg-shell of water to each yolk. Beat yolks with a wooden spoon until creamy. Whisk whites until stiff enough to stay in basin when turned upside down. Gently fold whites into yolks. Heat butter, pour in egg mixture and cook until golden brown on the underside, without drawing up mixture as in a plain omelette. Spread filling on cooked omelette and with a spatula fold over omelette and slip on to hot dish. This type of omelette is delicious with home-made jam, or with fresh fruit (raspberries, strawberries, peaches, apricots) which has been sliced and left to stand in a little liqueur and sugar to taste.

Simple Soufflés

There's nothing like a soufflé to create a cordon bleu reputation, and it's dead easy to get terrific results if you remember the supreme soufflé secret – Be Accurate. In farm kitchens, when time is short, most of us tend to get a bit slap-happy about weighing, measuring and timing, and somehow, although the results are jolly good, they don't always reach perfection in the blending of flavours or the right texture. But it's easy if you stick to these simple rules: be sure to follow a soufflé recipe exactly; make sure your oven is set to the correct temperature and is pre-heated; time your cooking exactly; and weigh ingredients scrupulously.

There's only one real problem – this is a dish that cannot be kept waiting. Don't attempt a hot soufflé unless you are absolutely certain of the very minute it can be eaten. One compensation here, though, is that the basic mixture can be prepared hours in advance, leaving only whipped egg whites to be added before cooking time. A soufflé can be as cheap to prepare as you like to make it, consisting often of leftovers and a few eggs – but it is always highly digestible, astonishingly filling and very nourishing.

The dish can be savoury or sweet, basically consisting of a white sauce or 'panada', some kind of flavouring and eggs. A savoury soufflé needs a salt and pepper seasoning, while a sweet soufflé needs 2 oz (50 g) caster sugar. A three-egg soufflé, which is enough for four people, needs about 4–6 oz (100–175 g) of flavouring material in the form of meat, fish, cheese, or vegetables, while a sweet soufflé can be flavoured with four tablespoons of sweetened fruit purée.

Equipment is very simple. You need a thick saucepan for making the basic sauce, a good egg-beater, and a straight-sided soufflé dish. For a three-egg soufflé, a 2-pint (1 l) capacity dish is needed. The classic French shape has fluted sides. If the dish is rather shallow, a buttered 2–3 in (5–7.5 cm) paper collar can be fastened round the rim to increase height. The French like their soufflés with a soft centre, which serves as a kind of sauce to the remainder. The Americans, on the other hand, like an almost cake-like texture, cooked evenly right through, but too long cooking makes the result tough and dry.

Basic soufflé

Step one : heat your oven to the correct temperature. This should be a moderate heat, with the soufflé cooked in the middle of the oven at 375°F/190°C/Gas Mark 5.

Step two : grease your soufflé dish, using olive oil. If a very large soufflé is needed, make and bake two sets of mixture in two smaller dishes, rather than double the quantity and upset the baking time.

For a savoury soufflé, a coating of dry breadcrumbs or grated cheese makes a pleasant embellishment, or use caster sugar for a sweet soufflé.

Make a paper or foil collar to give height to the dish, folding the paper two or three times to give stiffness. Brush with oil, and clip round the outside of the dish with a paper clip and string. This collar is removed before serving by running a knife quickly inside.

Step three: assemble all ingredients, and prepare the flavouring mixture. You will need 3 oz (75 g) butter, 2 oz (50 g) plain flour, ½ pint (300 ml) milk, and three large eggs, separated, to make the basic mixture. Meat, fish or vegetables should be cooked, then chopped finely or made into a purée. Cheese is best grated, and should be firm and dry, such as Cheddar, Parmesan or Gruyère. Use strong seasoning to give a good flavour when cooked. For a sweet soufflé, a tablespoon of liqueur will improve the flavour.

Step four: make a white sauce by melting butter in a thick saucepan over gentle heat. Stir in sifted flour, and slowly add milk, blending the mixture smoothly (this is much easier if the milk is warm). Bring the mixture to the boil, stirring carefully, and cook for three minutes. In some recipes, you will find this described as a 'panada' but it is really just a basic white sauce. Now add the filling you have prepared, and thoroughly mix in three large beaten egg yolks. You may then leave the mixture until baking time, when it should be gently reheated before the next step.

Step five: just before cooking time, beat three large egg whites until they are so stiff they stay in a basin turned upside down. Fold the whites very gently but thoroughly into the mixture.

Step six: fill the prepared dish with the mixture and put into the middle of your preheated oven for forty-five minutes exactly. The mixture may be used for individual soufflés, allowing fifteen minutes' cooking time. If a crisp crust is wanted, the soufflé can be put straight in the oven, but for an even texture without crust, stand the dish in a pan of hot, but not boiling, water.

When ready for eating, the soufflé should be well risen, firm to the touch and a good colour, fluffy and lightly set.

Apple soufflé: add four tablespoons thick apple purée, flavoured with lemon juice and 2 oz (50 g) caster sugar.

Asparagus soufflé: add 6 oz (175 g) fresh or

tinned asparagus, finely chopped, salt and pepper.

Cheese soufflé: add 4 oz (100 g) grated Cheddar cheese, salt, pepper and ½ teaspoon dry mustard.

Chicken soufflé: add 4 oz (100 g) minced cooked chicken, salt and pepper, a grating of lemon rind and a teaspoon of chopped parsley.

Chocolate soufflé: melt 2 oz (50 g) plain chocolate in the milk with 2 oz (50 g) sugar before making white sauce. Add ½ teaspoon vanilla essence with the egg yolks.

Crab soufflé: add 4–6 oz (100–175 g) chopped crabmeat, salt and pepper.

Fish soufflé: add 4–6 oz (100–175 g) cooked flaked fish, salt and pepper (smoked haddock is very good).

Ham soufflé: add 4–6 oz (100–175 g) chopped cooked ham, salt and pepper and a pinch of dry mustard.

Lemon soufflé: add 2 oz (50 g) caster sugar, the finely grated rind of a whole lemon, and juice of ½ lemon.

Mushroom soufflé: add 6 oz (175 g) chopped mushrooms lightly cooked in butter, seasoned with salt and pepper.

Prune soufflé: add four tablespoons thick prune purée and 2 oz (50 g) caster sugar.

Raspberry soufflé: add 8 oz (225 g) raspberries flavoured with lemon juice and 2 oz (50 g) caster sugar.

Shrimp soufflé: add 4 oz (100 g) shelled fresh or frozen shrimps, a squeeze of lemon juice, salt and pepper.

Surprise soufflé: make a cheese soufflé, and put half the mixture into the dish. Break in four eggs, and cover with the remaining mixture. The eggs will cook inside the soufflé, and give a very substantial main dish, preferably served with a green salad.

Dairy
Produce

Say Cheese

Most people know the pleasure of a good hunk of Cheshire or Cheddar with a corner of new bread, creamy butter, and perhaps a crisp radish or onion. Not so many of us have enjoyed experimenting with Wensleydale, Stilton, Double Gloucester, Derby, Lancashire, Leicester and Caerphilly, with the rare Dorset Blue Vinney, and the more difficult to find Dunlop and Orkney. Perhaps we tend to forget, or never knew, how good these British cheeses can be for cooking, too. Most of us use Cheddar, but Double Gloucester, Wensleydale and Cheshire also give excellent results and best of all is Lancashire, known to so many as the only cheese for toasting. Orkney is rather like a mild Cheddar, and though it is too soft for grating well, it is creamy and delicious for Welsh Rarebit.

Today the trend is towards neat even slices of cheese tightly wrapped in plastic; excellent for the bed-sitter or the occasional picnic when you can't be bothered with leftovers, but useless for the normal family. To get the best cheeses in perfect condition, with full flavour, seek out a grocer who really knows his business. There are still quite a lot of them about. When you can see large pieces of cheese side by side, it's so much easier to compare texture and flavour (no good cheese merchant will begrudge you a small 'taster' when you're comparing and buying).

Buy only enough cheese for a week's supply at a time, because cheese will deteriorate after cutting. Keep cheese away from draughts or too much air circulation, which will dry it out, in a polythene bag, foil, or greaseproof paper and store it in a cool place. It can be kept in the refrigerator away from the ice-making compartment, but should be taken out at least an hour before eating to regain temperature and full flavour.

If you get a lot of cheese ends, grate them finely (easier if the cheese is dried out naturally in a cool airy place), and store the grated cheese in a loosely covered jar in a cool place, or in a polythene bag or rigid container in the freezer. This makes an excellent standby for quick and easy cooking, and for adding extra flavour to soups, salads and pasta.

Welsh rarebit

This mixture also makes a delicious sauce, over cooked cod or halibut steaks, or smoked haddock, finished off with a little browning under the grill.

4 oz (100 g) cheese
½ oz (15 g) butter
Salt and pepper
Made mustard to taste
3 tablespoons ale (or milk)

Cut the cheese in small pieces. Melt the butter over very low heat. Gradually add cheese, seasonings and ale or milk. When just melted, put on toast and just brown. Do not overcook, or use anything but the lowest heat, or the cheese will get tough and stringy.

Serves 4

Lancashire scones

8 oz (225 g) self-raising flour
1 oz (25 g) butter
3 oz (75 g) crumbled Lancashire cheese
Pinch of salt
¼ pint (150 ml) milk

Mix flour with salt, rub in butter and add cheese. Make into a soft dough with milk. Roll out mixture ¾ in (2 cm) thick and cut in small circles. Bake at 425°F/220°C/Gas Mark 7 for twelve minutes. Split, spread with butter and eat hot.

Serves 4

Potato cakes

They're delicious for teatime, and very good with the breakfast bacon.

8 oz (225 g) cooked potatoes
2 oz (50 g) plain flour
2 oz (50 g) grated Double Gloucester cheese
1 egg
Butter

Mash the potatoes thoroughly with a little butter and work in flour and cheese. Beat egg and add to mixture. Roll out and cut into small rounds. Bake at 325°F/170°C/Gas Mark 3 until golden, or cook on a griddle or heavy frying pan.

Cheese and ale

4 oz (100 g) Cheshire cheese
6 tablespoons ale

Cut the cheese into thin slices and put into a thick bottomed saucepan. Cover with the ale and heat very gently until the mixture is like custard. Serve hot on toast.

Serves 4

Baked cheese and onions

4 large onions
4 slices buttered toast
4 oz (100 g) grated
   Cheddar cheese
1 egg
¼ pint (150 ml) milk
1 teaspoon salt
Pinch of pepper
½ oz (15 g) butter

Serves 4

Peel the onions and cook them until almost tender in boiling salted water. Drain and cut into rings. Make the toast, cut into triangles and arrange in a fireproof dish. Pile on the onion rings and sprinkle with the cheese. Beat the egg, add the milk and seasonings, and pour over the onions. Dot with butter and bake at 350°F/180°C/Gas Mark 4 for thirty minutes.

Dale pudding

Breadcrumbs
2 large apples
4 oz (100 g) grated
   Wensleydale cheese
¼ pint (150 ml) milk

Serves 4

Grease a pie-dish, and line with breadcrumbs. Peel, core and slice apples into rings, and put half of them into the bottom of the dish. Cover with half the cheese, remaining apples and the rest of the cheese. Pour on the milk, and sprinkle the top with breadcrumbs and dot with flakes of butter. Bake at 375°F/190°C/Gas Mark 5 for thirty minutes. A good way of combining the traditional apples and cheese.

Potted cheese

Traditional potted cheese was made by mixing grated cheese with double its weight in butter, a little mace or nutmeg, and port or sherry to moisten. This type of cheese can be pressed into pots, sealed with clarified butter and stored in a cold place for some weeks.

4 oz (100 g) unsalted
   butter
Salt and pepper
½ teaspoon home-made
   mustard
8 oz (225 g) cheese
3 tablespoons milk
Few drops
   Worcestershire sauce

Cream the butter and season with salt, pepper and mustard, and mix with finely grated cheese. Gradually work in the milk and sauce. Pack into small pots and chill before serving with biscuits, crusty bread or toast. If liked, work some chopped chives or mixed fresh herbs or nuts into the cheese.

Serves 4

Cheese pudding

This is good to eat with a crisp green salad to which a few slices of radish and raw onion have been added.

1 pint (600 ml) milk
4 oz (100 g) fresh white
  breadcrumbs
1 tablespoon butter
2 eggs, beaten
4 oz (100 g) grated Double
  Gloucester cheese
Salt and pepper

Heat the milk and pour on to breadcrumbs, add butter and leave to cool. Add beaten eggs, cheese and seasonings. Put into a greased pie dish and bake at 350°F/180°C/Gas Mark 4 for forty minutes until set and brown.

Serves 4

Egg rarebit

6 oz (175 g) Cheddar
  cheese
1 teaspoon mustard
  powder
Pepper
2 tablespoons brown ale
  or milk
4 eggs
4 slices bread

Grate the cheese and put into a saucepan with the mustard, pepper, ale or milk. Heat very gently until the cheese has melted. Poach the eggs and put on buttered toast. Pour on the cheese mixture and brown under the grill.

Serves 4

Lancashire cheese and eggs

1 oz (25 g) butter
1 teaspoon cooking oil
8 oz (225 g) Lancashire
  cheese
4 eggs
Pepper

Serves 4

Melt the butter and oil in a shallow dish on top of the stove. Cut the cheese into slices, reserving 1 oz (25 g) for grating. Put the cheese into the dish and melt it gently. Break the eggs on top and cook at 350°F/180°C/Gas Mark 4 for eight minutes. Sprinkle with pepper and grated cheese and brown under the grill.

Cheese and onion flan

6 oz (175 g) shortcrust
  pastry (recipe p. 97)
1 large onion
1 oz (25 g) butter
6 oz (175 g) cheese
1 egg
½ pint (300 ml) milk

Serves 4

Line a 7 in (17.5 cm) flan ring or sponge tin with the pastry. Chop the onion and soften it in the butter until golden. Put half the onions on the pastry, then the grated cheese. Add the remaining onions. Whisk the egg into the milk, season to taste, and pour into the pastry case. Bake at 400°F/200°C/Gas Mark 6 for thirty minutes. This is good hot or cold; a few scraps of bacon can also be added.

Make a Meal of Yogurt

Not so long ago, few of us were able to enjoy yogurt unless we made it ourselves, but now there's a wide range of plain and fruit-flavoured varieties available. While children particularly enjoy the flavoured kinds, the unflavoured variety can be used in many ways in the kitchen.

In eastern and near-eastern countries, yogurt has been eaten for centuries, and people use it with meat, fish and poultry, stews and curries. The Scandinavians, on the other hand, like to eat the unflavoured variety with brown sugar and cinnamon, accompanied by thin, crisp ginger biscuits. At home, we can add it to savoury dishes near the end of cooking to make a smooth, creamy sauce with a slight tang.

Just stir natural yogurt into a pan of minced beef and heat it through, or add to the pan juices when cooking liver or kidneys. Let it brown slightly and season with a little Worcestershire sauce.

Baked fish cooked in yogurt is creamy with an extra flavour or the yogurt can be used as a sauce for grilled or steamed fish.

Young carrots, spinach, broccoli and baby turnips are good if cooked in a little stock (or in a casserole with a little butter) with yogurt added just before serving.

A quick sauce can be made by flavouring yogurt with fresh herbs, or with chopped capers or gherkins or delicious potato salad, by tossing potatoes in natural yogurt with finely chopped onion and plenty of salt and pepper.

Try it too for making dips, cheesecakes and soups, and even ice-cream.

If your family likes to eat a lot of it, you may find it worth while to invest in one of the many machines which maintain the milk at an even temperature while it is transformed into yogurt, but you can make your own yogurt without special equipment, and it is worth trying a batch to see how you like it.

Raspberry fool

1½ lb (700 g) raspberries
Sugar
½ pint (300 ml) double
    cream
¼ pint (150 ml) natural
    yogurt
Rind of 1 orange

Serves 4

Save a few raspberries for decoration and sieve the rest. Sweeten with a little sugar if necessary. Whip half the cream until just stiff and beat in the yogurt. Fold in the raspberry pulp and grated orange rind. Put into a bowl and chill. Whip remaining cream to decorate the top and put on the reserved raspberries. Serve very cold.

Home-made soft yogurt

1 pint (600 ml)
    pasteurized, sterilized
    or Channel Island milk
¼ pint (150 ml) natural
    yogurt

Warm the milk to blood heat (98°F) and remove from heat. Gently whisk in the yogurt with a wire whisk or fork. Transfer to a bowl and cover with a plate. Leave in a warm place for 8–12 hours until set. If liked, put into the refrigerator after setting. For firmer yogurt, the Milk Marketing Board recommends using ultra-heat-treated (UHT) milk.

If you like flavoured yogurt, stir small pieces of fresh, canned or thawed frozen fruit into the mixture when it has set. To start another batch of yogurt, some home-made yogurt can be used with the fresh milk in the same proportions.

Yogurt scones

Split and serve with butter to eat with salads, or sandwich together with jam and cream. Wholemeal flour can be used for these scones and they are then good with cheese.

8 oz (225 g) plain flour
½ teaspoon salt
1½ teaspoons baking
    powder
1 oz (25 g) butter
¼ pint (150 ml) natural
    yogurt

Sift together the flour, salt and baking powder. Rub in the butter and stir in the yogurt to make a soft dough. Knead lightly until smooth. Roll out ½ in (1.25 cm) thick and cut into 3 in (7.5 cm) rounds. Put on a greased baking sheet and bake at 400°F/200°C/Gas Mark 6 for twelve minutes.

Serves 4

Yogurt salad dressing

3 tablespoons natural
    yogurt
1½ tablespoons salad oil
¼ teaspoon salt
Pepper
2 teaspoons chopped
    chives
2 tablespoons finely
    chopped parsley

Mix together all the ingredients and serve on salads.

Chicken curry

1 small chicken
Flour
Salt and pepper
Ground ginger
4 oz (100 g) butter
3 medium onions
2 lb (1 kg) peeled
 tomatoes
1 tablespoon curry
 powder
½ pint (300 ml) yogurt
2 oz (50 g) blanched
 almonds

Serves 4

Cut the chicken in four pieces (if preferred, four chicken joints can be used instead). Dip the pieces in flour seasoned with salt and pepper, and then sprinkle them generously with ground ginger. Brown the chicken in 2 oz (50 g) hot butter and, when well browned, remove the chicken into a casserole, or a heavy saucepan.

Slice the onions and fry them in the rest of the butter until lightly golden. Add the sliced tomatoes and cook for five minutes and then stir in the curry powder. Cook for three minutes and then add the yogurt. Mix well and pour over the chicken. Cover and cook gently for thirty minutes. Serve hot, sprinkled with almonds, with an accompaniment of rice and chutney.

Yogurt meatballs

1½ lb (700 g) minced beef
3 tablespoons
 breadcrumbs
2 tablespoons very finely
 chopped onion
1 egg
¼ teaspoon pepper
½ teaspoon salt
3 tablespoons flour
2 oz (50 g) butter
14 oz (400 g) can tomatoes
1 teaspoon paprika
½ pint (300 ml) yogurt

Mix together the meat, breadcrumbs, onion, egg, pepper and salt, and form into small balls. Roll in the flour and brown in the butter or other fat if you prefer. Add the tomatoes and simmer gently for thirty minutes. Stir in the paprika and yogurt and cook gently for five minutes.

Serves 4

Kidneys in yogurt sauce

8 lamb kidneys
¼ pint (150 ml) beef stock
4 oz (100 g) sliced
 mushrooms
1 tablespoon tomato
 purée
2 teaspoons made mustard
¼ pint (150 ml) natural
 yogurt
Salt and pepper
1 tablespoon chopped
 parsley

Pour a little boiling water on the kidneys and leave them to soak for thirty minutes. Skin kidneys, cut them in half and remove the cores. Put into a pan with the stock, mushrooms and tomato purée. Cover and cook for twenty minutes. Stir in the mustard and yogurt, and season with salt and pepper to taste.

Put the kidneys into a ring of rice, spaghetti, noodles or mashed potatoes, and sprinkle with fresh parsley just before serving.

Serves 4

Yogurt and apricot flan

Pastry:

3 oz (75 g) butter
4 oz (100 g) plain flour
3 oz (75 g) ground
  almonds
2 oz (50 g) caster sugar
2 teaspoons water
1 egg yolk
Few drops of almond
  essence

Filling:

½ pint (300 ml) natural
  yogurt
2 egg yolks
2 oz (50 g) sugar
1 lb 13 oz (900 g) can
  apricot halves

To make the pastry, rub the butter into the flour until the mixture looks like fine breadcrumbs. Stir in the ground almonds and sugar. Mix the water, egg yolk and almond essence. Add to the rubbed-in mixture and mix to a stiff dough. Knead lightly on a floured surface, wrap in foil or greaseproof paper, and chill for at least an hour. Roll out on a floured surface and use to line a lightly greased 8 in (20 cm) flan ring.

Prick the base of the pastry and line with foil and baking beans. Bake at 375°F/190°C/Gas Mark 5 for ten minutes. Remove the foil and baking beans and bake for ten minutes until the base of the pastry is cooked.

To make the filling, combine the yogurt, egg yolks and sugar and spoon half the mixture into the flan case. Cook at 350°F/180°C/Gas Mark 4 for twenty minutes. Drain the apricot halves and place them on top, cut side downwards, and spoon the remaining yogurt mixture around them. Return to the oven for ten minutes. Serve hot or cold.

Lemon and honey whip

2 tablespoons lemon juice
2 tablespoons clear honey
¼ pint (150 ml) natural
  yogurt
1 egg white

Chill the yogurt before mixing the pudding. Mix the lemon juice, honey and yogurt. Whip egg white stiffly and fold in just before serving. Pile into four glasses and decorate with lemon slices.

Serves 4

Grapefruit whip

¼ pint (150 ml) natural
  yogurt
2 tablespoons freshly
  chopped mint
Juice of ½ grapefruit
Sugar to taste
1 egg white

Mix the chilled yogurt, mint, grapefruit juice and sugar. Whip egg white stiffly and fold in just before serving. Pile into glasses and decorate with sprigs of fresh mint.

Serves 4

Vegetables

First of the Season

Is there anything more rewarding than gathering the first early vegetables from the garden? At their best when simply cooked and served with crisp bacon or sweet ham, topped off with new bread, a lot of butter and some English cheese, they can also be used as 'starter' dishes on their own, to be followed by a more substantial meat or fish course.

There's no need to drown these tender young babies. Just cover them with water (and only just), cook them quickly, dress them with plenty of fresh butter, and the best of all seasonings – sea salt and freshly ground pepper.

Beetroot are nicest baked in foil on a rack in a moderate oven for an hour; they're done when the flesh yields and the skin slips off easily.

Broad beans should be cooked in boiling salted water for only fifteen minutes (thirty minutes as they get older when they are nicest with skins slipped off); the perfect herb to enhance broad beans is savory, used with a light hand.

French beans are best used very young so they can be cooked whole. Otherwise cut them in chunks (the same applies to *runner beans*, whose flavour is lost in shredding into water). Cook the beans with a lump of sugar and a pinch of salt in the water for just fifteen minutes; season with salt, pepper and a squeeze of lemon juice, or mix with a few tiny button mushrooms or shredded almonds.

Peas of course need sugar and salt in the cooking water, and most people like a hint of mint; cook the peas with the lid off.

Carrots only need scrubbing, and cooking in very little water, and are nice glazed before serving in a little butter with a sprinkle of brown sugar.

Turnips are best peeled thickly and cooked for twenty minutes in boiling salted water; they, too, can be glazed with a little meat extract dissolved in hot water and a pinch of sugar (particularly good with a piece of rare beef).

Potatoes: the first tiny ones like marbles, seem more precious than any other vegetable, with a subtle flavour so quickly lost as they swell to manageable proportions. Make the best of them by cooking in the skins in boiling salted water for fifteen minutes, removing the skins, and tossing in melted butter; it's a fiddling and finger-burning business, but worth the trouble. Those who love the flavour and texture of cold potato will enjoy new potatoes tossed in a little olive oil with salt and pepper and a sprinkling of green pepper and onion, then left to cool and take up the oil.

Freezer reminders

Broad beans: use small young beans with tender outer skins. Remove from shell, blanch $1\frac{1}{2}$ minutes, cool and pack in bags or cartons.

French beans: top and tail tender young beans without strings. Leave whole or cut into 1 in (2.5 cm) pieces. Blanch whole beans three minutes, cut beans two minutes. Cool and pack in bags or cartons.

Runner beans: use tender young beans cut in pieces. Do not shred finely, or result will be pulpy and tasteless. Blanch two minutes, cool and pack in bags or cartons.

Beetroot: use very young beetroot, not more than 3 in (7.5 cm) in diameter. Freeze very small ones whole, larger ones sliced or diced. Pre-cook, as short blanching and long storage makes them tough and rubbery. Cook in boiling water until tender, grading sizes so they are cooked through. Cool quickly in running water, rub off skins and pack, preferably in cartons.

Carrots: freeze only very young carrots. Wash thoroughly and scrape and blanch for three minutes. Pack whole, sliced or diced.

Parsnips: use small young parsnips, trim and peel, and cut into strips or dice. Blanch two minutes and pack in bags or cartons.

Peas: use young, sweet peas, not those which are old and starchy. Shell, and blanch one minute, lifting basket in and out of water to distribute heat evenly through layers. Chill and pack in bags or cartons.

Potatoes: scrape small new potatoes, blanch for four minutes, cool and pack in bags (at serving time, cook for fifteen minutes). Or, slightly undercook, drain, toss in butter, cool quickly and pack (at serving time, plunge freezing bag in boiling water, remove pan from heat and leave ten minutes).

Turnips : use small young mild turnips, trim and peel, and dice. Blanch 2½ minutes, cool and pack in bags or cartons.

Buttered carrots

1 lb (450 g) new carrots
2½ oz (65 g) butter
2 teaspoons sugar

Serves 4

Scrape carrots, wash and drain and cut into ¼ in (65 mm) slices. Melt 1½ oz (40 g) butter, and add a pinch of salt, carrots and sugar. Add water just to cover, bring to the boil and simmer uncovered until almost all liquid has evaporated and carrots are tender (about twenty-five minutes). Add remaining butter and a little finely chopped parsley.

Creamed broad beans

Good as an individual dish, or with ham or poultry.

2 lb (1 kg) young broad beans
4 oz (100 g) butter
1 teaspoon sugar
1 sprig savory
4 tablespoons double cream
1 egg yolk
Salt and pepper

Shell beans and boil ten minutes in salted water. Drain well. Melt butter, add sugar, savory, beans, salt and pepper. Cover and simmer gently for fifteen minutes. Remove from heat. Mix cream and egg yolk, and stir into beans. Test seasoning and serve.

Serves 4

Creamed beetroot

This is very good with beef. A grating of fresh horseradish is a delicious addition.

4 large beetroots
1½ oz (40 g) butter
¼ pint (150 ml) double cream
Salt and pepper

Cook the beetroot whole by boiling, or better still by baking at 325°F/170°C/Gas Mark 3 for an hour until tender. Peel and cut in slices. Heat butter until frothy, and reheat beetroot on a low heat for ten minutes. Put into serving dish. Heat cream gently in same pan, mixing with juices. Season with salt and pepper and pour over beetroot. Serve very hot.

Serves 4

Braised lettuce

This is very good with lamb. Most people are surprised at cooking lettuce, but it's a useful answer to the glut and delicious.

4 small well-hearted lettuce
1 small onion
1 rasher lean bacon
1 tablespoon olive oil
1 tablespoon butter
4 tomatoes
2 teaspoons chopped parsley
Salt and pepper
1 cube of sugar
Pinch of nutmeg

Wash the lettuce but keep them whole. Plunge into boiling salted water and bring water to boil again, then take out lettuce and drain them thoroughly. Heat oil and butter and add chopped bacon and onion, stir until lightly coloured, and add skinned and chopped tomatoes. Stir until the mixture begins to form a sauce, then put in lettuce, parsley and seasonings. Cover pan tightly and simmer very gently for thirty minutes. If liked add a dozen stoned olives before serving.

Serves 4

Spinach and eggs

A good way of treating a much-maligned vegetable, delicious when young. The secret lies in the short cooking time and the lack of cooking water.

1 lb (450 g) spinach
2 tablespoons thick cream
2 hard-boiled eggs

Wash the spinach very thoroughly, drain it well, and cook it without water for five minutes, adding a pinch of salt. Press the water out, and reheat gently; just before serving add cream and sliced eggs, and serve very hot.

Serves 4

Spring onions vinaigrette

These onions are good eaten hot or cold, and young leeks may be prepared in the same way.

1 bunch spring onions
Olive oil
Vinegar
Salt and pepper
Tarragon

Wash and trim the onions, and tie into a bundle. Cook until tender in boiling salted water. Mix a vinaigrette sauce, using two parts oil to one part vinegar, and season with salt, pepper and chopped tarragon. Serve the sauce separately.

Serves 4

Hot potato salad

Very good with fish or meat.

1 lb (450 g) new potatoes
4 tablespoons chutney
2 tablespoons wine
  vinegar

Serves 4

Cook potatoes in their skins, then peel and cut in dice. Warm them gently with chutney and vinegar, and season to taste if necessary.

Brandied carrots

1 lb (450 g) young carrots
4 oz (100 g) butter
1 teaspoon sugar
Salt
2 tablespoons brandy
  (optional)

Serves 4

Clean carrots and cut into thin slices. Melt butter in an ovenware dish, add sugar and salt, and put in the carrots. Pour over brandy (or water), cover tightly and cook in a moderate oven (350°F/180°C/Gas Mark 4) for an hour. Do not stir while cooking, but look at the carrots occasionally to see that they do not get hard and brown.

French peas

12 spring onions
1 sprig parsley
3 sprigs basil
Salt
½ teaspoon sugar
1 crisp lettuce
2 lb (1 kg peas) (in pods)
4 oz (100 g) butter

Serves 4

Put all the ingredients into a saucepan with half the butter, shredding the lettuce finely and shelling the peas. Add four tablespoons of water. Bring to the boil, cover and simmer over a low heat. When the peas are cooked take out the parsley and basil, and add the remainder of the butter to the saucepan.

Glazed turnips

12 young turnips
2 oz (50 g) butter
Salt and pepper
Granulated sugar
1 teaspoon meat extract

Serves 4

Peel the turnips and boil them in salted water until almost done. Drain and put into a frying pan with very hot butter to brown. Season well, adding the granulated sugar. When the turnips are well browned, drain off the fat and add the meat extract dissolved in four tablespoons hot water. Simmer until the turnips are glazed, and serve sprinkled with chopped parsley.

French beans in lemon butter

1 lb (450 g) French beans
3 oz (75 g) butter
1 tablespoon lemon juice
Salt and pepper

Serves 4

Cover beans with cold water and bring to the boil. Boil for two minutes only, then drain. Melt butter in a heavy saucepan, add lemon juice and plenty of salt and pepper, and four tablespoons water. Add the beans, cover and cook slowly for ten minutes.

Summer Salad Days

Crisp salad vegetables are delicious but all too often the English salad is a sad mixture of lettuce leaves, pippy tomatoes, bits of radish and cucumber, a spiking of spring onions, egg slices crumbling all over the place, and beetroot turning the whole mixture an unappetizing shade of pink. This kind of mixed salad is nearly always a disaster because its appearance deteriorates as various members of the family avoid the things they don't like and fork over the rest. It is much better to prepare the ingredients in separate bowls so that they look really refreshing and appetizing, and to offer a bowl of home-made dressing. Such a salad becomes a meal in itself, not just a dreary accompaniment to a slice of cold meat.

Green Salad

Wash lettuce thoroughly and drain in a salad shaker. Tear leaves but do not cut them. Put into a bowl rubbed with a cut clove of garlic. Slices of cucumber may be mixed with the lettuce, or a sprinkling of chopped fresh herbs – parsley or chervil, thyme, mint, chives. This salad is good with French dressing, which should be added just before serving.

French bean salad

2 lb (1 kg) cooked French
  beans
1 medium onion
4 tablespoons lemon juice
12 tablespoons salad oil
Salt and pepper
Chopped chives

Serves 4

Cut the beans into chunks for cooking. Cool and mix with finely chopped onion. Shake together the lemon juice, oil, salt and pepper and pour over the salad, then sprinkle with chives.

43

Yorkshire ploughman's salad

1 lettuce
Small handful of chives
1 saltspoon salt
1 saltspoon pepper
2 tablespoons vinegar
1 tablespoon black treacle

Wash the lettuce and drain and dry it well. Shred the lettuce and add finely chopped chives. Mix the salt, pepper, vinegar and treacle, and toss the lettuce just before serving.

Serves 4

Nutty salad

1 cabbage lettuce
4 oz (100 g) cooked peas
2 spring onions
1 teaspoon fresh parsley
3 teaspoons chopped nuts
French dressing

Use a really 'hearty' lettuce for this and cut the heart in quarters. Put into a bowl and sprinkle with the peas, chopped spring onions and parsley and nuts. Pour on French dressing.

Serves 4

Broad bean salad

Young broad beans
French dressing

Cook the beans and quickly slip them out of their skins. Cool and toss in French dressing. This is particularly good with cold pork or ham.

German potato salad

1 lb (450 g) potatoes
2 teaspoons grated onion
2 tablespoons hot bacon fat
1 slice crumbled fried bacon
French dressing

Cook potatoes, keeping them firm. Cut in cubes and mix with onion, bacon fat and bacon. Leave until cold, then toss in French dressing.

Serves 4

Tomato salad

Tomatoes
French dressing
Chopped mint or basil

Slice the tomatoes very thinly and put into a serving dish. Pour over French dressing and garnish with chopped mint or basil.

New potato salad

1 lb (450 g) small new potatoes
Chives
Parsley
French dressing
Salt and pepper

Cook the potatoes in their skins and peel them. When they are nearly cool, sprinkle thickly with chopped chives and parsley and pour on French dressing. Toss well before serving.

Serves 4

Carrot salad

This is very good with cold beef.

1 lb (450 g) new carrots
3 tablespoons white wine
  vinegar
1 small onion
2 bay leaves

Scrape the carrots and cook them until tender. Meanwhile, mix the vinegar, finely chopped onion and the bay leaves. Cool the carrots and pour over the dressing.

Serves 4

Cauliflower salad

Cauliflower
1 small onion
1 teaspoon fresh parsley
French dressing
Mustard

Cut the cauliflower into flowerets before cooking them until they are only just tender. Cool and mix with finely chopped onion and parsley, and French dressing with a little mustard.

Serves 4

Cucumber salad

The cucumber remains fresh and crisp, and may be served with other salads, with hot meat or fish dishes and with paté.

1 cucumber
$\frac{1}{4}$ pint (150 ml) white
  distilled vinegar
2 tablespoons water
2 tablespoons sugar
$\frac{1}{4}$ teaspoon salt
Dash of pepper
1 tablespoon chopped
  parsley

Slice the cucumber thinly without peeling. Mix together vinegar, water, sugar, salt and pepper and pour over the cucumber. Sprinkle with parsley, and leave in a very cold place for three hours before serving.

Serves 4

French dressing

2 parts oil
1 part vinegar
Salt and pepper

If you don't like olive oil, use salad oil. Lemon juice may be substituted for vinegar. Put the oil and vinegar into a screwtop jar with salt and pepper to taste and shake well before serving. Some people like to add a pinch of sugar and a little made mustard (particularly good with lettuce salad) or some chopped fresh herbs. The dressing will store in the refrigerator for about a week. Add it to the salad just before serving.

Salad cream

4 oz (100 g) butter
4 tablespoons plain flour
3 tablespoons sugar
1 tablespoon mustard
1½ pints (900 ml) milk
¾ pint (450 ml) vinegar
2 eggs

Melt the butter and take off the heat. Stir in the flour, sugar and mustard and work in the milk. Stir over a gentle heat until the mixture begins to thicken. Cool and then beat in the eggs and vinegar. This will keep for up to six weeks in a covered jar in the refrigerator.

Mayonnaise

1 egg yolk
¼ teaspoon salt
Pinch of pepper
½ teaspoon dry mustard
1 tablespoon vinegar
¼ pint (150 ml) olive oil
  or salad oil
1 tablespoon lemon juice

Mix together egg yolk and seasonings, then add vinegar. Beat oil into this, a few drops at a time. When the mixture has thickened, blend in the lemon juice.

Slowness is the operative word when making mayonnaise, as the too rapid addition of oil usually brings disaster. If the mixture curdles, put an egg yolk into a clean bowl, and add the mayonnaise very slowly. Keep mayonnaise in a cold place until serving, but not in a refrigerator.

Sour cream dressing

This dressing is excellent with potatoes, green salad or tomatoes. (A tablespoon of lemon juice will sour ¼ pint (150 ml) fresh cream.)

¼ pint (150 ml) sour
  cream
2 teaspoons finely
  chopped onion
¼ teaspoon salt
¼ teaspoon sugar
2 teaspoons grated
  horseradish
Dash of Tabasco sauce

Mix together all the ingredients and chill.

Winter Vegetables

The trick with using winter vegetables is to stop pretending they're just rather poor accessories to the meat course, to take a little extra trouble and spend a few pence more on butter, cream, bacon or mushrooms to transform the traditional 'two veg.' into luscious soups, tempting supper savouries, or piquant garnishes.

Potatoes

Instead of serving potatoes plain boiled, cut them in thin slices, dot with butter and cook them for the last half hour on top of the oven stew or mince. For the Sunday joint, put the thin slices under a joint of lamb so they cook in the meat juices. To serve with cold meat, layer thin slices of potato with melted butter, plenty of salt and pepper in an oven dish, pour on the cream from the top of a pint of milk, cover and bake in a moderate oven until browned, then cut the potatoes in wedges like a cake. Try lining a 2 lb (1 kg) loaf tin with about 2 lb (1 kg) of buttery mashed potato which has been blended with flour and a little milk to make a stiff dough. Fill the centre with minced meat and chopped leftover vegetables and top up with thick gravy; cover with more potato dough and bake in a moderate oven until golden brown. Try serving the last of the large 'oven-busters' baked in their jackets, the fluffy insides mashed up with a lot of butter, salt and pepper, and with a surprise bonus like a few ounces of flaked smoked haddock, or a grilled kidney wrapped in crisp bacon tucked into the centre.

Onions

Small onions are delicious when glazed and served with roast beef. Just toss them very gently in a pan, allowing 2 oz (50 g) butter and 2 oz (50 g) sugar, with salt and pepper, to each 1 lb (450 g) tiny onions; continue tossing until they are tender and well glazed. Really large onions can be boiled in salted water, then the centres hollowed out to be filled with savoury mince, and the onions finished off in a moderate oven with a glazing of good beef dripping, or some rich gravy. A delicious supper dish, or a first course for dinner can be a pastry flan case filled with sliced onions lightly poached in water, then mixed with slivers of bacon, plenty of herbs, salt and pepper, and finished with a mixture of two egg yolks beaten with the top of the milk, and a good knob of butter, then baked in a moderate oven for forty-five minutes. If you ever find a joint of mutton, serve it with onion sauce to which a tablespoon of cream and a pinch of mace have been added. You don't have to wait for mutton; the sauce is just as good with some thick grilled lamb chops. Pork chops are delicious if put on a bed of mixed chopped apple, onion and sage, and cooked in a moderate oven until done.

Leeks

Leeks are good in a flan, using pastry made with butter. Only use the white parts of 2 lb (1 kg) leeks, slice them thinly and toss in butter before putting in the pastry case. Cover them with a mixture of three egg yolks and $\frac{1}{4}$ pint (150 ml) single cream with plenty of salt and pepper, dot with butter, and bake in a moderate oven for forty minutes. Leeks, of course, give a subtle flavour to winter soups; try softening them in butter, then mixing with an equal quantity of diced raw potato and simmering in chicken stock until soft, sieving the soup and serving it very hot with a knob of butter and a grating of black pepper in each bowl. If you have some rather undersized leeks, poach them gently in water, drain and serve with an oil and vinegar dressing (three parts olive oil to two parts wine vinegar, salt and pepper).

Cabbage

Cabbage is at its best only lightly cooked, so it still has a 'bite', and it is excellent whipped up with mashed potato and served with slices of crisp bacon; a little chopped boiled onion can be added. For a simple supper savoury, try covering just-cooked cabbage in a rich cheese sauce flavoured with an onion and a bay leaf, then sprinkling with grated cheese and brown breadcrumbs before browning in the oven or under a hot grill. Cabbage soup is simply made if the cabbage is shredded finely and cooked gently in bacon or ham stock, then finished with a little butter and seasoning; another type of cabbage soup can be made if the shredded vegetable is first cooked lightly in butter, made into a purée, then simmered with milk, and finished with a little cream.

Cauliflower

Instead of the usual cauliflower cheese, try dressing the cooked vegetable with fresh white breadcrumbs fried until golden brown in butter, scattered with a chopped hard-boiled egg and a little chopped parsley. Another way of making a complete supper dish, is to cover the cauliflower with a white sauce containing a couple of chopped hard-boiled eggs and four rashers of chopped crisply fried bacon. Cauliflower is much nicer if cooked in flowerets rather than whole; if the little heads are only just tender, they are delicious tossed in a dressing of three parts olive oil to three parts vinegar, well seasoned and garnished with anchovy fillets (this makes a good winter salad).

Parsnips

Parsnips are not to everyone's taste as a vegetable, though they are vastly improved if cut into large dice, steamed and drained, then tossed in plenty of butter and sprinkled lightly with Demerara sugar before serving. They make an excellent supper soup if chopped and tossed in butter with pepper, salt and nutmeg, then mashed and heated with equal quantities of consommé or stock and milk, and served with plenty of cubed fried bread, toast and a bowl of grated cheese.

Turnips

Turnips arouse even stronger feelings than parsnips. Older ones are greatly improved by mashing into a thick white sauce finished with a little cream and a dash of sherry. To serve with beef, a casserole can be made by cubing 1 lb (450 g) turnips and putting in a casserole with 2 oz (50 g) butter, plenty of salt and pepper, a teaspoon of sugar and six tablespoons stock, cooking in a moderate oven until tender.

Carrots

Carrots are endlessly useful in stews, but they also can be cooked in a casserole like turnips. They are good combined with chopped celery in a white sauce, and particularly delicious if the sauce is made with chicken stock. To serve with the Sunday joint, try tossing them in butter in which a small onion has been finely chopped and cooked until golden; or glaze them in a heavy pan with a mixture of 4 oz (100 g) butter and 3 oz (75 g) brown sugar until the pieces of carrot are shiny.

Celery

Celery need not be plainly boiled: it is much nicer if cooked in consommé or stock in the oven; it's best to toss the chunks of celery in butter first, only add a spoonful of stock, season well and cook in a covered dish. If the celery is cooked in boiling salted water, then carefully drained and dressed with melted butter, salt, pepper and grated Parmesan cheese, grilled until the topping is golden and bubbling, you have a delicious vegetarian meal. Another supper savoury can be made by mixing 8 oz (225 g) grated Cheddar cheese with six sticks of finely chopped celery, 2 oz (50 g) self-raising flour, salt, pepper, nutmeg and an egg, then frying the mixture as little fritters until golden in butter.

Onion dumplings

8 oz (225 g) self-raising
  flour
4 oz (100 g) shredded suet
Pinch of salt
4 large onions
2–3 oz (50–75 g) cooked
  ham or bacon
1 tablespoon chopped
  parsley

Mix pastry with flour, suet, salt and enough cold water to make a firm paste. Roll out and cut into four large squares which will cover the onions. Scoop out the centre of each onion and fill with a mixture of finely chopped ham or bacon and parsley. Wrap each onion in a piece of suet pastry. Tie in cloths and boil for 1½ hours. Serve with a brown gravy.

Serves 4

Onion cake

1 lb (450 g) potatoes
8 oz (225 g) onions
4 oz (100 g) butter
Salt and pepper

Serves 4

Use a well-buttered cake tin. Peel the potatoes, slice them fairly thinly and arrange in a layer on the bottom of the tin. Sprinkle a layer of finely chopped onion on the potatoes, and add flakes of butter, salt and pepper. Continue in layers until the tin is full, finishing with a layer of potatoes and a few flakes of butter. Cover with a lid and bake at 350°F/180°C/Gas Mark 4 for one hour. Eat with hot or cold meat.

Baked cheese marrow

1 large marrow
4 oz (100 g) grated cheese
4 oz (100 g) breadcrumbs
1 teaspoon mixed herbs
Salt and pepper
Butter

Serves 4

Peel the marrow, steam until tender (testing with a skewer) and cut in thick slices, removing the seeds. Put into a greased baking dish, and sprinkle with a mixture of cheese, breadcrumbs, herbs and plenty of salt and pepper. Dot with butter and bake at 400°F/200°C/Gas Mark 6 until golden brown.

Stuffed onions

4 large onions
4 carrots
½ pint (300 ml) white
    sauce
2 oz (50 g) breadcrumbs
1 tablespoon butter
Salt and pepper

Serves 4

Boil the onions until they are tender and scoop out the centres carefully. Cook the carrots and cut them into small pieces. Dip them into melted butter, season with salt and pepper, and mix them with the scraped-out onion pieces. Put the whole onions into a buttered dish, fill with the mixture of carrots and onions, and pour on the white sauce. Sprinkle with the breadcrumbs and dot with a few bits of butter. Grate on a little nutmeg if you like. Put in the oven until the breadcrumbs are just brown, and serve very hot. You can add a little grated cheese and chopped parsley.

Leek pudding

4 oz (100 g) self-raising
    flour
2 oz (50 g) suet
Salt and pepper
2 leeks (or onions)

Serves 4

Sieve the flour and stir in suet and seasoning. Mix to a stiff dough with cold water. Roll out thinly and use two-thirds to line a greased pudding basin. Chop the leeks or onions, season with salt and pepper, and fill the centre, and top with a pastry lid (if preferred, simply mix the leeks with the suet pastry and put straight into the basin). Cover and boil in a pan of water for 2 hours. Serve in slices with meat dishes.

Cauliflower crown

2 small cauliflowers
½ pint (300 ml) white
    sauce
Buttered breadcrumbs
2 oz (50 g) walnut kernels

Serves 4

Cook the cauliflowers in very little salted water. Drain well and put one whole cauliflower in the centre of serving dish. Break the other into flowerets and put these round the dish. Pour over the white sauce and sprinkle well with breadcrumbs and finely chopped walnuts. Put into an oven set at 350°F/180°C/Gas Mark 4 until the crumbs are brown.

Red cabbage with apples

1 small red cabbage
2 cooking apples
1 small onion
3 tablespoons bacon fat
½ pint (300 ml) stock
3 tablespoons vinegar
1 tablespoon brown sugar
¼ teaspoon mixed spice
Salt and pepper

Shred cabbage finely and add thinly sliced apples. Slice the onion and cook until golden in bacon fat. Add to cabbage and apples together with stock and cook very gently with a lid on for 1½ hours. Add vinegar, sugar, spice and seasoning, and simmer for five minutes. Serve with pork or ham.

Serves 4

Carrots and celery in cider

This is particularly good with beef and with boiled bacon.

1 pint (600 ml) dry cider
1 lb (450 g) carrots
½ head celery
Salt and pepper
Chopped parsley

Serves 4

Bring the cider to boiling point. Prepare the vegetables and cut them into 2 in (5 cm) strips, using all the celery stalks. Put the carrots into the cider and boil gently for fifteen minutes. Add the celery, salt and pepper and cook for thirty minutes. Drain the vegetables and keep them hot. Boil up the cider until it has been reduced to about four tablespoonfuls. Pour over the vegetables and sprinkle with parsley.

Mushroom Meals

What would we do without mushrooms? Their price has changed little in the past few years, they are always in abundant supply, and their flavour turns a simple meal into a luxury dish. Another joy is that they need so little preparation, only a wipe to clean off any soil, and very short cooking.

Steak pockets

This is an expensive dish, but very good for a small party.

4 thick fillet steaks
2 oz (50 g) finely chopped onion
3 oz (75 g) finely chopped mushrooms
1 teaspoon French mustard
6 oz (175 g) whole mushrooms tossed in butter

Serves 4

Slit each steak to form a pocket. Toss the chopped mushrooms and onion in a little hot oil, add a little mustard and put this mixture into the pockets. Sew up firmly and brush the steaks with oil. Season well and cook quickly under a hot grill. Remove thread and serve on a hot dish, garnished with whole mushrooms.

Beef and mushroom casserole

1½ lb (700 g) stewing steak
4 oz (100 g) salted pork
1 large onion
3 shallots
2 leeks
3 carrots
1 garlic clove
Parsley, thyme and bay
    leaf
Beef stock
½ pint (300 ml) red wine
8 oz (225 g) button
    mushrooms

Cut steak and salted pork in dice. Cut onion, shallots, leek and carrots in large pieces. Crush the garlic, and toss the vegetables and garlic in a little hot fat. Toss steak and pork in fat, and put into casserole with vegetables. Pour in wine and enough stock to cover. Season well with salt and pepper. Cover tightly and cook at 300°F/150°C/Gas Mark 2 for three hours. If liked, thicken gravy with a little flour or corn-flour. Toss mushrooms in a little hot butter and serve as a border to the casserole. Garnish with chopped parsley.

Serves 4

Creamed field mushrooms

This simple dish is best made with field mushrooms and is very good for breakfast or supper. The mushrooms may be served with crisp bacon, or on toast.

Field mushrooms
Butter
Creamy milk
Salt and pepper

Wipe and slice the mushrooms and cook gently in a little butter until it is almost absorbed. Add a teacup of creamy milk and continue cooking for about ten minutes. Add a little more milk and cook two or three minutes longer, so the mushrooms are in a light creamy sauce. Season to taste.

Mushroom salad

Many people have not tried raw mushrooms, but they are delicious served as a salad, particularly with shellfish.

8 oz (225 g) mushrooms
8 tablespoons olive oil
2 tablespoons lemon juice
1 garlic clove
Salt and black
    peppercorns
Chopped parsley

Wipe mushrooms and slice thinly, including the stalks. Mix oil and lemon juice, crushed garlic and freshly ground black pepper. Pour over mushrooms. Leave for a couple of hours until they have absorbed most of the dressing. Just before serving, season with salt and sprinkle with chopped parsley.

Serves 4

Cheese and mushroom flan

6 oz (175 g) shortcrust
  pastry (recipe p. 97)
8 oz (225 g) mushrooms
1 oz (25 g) butter
¼ pint (150 ml) single
  cream
2 eggs and 1 egg yolk
2 oz (50 g) grated
  Parmesan cheese
Salt and pepper

Line an 8 in (20 cm) flan ring with pastry. Fry sliced or chopped mushrooms in butter. Beat up cream, eggs and egg yolk, and add drained mushrooms and cheese. Season with salt and pepper, and pour into pastry case. Sprinkle with a little cheese, and bake at 375°F/190°C/Gas Mark 5 for forty minutes.

Serves 4

Perfect Potatoes

Potatoes are marvellous for a cold winter evening, with a spot of crisp bacon or some boiled ham if meat is a bit short. Or how about a good winter potato salad of diced, cooked potatoes with grated raw onion, crumbled fried bacon, a spoonful of hot bacon fat, and a good dressing of oil and vinegar?

Really big potatoes – the oven-busters – make a meal on their own. They are a supper-time treat for the children, spin out the leftovers, and occupy that spare shelf when the oven is on. To serve them just cut the tops crosswise and squeeze them open, fill with knobs of butter, plenty of sea salt and a grind of black pepper. The jacket is often the best bit. For a complete meal, try a spoonful of thick cream and chives in the top, a kidney wrapped in bacon, chopped buttered mushrooms, cooked mince with a pinch of curry powder, grated cheese, scrambled eggs with plenty of chopped parsley, or cooked, flaked smoked haddock or kipper.

Another useful oven-filler, which cooks itself while you are doing something else, is the potato cake. Cut 1 lb (450 g) peeled potatoes into thin slices and put them in layers in a buttered oven dish, seasoning each layer with salt and pepper, and brushing with melted butter (about 2 oz (50 g) altogether). Cover with buttered paper and bake at 375°F/190°C/Gas Mark 5 for 1–1¼ hours until soft and golden. Turn out on a hot dish and cut in wedges to serve. (You could also add a little onion, or put in ½ pint (300 ml) creamy milk and a grating of cheese, but you won't be able to turn it out then.)

Everyone likes fried potatoes and real sauté potatoes are hard to beat. This easy method is a souvenir from a French girl who enjoyed a school holiday with us, and spent most of the summer turning out platefuls for a bunch of appreciative children. Peel the potatoes and cut into small cubes. Dry well in a tea towel and coat the cubes with flour. Put a few at a time into hot oil in a frying pan; they must not be covered with the oil. Turn often until nearly brown, and cooked inside. When they start to brown, turn heat down, put on a cover and turn occasionally.

Farmhouse potatoes

1½ lb (700 g) potatoes
4 oz (100 g) mushrooms
4 oz (100 g) grated cheese
8 fl.oz (225 ml) double cream
2 oz (50 g) butter
Salt and pepper
Chopped parsley

Serves 4

Peel the potatoes and cut into thin slices. Wash the mushrooms, dry them and cut into slices. Put the potatoes on a large sheet of foil, cover evenly with the mushrooms, sprinkle with the cheese, pour over the cream and dot with pats of butter. Season well with salt and pepper. Make a parcel with the foil and place in a roasting tin. Bake at 400°F/200°C/Gas Mark 6 for 1–1½ hours until the potatoes are cooked. Serve very hot, sprinkled with chopped parsley.

Poten ben fodi

This is a sort of Welsh washday dish, excellent for dealing with oddments from the weekend joint.

2 lb (1 kg) potatoes
8 oz (225 g) minced cooked meat
1 rasher bacon
1 medium onion
1 oz (25 g) butter
1 tablespoon wholemeal flour

Boil the potatoes and mash them with the butter and flour, then mix in the meat. Chop bacon and onion and cook in the fat which runs from the bacon until golden. Mix well into the potatoes, season to taste, and turn into a greased pie dish. Bake at 350°F/180°C/Gas Mark 4 for thirty minutes until the top is golden.

Serves 4

Rumbledthumps

1 lb (450 g) cooked cabbage
1 small onion
4 oz (100 g) Cheddar cheese
1 lb (450 g) mashed potatoes
Salt and pepper

Shred the cabbage, chop the onion and grate the cheese. Mix together with potatoes, cabbage, onion, salt and pepper, and put into a greased ovenproof dish. Cover with grated cheese and bake at 400°F/200°C/Gas Mark 6 until the cheese is golden.

Serves 4

55

Devonshire potato cake

Potatoes are a traditional country ingredient of light scones and cakes, and this is one of the most delicious recipes.

1 lb (450 g) boiled
  potatoes
2 oz (50 g) butter
2 oz (50 g) sugar
2 oz (50 g) dried fruit
Pinch of ground
  cinnamon
6 oz (175 g) self-raising
  flour

Sieve the potatoes while hot and add the butter, sugar, fruit and cinnamon. Knead in the flour to make a stiff dough, and roll out to a circle 1½ in (3.5 cm) thick. Shape into a round and mark into segments across the top, but do not cut right through. Place on a baking sheet and bake in a moderately hot oven, 375°F/190°C/Gas Mark 5 for thirty minutes. Sprinkle with caster sugar and serve hot.

Serves 4

Welsh potato cakes

Delicious hot – or cold potato cakes can be fried with the breakfast bacon.

1 lb (450 g) boiled
  potatoes
4 oz (100 g) plain flour
1 teaspoon baking powder
1 egg   .
1 oz (25 g) butter
1 tablespoon sugar
Pinch of salt

Mix all the ingredients except the butter. Melt the butter and mix thoroughly with the rest. Roll out 1 in (2.5 cm) thick. Bake on a girdle, or at 425°F/220°C/Gas Mark 7 for twenty minutes. Serve hot with a lot of butter.

Serves 4

Kidney potatoes

4 large potatoes
4 thin streaky bacon
  rashers
4 lambs' kidneys
Salt and pepper
1 oz (25 g) butter

Serves 4

Scrub the potatoes and rub salt into the skins. Bake at 350°F/180°C/Gas Mark 4 until just soft, which will take about 1¼ hours. Remove the rind and bone from the bacon rashers and flatten out the bacon with a flat-bladed knife. Skin and core the kidneys, and wrap each one in a rasher of bacon. Cut off the tops of the potatoes and scoop out enough potato to make room for the kidney. Season the insides with pepper and a knob of butter. Put in the kidneys and replace the tops. Return to the oven for a further twenty minutes or until the kidneys are cooked. After ten minutes, remove the lids to allow the bacon to become crisp. Serve very hot.

Champ

This is known as thump in Ireland, and another version, called colcannon, includes chopped boiled curly kale or cabbage. The Welsh version is a stwns, being a mixture of vegetables – potatoes and swedes; potatoes and peas; or potatoes and broad beans, sometimes with buttermilk poured over.

8 large potatoes
6 spring onions
½ pint (300 ml) milk
Salt and pepper
Butter

Let the peeled potatoes stand in cold water for an hour. Drain and cover with cold salted water, and boil until tender. Drain well and dry off by putting a folded cloth on top and returning the pot to a gentle heat for a few minutes. Chop the spring onions very finely, using the green tops as well as the bulbs, put them into a bowl and pour on boiling water to cover them, for five minutes. Drain the onions and add to the milk. Bring to the boil and pour on to the mashed potatoes, with pepper and salt to taste. When very light and fluffy, pile up on individual plates, making a well in the middle, and put a piece of butter in the 'well'. The potato is scooped up into the melted butter as it is eaten.

Serves 4

Boxty

2 large raw potatoes
12 oz (350 g) mashed potatoes
2 tablespoons plain flour
1 teaspoon bicarbonate of soda
1 teaspoon salt

Serves 4

Grate the raw potatoes and squeeze out the liquid. Add to the mashed potatoes and salt. Mix the soda with the flour and add to the potatoes. Roll out ½ in (1.25 cm) thick in a circle. Cut in four quarters and put on an ungreased girdle. Cook on gentle heat for thirty to forty minutes, turning bread once. The farls or quarters should be well browned on both sides. A teaspoon of caraway seeds can be added to the dough.

Stovies

Serve with roast beef or a casserole.

1 oz (25 g) bacon fat or dripping
8 oz (225 g) onions
2 lb (1 kg) potatoes
½ pint (300 ml) hot water
Salt and pepper

Melt the fat. Slice and fry onions without browning. Add sliced potatoes, hot water and seasoning. Cover and cook slowly for 1–1½ hours, stirring and shaking the pan occasionally to prevent burning.

Serves 4

Pan haggerty

2 lb (1 kg) potatoes
1 lb (450 g) onions
1 tablespoon dripping
3 oz (75 g) grated cheese
Salt and pepper

Serves 4

Cut the potatoes and onions in slices. Melt the dripping in a heavy frying pan. Put in layers of potatoes, onions and grated cheese, seasoning each layer. Fry gently until brown. Keep a lid on the pan until the vegetables are cooked right through.

Increase your Pulse Rate

The taste for pulses – dried peas and beans – seems to have died, yet pulses provide tasty eating, they are full of protein and can fortify a meal when meat is short. It is worth looking at the seed catalogues a bit more carefully to see which varieties are suitable for home-drying, but if you have to rely on shops, look for the varieties of peas and beans which are packed loose, particularly in health food shops. The most traditional types of lentils and beans are also sold in boxes by most grocers. Soak them in plenty of water for twenty-four hours, then simmer until tender before adding salt. They can be used as a plain vegetable with butter, or put into a curry sauce or a parsley sauce.

A lot of people think of pulse dishes as being fit only for vegetarian cranks, but many of our traditional dishes are based on these dried vegetables. Many northerners still enjoy a 'mushy pea'. Pulses are even packed under that name in the frozen food cabinets, for those who cannot be bothered with traditional soaking and slow cooking.

Butter bean roll

1 lb (450 g) cooked butter
  beans
6 oz (175 g) cheese
1 onion
4 oz (100 g) fresh
  breadcrumbs
1 oz (25 g) butter
Salt, pepper and nutmeg

Serves 4

Soak the beans for twenty-four hours, and cook until tender. Put the cooked beans and the cheese through a mincer. Grate the onion and soften by cooking in 1 oz (25 g) butter. Add 2 tablespoons water. Remove the onion, and mix it with the breadcrumbs, beans and cheese, and plenty of seasoning. Form into a roll and place in a baking dish. Brush over with the butter and water from the frying and scatter with a few more breadcrumbs. Bake at 350°F/180°C/Gas Mark 4 for an hour, adding a little hot dripping if it seems a little dry. Serve with gravy or mushroom sauce.

Pork and pea soup

This is almost a stew and excellent for cooking in a slow oven. It can be served in the iron or earthenware casserole in which it has been cooked. You only need some crusty bread for a complete meal. If trotters are not available, or do not appeal to you, use a bit of belly pork, or ask the butcher for a hock, or hand and spring, which are often cheap. There will then be enough meat to serve cold for a second day as well.

8 oz (225 g) split peas
Pinch of salt
2 pig's trotters
4 onions or leeks
2 oz (50 g) butter

Soak the peas in 4 pints (2.5 l) of water overnight. Simmer slowly in the same water for two hours and add salt. Put through a sieve, then simmer the pig's trotters or meat in this liquid for an hour. Add chopped onions or leeks and butter, and continue simmering until tender. Adjust seasoning and add pepper to taste. Serve very hot.

Serves 4

Pease pudding

Serve with boiled or roast pork, boiled bacon or boiled beef.

1 lb (450 g) split peas
Salt and pepper
½ oz (15 g) butter

Serves 4

Put the peas into a clean cloth, leaving them plenty of room to swell, and tie ends of cloth together. Put in cold water and boil until tender, which should take about 2½ hours. Take them out of the cloth, sieve and season well. Beat for five minutes with the butter, put into a floured cloth, tie tightly and boil again for forty-five minutes.

A richer pudding used to be made with the addition of two beaten eggs and 2 oz (50 g) dripping to sieved peas. Another version mixes the mashed peas with seasoning, chopped onion and dripping, and then bakes the 'pudding' in a hot oven for thirty minutes to serve with cold meat. It must have been a staple dish for many families, judging by the old rhyme:

Pease pudding hot, pease pudding cold,
Pease pudding in the pot nine days old.

Lentil or pea soup

6 oz (175 g) lentils or peas
1 carrot
1 small turnip
1 onion
1 oz (25 g) dripping
Salt and pepper

Serves 4

Wash the lentils or peas and if possible soak them overnight, in 2 pints (1 l) water. Melt the dripping and cook the chopped vegetables until soft. Add the lentils or peas and make up the liquid to 2 pints (1 l) again with water, or some stock. Simmer for two hours.

The soup may be sieved or not, as preferred. Season well and serve with squares of toasted or fried bread and a sprinkling of chopped parsley. A little chopped ham is a good topping.

Bean curry

This is good if served over hard-boiled eggs, with some plainly boiled rice.

4 oz (100 g) haricot beans
½ oz (15 g) butter
1 small apple
1 teaspoon flour
½ teaspoon ginger
1 teaspoon curry powder
½ teaspoon brown sugar
Squeeze of lemon juice
Salt

Soak the beans, then boil them until tender, retaining the water. Chop the peeled apple and fry it in the butter until soft. Stir in the flour, ginger and curry powder, sugar, salt and cooked beans. Add ½ pint (300 ml) water in which the beans were cooked and season with salt. Bring to the boil and simmer for thirty minutes. Add the lemon juice.

Serves 4

Potato and bean salad

This is a good winter salad when greenstuff is short.

1 lb (450 g) cooked
    potatoes
4 oz (100 g) cooked butter
    beans
1 teaspoon finely chopped
    onion
1 oz (25 g) chopped nuts
    or celery
Salt and cayenne pepper
Chopped parsley
Mayonnaise

Chop the potatoes neatly and mix with the beans, onion, nuts or celery. Season with salt and cayenne pepper and toss lightly in mayonnaise. Sprinkle with chopped parsley.

Serves 4

Fish

Delicious Fish

Why do so many of us find it difficult to include much fish in our meal-planning? Once a week is usually about as much as we manage, and even that one meal is seldom anything more adventurous than the favourite fish and chips, or a bit of smoked haddock.

For many of us in the country, it's a problem of finding a good supplier within easy distance. Second big problem is that some men imagine they don't find fish filling enough, and tend to look searchingly at their plates and ask plaintively what there is for the meat course. The supply problem may be solved to a certain extent by using frozen fish: a little time and trouble can produce a tasty dish. That same time and trouble may be needed with the fresh variety, too, to persuade the family they are eating a real meal and not just a prelude to the main course.

Make even simple fish dishes colourful, serving them with carrots, peas or tomatoes and add an easy garnish of parsley, watercress, lemon wedges or radishes. A sauce does wonders for fish (cheese, mushroom and home-made tomato sauce are particularly good), and cold fish gives an opportunity to show off a good mayonnaise. If you can't be bothered to go that far, just garnish with butter flavoured with lemon or parsley. Above all, never over-cook fish – that will make it dry and tough. Whole fish and fish on the bone are cooked when the flesh comes away cleanly from the bone; fillets and cutlets are cooked when you see a creamy white substance oozing out between the flakes.

Kipper grill

1 lb (450 g) kipper fillets
2 oz (50 g) butter
2 oz (50 g) plain flour
1 pint (600 ml) milk
2 egg yolks
2 teaspoons made mustard
6 oz (175 g) grated
   Cheddar cheese
2 tablespoons chopped
   capers
Pepper

Serves 4

Cook kipper fillets, drain and flake them. Melt butter, add flour and cook for one minute without browning. Remove from heat and gradually add milk. Return to heat and bring to boil, stirring well for two minutes. Add beaten egg yolks, mustard, 4 oz (100 g) of the cheese and pepper, and heat very gently just to melt cheese. Stir in flaked kippers and capers and put mixture into shallow 1 pint (600 ml) dish. Sprinkle with cheese and brown under grill.

Cheese-topped cutlets

4 cod cutlets
6 oz (175 g) grated cheese
1 small finely chopped
    onion
1 oz (25 g) butter
Juice of a lemon
Mixed herbs
Salt and pepper

Serves 4

Wash and dry cutlets. Season each with salt and pepper and a squeeze of lemon. Mix cheese, onion, herbs and remaining lemon juice and form into four balls. Place one on each cutlet with a small knob of butter. Cook seven minutes under a hot grill, and serve with a wedge of tomato and sprig of parsley, and creamy mashed potatoes. The cheese must be formed in balls or it will melt before the fish is cooked.

Cod skewers

Serve with salad and buttered boiled rice.

1½ lb (750 g) thick cod or
    coley fillet
1 small green pepper
4 small onions
2 tomatoes
4 button mushrooms
2 oz (50 g) melted butter
Salt and paprika

Serves 4

Cut fish into large cubes. Blanch green pepper and onions by pouring on boiling water and leaving for five minutes. Drain and cut the pepper into cubes. Cut the tomatoes into quarters. Thread fish cubes, vegetables and bay leaves on to four long skewers and brush with melted butter. Season with salt and paprika and grill under moderate heat for six to eight minutes, turning carefully once and brushing with more butter. Sprinkle with chopped parsley before serving.

Fish salad with chive dressing

4 cod or coley fillets
¼ pint (150 ml) milk
Salt and pepper
Juice of 1 lemon
Salad greens

Dressing:
¼ pint (150 ml) thick
    mayonnaise
1 tablespoon chopped
    gherkins
1 tablespoon chopped
    capers
2 tablespoons chopped
    chives
1½ tablespoons vinegar
1 teaspoon lemon juice

Clean fish, cut into portions and put into shallow baking dish. Season well with salt and pepper and a squeeze of lemon juice, pour over milk and cover dish with lid or foil. Bake at 350°F/180°C/Gas Mark 4 for twenty minutes. Remove fish from dish and leave to cool, then place cold fish on salad greens. Make dressing by adding vinegar and lemon juice to mayonnaise and adding chopped gherkins, capers and chives. Pour a little dressing over fish, and serve the rest of the dressing separately.

Serves 4

Mackerel in foil

4 mackerel
Salt and pepper
2 tomatoes
1 lemon
Parsley
1 oz (25 g) butter

Serves 4

Clean fish and remove heads. Season well with salt and pepper. Put each fish on a piece of buttered kitchen foil. Cut tomatoes and lemon into slices and arrange on fish, put a piece of parsley on each, and dot with butter. Fold foil into neat parcels. Put parcels on baking sheet and bake at 350°F/180°C/Gas Mark 4 for thirty minutes. Serve in foil, or transfer to serving dish together with cooking juices.

Whiting with mustard sauce

This is very good with rather floury boiled potatoes.

4 whiting
Salt and pepper
2 small shallots
1 tablespoon French mustard
4 tablespoons dry white wine
Juice of ½ lemon
1 oz (25 g) butter
1 tablespoon finely chopped parsley

Put fish in buttered oven dish and season with salt and pepper. Chop shallots very finely and scatter over fish. Blend together mustard and wine and pour over fish. Cover and bake at 350°F/180°C/Gas Mark 4 for twenty minutes. Pour cooking liquid into saucepan, add lemon juice and heat three minutes, stirring well; add butter and chopped parsley, and pour over fish.

Serves 4

Home-made rollmops

These are particularly good with a potato salad and shredded raw cabbage.

6 boned and cleaned herrings
Brine (2 oz (50 g) salt and 1 pint (600 ml) water)
1 pint (600 ml) white distilled vinegar
1 tablespoon mixed pickling spice
4 medium onions (sliced in rings)
1 chilli pepper
1 bay leaf

Soak herrings in brine for two hours. Prepare spiced vinegar by slowly bringing to the boil vinegar and mixed spice. Remove from heat and leave to infuse for thirty minutes, then strain and cool. Roll up each herring, skin side outside, including a few shredded raw onion rings with each herring. Pack into a wide-necked jar, add chilli and bay leaf. Cover with spiced vinegar. Cover and leave for five or six days before serving.

6 rollmops

Baked stuffed haddock

Serve with mashed potatoes and a garnish of lemon slices.

2 medium haddock
2 oz (50 g) butter
1 onion
2 oz (50 g) mushrooms
4 oz (100 g) dry
  breadcrumbs
1 egg

Remove the head and fins from the fish and trim the tail. Make an incision with a sharp knife down the back of the fish. Melt the butter and fry the chopped onion and mushrooms, add the breadcrumbs, and mix all the ingredients together. Put the stuffing in the cavity of each fish, and put fish in a buttered roasting tin. Bake at 400°F/200°C/Gas Mark 6 for thirty minutes.

Serves 2

Stuffed plaice

Serve very hot with mashed potatoes and a cream sauce.

4 large fillets skinned
  plaice
Salt and pepper
4 rounded tablespoons
  parsley and thyme
  stuffing
1 tablespoon chopped
  parsley
2 tablespoons melted
  butter
Grated rind and juice
  of $\frac{1}{2}$ lemon
4 thin rashers streaky
  bacon

Season plaice with salt and pepper. Put stuffing, parsley, salt and pepper, butter, lemon rind and juice into a basin and add enough boiling water to give a fairly stiff mixture. Spread stuffing over the skinned side of each fillet and roll up carefully. Remove rind from bacon and roll each fillet in bacon. Put a sheet of foil on a baking tin and grease the centre with a little melted butter. Put the fillets in the middle of the foil, making sure the ends of the bacon are underneath. Fold over foil to make a loose parcel, and bake in the centre of the oven (400°F/200°C/Gas Mark 6) for forty minutes.

Serves 4

Lemon cod

4 cod fillets
3 large onions
2 oz (50 g) butter
1 lemon
Bay leaf
Chopped parsley

Serves 4

Put cod fillets in a buttered oven dish. Slice the onions very thinly and put in a saucepan with very little water. Quickly boil this water away and stir in butter. Cover the fish with onion rings, seasoning with salt and pepper. Cut half the lemon, remove the peel and cut flesh into thin slices. Put these slices and the bay leaf on to the cod. Cover with greaseproof paper and bake at 375°F/190°C/Gas Mark 5 for twenty minutes. Serve with juice squeezed from the rest of the lemon, and with chopped parsley sprinkled over.

Fish and mushroom bake

1 lb (450 g) cod or
    haddock fillet
Squeeze of lemon juice
1 oz (25 g) butter
4 oz (100 g) button
    mushrooms
1 egg
½ pint (300 ml) milk
    infused with 1 slice of
    onion
Bay leaf, thyme and
    parsley
1 oz (25 g) butter
¾ oz (20 g) plain flour
1 lb (450 g) potatoes
1 oz (25 g) grated cheese

Put fish in an oven dish with lemon juice, cover with a buttered paper and cook at 350°F/180°C/Gas Mark 4 for fifteen minutes. Toss mushrooms in hot butter. Make a sauce with milk, herbs, butter and flour, and stir in beaten egg, mushrooms and fish. Put into baking dish, and cover with potatoes cooked and mashed to a purée with some hot milk and a knob of butter. Scatter with grated cheese and brown in a hot oven.

Serves 4

Orange pickled herrings

Serve with watercress
and orange tossed in
French dressing.

4 large herrings
1 large orange
¼ pint (150 ml) white
    vinegar
2 bay leaves
1 small sliced onion
4 peppercorns
1 teaspoon salt

Fillet herrings, wash them, and roll up firmly, securing with a cocktail stick. Put herrings into a deep casserole dish with thinly peeled orange rind, vinegar, bay leaves, onion, peppercorns, salt and ¼ pint (150 ml) cold water. Cover the dish with foil and cook in the centre of the oven at 375°F/190°C/Gas Mark 4 for thirty minutes. Leave to cool in liquid, then drain.

Serves 4

Stuffed mackerel

Serve with green salad.

4 mackerel
4 oz (100 g) mushrooms
1 cooking apple
2 medium slices brown
    bread
1 lemon
Salt and pepper
Pinch of basil
1 egg
Oil

Split and bone mackerel. Put mushrooms, apple and bread through the mincer, and add salt, pepper, basil, and juice and grated rind of lemon. Bind with the egg. Put stuffing in mackerel and close up. Put in baking dish, sprinkle with salt and pepper and a little oil. Cover with greased paper and bake at 325°F/170°C/Gas Mark 3 for forty-five minutes.

Serves 4

Baked haddock in cider

Serve with mashed potatoes and peas.

2 lb (900 g) haddock
Salt and pepper
1 lemon
Small chopped onion
Crushed garlic clove
1 tablespoon olive oil
¼ pint (150 ml) water
½ pint (300 ml) dry cider
1 tablespoon chopped
    parsley
8 oz (225 g) sliced
    tomatoes

Put a tail-end of haddock in a baking dish. Sprinkle with salt and pepper and juice from half the lemon. Fry onion and garlic in oil until tender, then stir in water and simmer for five minutes. Pour over fish and add cider, remaining lemon cut in slices, parsley and tomatoes. Bake at 350°F/180°C/Gas Mark 4 for forty-five minutes.

Serves 4

Plaice in cheese sauce

4 large plaice fillets
2 tomatoes
1 small onion
½ red or green pepper
2 in (5 cm) piece of
    cucumber
1 oz (25 g) butter
1 oz (25 g) flour
¾ pint (450 ml) milk
3 oz (75 g) grated
    Cheddar cheese

Serves 4

Butter a shallow fireproof dish and put in fish. Chop roughly tomatoes, onion, pepper and cucumber and sprinkle on the fish. Season lightly with salt and pepper and with a sprinkling of fresh herbs (basil or parsley are good with this). Cover with greaseproof paper and bake at 350°F/180°C/Gas Mark 4 for twenty-five minutes. Melt butter, work in flour and milk and cook until thick and creamy. Add almost all the cheese, stir until melted and pour sauce over fish. Sprinkle with remaining cheese and return to oven, or put under grill until golden.

Super fish pie

1 lb (450 g) haddock or
    cod
2 hard-boiled eggs
2 oz (50 g) shrimps
1½ oz (40 g) butter
¾ oz (20 g) flour
½ pint (300 ml) milk
Salt and pepper
1½ lb (750 g) mashed
    potatoes

Serves 4

Put fillets or cutlets in a fireproof dish. Sprinkle with salt and pepper and dot with a little butter. Cover and bake at 350°F/180°C/Gas Mark 4 for twenty-five minutes. Remove skin and bones and flake fish, reserving liquid. Melt butter, stir in flour and add milk and liquid. Season and cook until thick and smooth. Put a little sauce in a fireproof dish, add a layer of fish with a few shrimps, some slices of egg and some sauce. Add remaining fish, shrimps, egg and sauce. Top with mashed potato. Cook at 350°F/180°C/Gas Mark 4 for twenty-five minutes and serve hot with watercress.

Meat

The Roast with the Most

Most families like a traditional joint at least once a week, but lazy cooking often results in a tough, under-done piece of meat or a crisp, grey lump with the attendant potatoes in a corresponding state of greasy softness or rock-hard brownness. It's all too easy to throw a joint into a roasting tin with a lump of dripping and a border of potatoes and trust to luck.

Before a joint can be successfully roasted, there are a number of factors to consider. Firstly, the type of meat such as beef, lamb, mutton, pork or veal. Secondly the cut, and every family has its favourite. Thirdly the amount of fat. Finally, the age and probable ancestry of the meat, and the length of time it has been hung. Only a friendly and well-trained butcher can help you, and there was never a more true shopping maxim than 'Make a friend of your butcher'.

In roasting, everything is done to preserve the dry quality of the heat, and meat should be cooked on a rack which allows air to circulate. Potatoes are best cooked separately in a few spoonfuls of pan drippings. To start the joint, just rub a little fat over the pan. Very lean meat may be larded with lengths of fat, or brushed with melted fat or oil, and then basted, but in top quality meat which has a good fat content, there is sufficient moisture in the meat, and no basting is necessary. Stock or water used in the pan creates excess steam and spoils the flavour. The best and safest method of basting is with a bulb-type baster rather than a spoon.

There are many theories about times and tempera-tures in roasting, but I feel that the flavour is best retained by quick browning, followed by cooking at medium heat. Be sure the meat is wiped dry, and use very little fat to brown the meat. Put it on a rack in a roasting pan into an oven pre-heated to 500°F/ 250°C/Gas Mark 10. After three minutes, reduce the heat to 350°F/180°C/Gas Mark 4 and cook for the required method. This initial hot searing of the meat seals in the juices: no basting is needed, and there is little pan juice. It is a particularly suitable method for really choice meat.

A really labour-saving and trouble-free method of roasting is to employ a meat thermometer, little used in this country. This is marked with the various temperatures and degrees of doneness for various joints. The thermometer is inserted right into the meat on the rack, put into the preheated oven, and checked from time to time until the correct temperature is recorded. If you do not use a meat thermometer, a 'touch test' will help to assess the doneness of the meat. If the meat feels firm, it is well done. If it responds like a cake, soft but resilient, the meat is medium rare. Pricking meat loses valuable juices, but if this is done, the meat is rare when the juice is red, medium rare when pink, and well done when colourless. Pork and fowl with light meat must be cooked until the juice is colourless, but most other meats are overdone at this point.

Timing in meat cookery must be a matter of choice depending on the doneness required. At the moderate temperature, beef needs twenty-five minutes per lb (450 g), but for a rare joint take off five minutes per lb (450 g). Lamb needs thirty minutes per lb (450 g) as this meat is usually preferred a little more cooked than beef; but it should not be overcooked, and should have a faint pinkness. Pork and veal must always be very well cooked so they need thirty-five minutes per lb (450 g).

If the joint has been carefully prepared to eat hot, it will also be very good cold. A joint brushed with salad oil, then liberally rubbed with dry mustard and sprinkled with pepper, salt and flour, will have a delicious brown and tender crust. While meat roasted on the bone has the reputation of being sweetest, a boned joint can be stuffed to extend the meat and make more servings.

A roast joint can be made more attractive by basting with a mixture which will give a rich glaze. A $\frac{1}{4}$ pint (150 ml) of fruit juice blended with a tablespoon each of brown sugar and made mustard and a spoonful or two of the pan dripping should be spooned over the roast twice during the last thirty minutes of cooking.

Well-chosen accompaniments add to the pleasure of a good joint. Yorkshire pudding and mustard, of course, with beef; mint sauce with lamb; redcurrant jelly with mutton; orange or apple with pork and veal. A quick piquant sauce for any hot roast can be made by whipping one tablespoon made mustard with three tablespoons redcurrant jelly. A creamy gravy is very good with veal or lamb, made by adding milk instead of water to the flour stirred into the pan drippings. Hot fruits are a very good extra, such as hot peach slices with baked ham, hot pineapple slices with lamb, and hot orange slices with veal. Everyone knows how good small baked apples are with pork, but they are equally good with beef.

After taking the roast from the oven stand it for fifteen to twenty minutes before carving; it will cut better and hold the juices.

Lamb from Top to Tail

Whether lamb is for the family or for a party, there are far more cuts than leg and shoulder. The loin, for instance, most usually asked for in the form of chops, can also be roasted whole, though there is a high proportion of fat. The joint can be divided into two sections, middle loin and chump end. A double loin, cut right across the spine, is the saddle. This is a large joint, but makes a superb roast for a party. A double loin chop, cut in the same way across the backbone, is considered by the knowledgeable to be the finest chop for a gourmet meat-lover.

The leg need not only be used for plain roasting, and a 'dressed-up roast' is particularly useful for the sort of dinner party where roast meat is formally correct, but your personal opinion is that it is rather dull. The leg can be divided into shank and fillet, with the shank used for braising, stews or pies. The fillet is lean and delicious when roasted, grilled or fried in slices. This is the easiest piece to cut in cubes for threading on skewers as kebabs which are a great favourite with children and all experimental eaters, and an excellent way of serving meat at a party.

The shoulder is also used for kebabs, and the greater proportion of fat bastes the meat during grilling and prevents the other ingredients from drying out. The shoulder can be divided into pieces for roasting, braising or pot-roasting. A boned shoulder of lamb with its good proportion of fat and lean is delicious stuffed, when the fat is absorbed into the stuffing. I find a good way of doing this is to put a piece of thin gammon down the centre of the boned meat, and then add the stuffing, as the bacon flavour points up the blandness of the lamb. Another idea with a lean shoulder is to fill the cavity with whole lambs' kidneys, well salted and peppered, and this does make the meat go a long way without using a heavy and filling stuffing.

The neck end of lamb, so often lumped together in one rather anonymous piece, can in fact be divided into three. Best end of neck is fine for grilling and makes the small meat cutlets which are so acceptable to those who like only a small quantity of choice meat; this is also the cut to buy for Lancashire hotpot. Middle-neck makes good casseroles and stews (the best cut for Irish stew), and can be cut into inexpensive chops. Scrag end of neck has little meat, but is good for soups and stews with plenty of flavour, and the meat can be taken from the bones for curries and goulash. Breast of lamb is very fatty, but very cheap. It is too fatty for some people to eat at all, but the flavour is excellent and the meat tender. The usual method of dealing with it is by boning, stuffing and roasting. A traditional French way of cooking the breast is to simmer the cut gently until tender, then bone and put under weights. When the meat is cold, it is cut into cubes, dipped in egg and breadcrumbs and fried crisply.

Lamb's offal is particularly delicious in flavour, and kidneys, liver, tongue and sweetbreads are all easy to prepare, very nourishing and useful for those on a diet who must eat lean meat. Most people serve tongue cold, but hot lambs' tongues are delicious cut in neat slices and served with a mushroom sauce or a rich spicy gravy.

Lamb must be either very hot or very cold, as lamb fat congeals quickly, and makes the meat taste positively unpleasant when lukewarm. Don't over-roast or the flesh will be dry and tough, but allow thirty minutes a lb (450 g) at 350°F/180°C/Gas Mark 4. The inevitable mint sauce usually drowns and spoils good lamb, and redcurrant jelly and onion sauce are traditional with mutton. Try using rosemary or garlic during roasting instead, and serve subtle-tasting mint jelly rather than sauce, with perhaps grilled pineapple slices.

Hot pot

Serve with pickled red cabbage or crumbled Lancashire cheese.

1½ lb (750 g) potatoes
1½ lb (750 g) neck of mutton
2 large onions
2 sheep's kidneys
Salt and pepper
½ pint (300 ml) stock

Trim meat and cut into neat pieces. Peel potatoes thinly and slice ¼ in (60 mm) thick. Slice onions and kidneys thinly. Put layers of meat and vegetables into a greased casserole, seasoning well and finishing with a layer of potatoes. Add stock, cover and bake at 325°F/170°C/Gas Mark 3 for 2½ hours, removing lid for last thirty minutes to brown potatoes, adding a few flakes of dripping or butter to prevent potatoes drying out.

Serves 4

Lamb and bean casserole

1 lb (450 g) best end neck of lamb
Dripping
3 large onions
8 oz (225 g) haricot beans
4 large carrots
Salt, pepper and rosemary
1 tablespoon tomato purée

Soak beans overnight. Trim meat, and dredge lightly with flour. Melt dripping and soften finely chopped onions, then brown meat. Put in casserole with sufficient water to cover, the drained beans, carrots cut in pieces, salt, pepper, a sprig of rosemary and tomato purée. Cover tightly and cook at 300°F/150°C/Gas Mark 2 for 2½ hours.

Serves 4

Spiced lamb roast

1 leg lamb
1 garlic clove
2 tablespoons plain flour
Salt and pepper
¼ pint (150 ml) bottled
  sauce (a brand like HP,
  or a home-made plum
  sauce)
2 tablespoons tomato
  sauce
1 tablespoon vinegar
2 tablespoons chopped
  mint

Rub meat with the cut garlic clove, and coat with flour, salt and pepper. Mix sauces, vinegar and mint and brush over meat. Wrap in aluminium foil and cook for thirty minutes a lb (450 g) at 350°F/180°C/Gas Mark 4, turning the joint every half hour. Serve with its own sauce and thick crusty bread.

Serves 4

Lamb skewers

1½ lb (750 g) lamb
  shoulder
¼ pint (150 ml) French
  dressing
1 garlic clove
8 oz (225 g) button
  mushrooms
4 bacon rashers
Salt and pepper

Serves 4

Cut lamb in 1 in (2.5 cm) cubes, and leave in French dressing for an hour, together with the split garlic clove. Cut bacon in 1 in (2.5 cm) pieces, and thread lamb, mushrooms and bacon alternately on skewers (turkey skewers are ideal for this), allowing a little space between each piece. Season with salt and pepper, and grill about 3 in (7.5 cm) from heat for fifteen minutes, turning to brown evenly. Chunks of green pepper, slices of kidney and pineapple pieces may also be used on the skewers, and a small firm tomato used at the end of each one. Serve with plain boiled rice.

Seven-hour lamb

5 lb (2.5 kg) leg of lamb
½ veal knuckle
Oil
2 pints (1 l) beef stock
10 large onions
1½ oz (40 g) butter
10 tomatoes
Salt and pepper

Wipe the leg of lamb and brown on all sides in hot oil. Cover with hot beef stock and season with salt and pepper. Bring back to the boil, reduce to low heat, cover and simmer for four hours (the bottom oven of an Aga can be used for this). Put the veal knuckle into a separate pan, cover with hot water and simmer.
  After four hours' simmering, add the knuckle to the lamb. Add thickly sliced onions which have been softened in the butter, and peeled and quartered tomatoes. Add to lamb, cover and continue simmering for three hours. To serve carefully lift lamb on to serving dish. Remove knuckle from sauce. Adjust seasoning, and if sauce is liquid, reduce by boiling (it should be quite thick, but not strained). Serve with this sauce and rice.

Stuffed lamb chops

6 thick chump chops with
all bones removed
4 oz (100 g) fresh
breadcrumbs
1 tablespoon chopped
parsley
1 tablespoon chopped
thyme
4 oz (100 g) mushrooms
tossed in butter
Salt and pepper
1 tablespoon lemon juice
1 egg

Make a slit in each chop to form a pocket.
Blend all other ingredients, chopping the
mushrooms finely. Fill the pocket of each chop.
Put into shallow baking tin and cover with foil.
Bake at 350°F/180°C/Gas Mark 4 for forty
minutes. Remove foil and bake ten minutes
longer. Serve with new potatoes, peas and
carrots, and mint jelly.

Serves 6

Herbed lamb shoulder

1 shoulder lamb
6 garlic cloves
6 sprigs rosemary
Salt and pepper
Juice of ½ lemon

Serves 4

Put garlic under the lamb in baking tin. Sprinkle
lamb with salt and pepper and put rosemary
sprigs on top. Put into oven set at 450°F/220°C/
Gas Mark 8 for five minutes, then reduce heat
to 375°F/190°C/Gas Mark 5 for twenty-five
minutes per lb (450 g). An hour before serving
time, put some fresh rosemary on top, pour off
the surplus fat, and add one wineglass of water
and the lemon juice to the pan juice. Baste well.
At serving time, put lamb on to a dish, and
boil up the pan juices for gravy.

Anchovy lamb

1 boned shoulder of lamb
1 oz (25 g) butter
1 small can anchovy fillets
1 teaspoon grated lemon
rind
2 teaspoons chopped
parsley
1 oz (25 g) plain flour
1 beef extract cube
dissolved in ½ pint (300
ml) hot water
Salt and pepper

Serves 4

Cut the lamb into 2 in (5 cm) pieces and
brown the meat in the butter. Drain off the fat
and mash the meat with the anchovies, lemon
rind, parsley, salt and pepper (go easy with the
salt if the anchovies are very salty). Add to the
pan and dredge with flour. Stir in the beef
extract liquid, and bring to the boil, stirring
until thickened. Cover tightly and simmer for
1¼ hours (or cook in a low oven, 325°F/170°C/
Gas Mark 3. Serve with mashed potatoes and
tomato salad.

Lamb breast with kidney stuffing

1 large breast of lamb
1 lamb kidney
4 oz (100 g) sausagemeat
1 egg
1 teaspoon salt
½ teaspoon Tabasco sauce
Pepper

Serves 4

Bone the lamb and put the breast on a board, boned side up. Chop the kidney and mix with the sausagemeat, egg, salt, sauce and pepper. Roll and tie the meat in four places. Weigh the joint and put in a roasting tin. Cook at 350°F/180°C/Gas Mark 4 for thirty minutes per lb (450 g).

Chops in orange sauce

4 thick chump chops
Seasoned flour
2 tablespoons fat
½ teaspoon grated nutmeg
½ pint (300 ml) orange
    juice
1 tablespoon grated
    orange rind
2 teaspoons vinegar

Coat the chops in seasoned flour and brown in hot fat. Add nutmeg, orange juice, orange rind and vinegar, cover and simmer slowly for two hours (or cook at 325°F/170°C/Gas Mark 3 in the oven). Serve with plainly boiled potatoes and a green salad.

Serves 4

Perfect Pork

The legend that pork should not be eaten in the summer months dies hard. In the days before refrigeration, it was obviously a chancy business to eat any meat or fish in the hot months, but now we know that pork is very versatile, and is equally delicious, hot or cold, winter or summer.

Too many people think only of pork in the form of a succulent joint topped by crisp crackling; they forget that the economy cuts are just as good for tasty quick meals, meat loaves, pies and all sorts of everyday dishes.

You can even have a good everyday joint with masses of crackling if you roast a piece of pork belly in its skin. I buy a large square of the belly, looking for a good proportion of lean to fat, and ask the butcher to score it very finely, deeply and evenly. Into a small baking tin goes a thick layer of stuffing – sage and onion with plenty of breadcrumbs and seasoning always tastes good – and then the pork, skin side up, on top. The trick with good crackling is to brush the skin with oil or melted lard and then rub over with plenty of salt. Roast at 325°F/ 170°C/Gas Mark 3, allowing thirty minutes a lb (450 g) and thirty minutes over. It's really good with plenty of apple sauce, a helping of roast potatoes and any seasonal vegetable, and just as good cold the second day. Use the same method with crackling on a larger joint, and follow the slow-roast method recommended for the pork belly, and you'll have a really good meal for any time of the year.

If you like something a bit more adventurous, try pouring ¼ pint (150 ml) orange juice or cider into the pan about twenty minutes before the end of cooking time – it makes a delicious gravy mixed with the pan juices.

Pork and sausage casserole

This is a delicious and unusual casserole which I've used very successfully for an informal buffet party.

It's easy to increase quantities according to numbers, and the casserole can stay in a low oven without harm. For a party, serve the casserole with rice and a salad; for every day, new or jacket potatoes and a green vegetable are suitable. I am able to buy sage-seasoned sausagemeat which is excellent for this recipe, but if you are using a rather bland variety, add ½ teaspoon chopped sage for this quantity of meat.

1 lb (450 g) lean pork
4 oz (100 g) pork
   sausagemeat
¼ pint (150 ml) dry cider
¼ pint (150 ml) stock
4 oz (100 g) button
   mushrooms

Cut the pork into pieces, toss in a little seasoned flour, and brown in a little lard. Put into a casserole with plenty of salt and pepper, cider and stock and cook with a lid on at 325°F/ 170°C/Gas Mark 3 for 1½ hours. Mix the sausagemeat with sage if needed and roll it into small balls. Toss the small whole mushrooms in a little butter until just soft. Add sausage balls and mushrooms to the casserole and continue cooking for twenty minutes.

Serves 4

Pork and kidney pie

1 lb (450 g) pork shoulder
  or hand of pork
3 pigs' kidneys
2 teaspoons basil
½ pint (300 ml) stock
Pinch of ground nutmeg
1 medium onion
2 medium carrots
8 oz (225 g) shortcrust
  pastry (recipe p. 97)

Cut the pork into cubes and chop the kidneys. Chop the basil (use sage if you like, but cut the quantity down to one teaspoon), and chop the onion and carrots. Mix all the ingredients with the stock and nutmeg and put into a casserole with the lid on. Bake at 325°F/170°C/ Gas Mark 3 for an hour. Remove the lid and cover with pastry. Bake at 400°F/200°C/Gas Mark 6 for thirty minutes.

Serves 4

West country chops

2 oz (50 g) butter
1 lb (450 g) cooking apples
1 large onion
1 tablespoon caster sugar
1 teaspoon sage
4 pork chops
¼ pint (150 ml) cider
Salt and pepper
4 tablespoons
  breadcrumbs
4 tablespoons grated
  cheese

Use half the butter to grease a shallow oven-ware dish. Peel, core and slice the apples and spread over the base of the dish, with the chopped onions. Sprinkle with sugar and sage. Trim the chops, removing any rind and surplus fat, and arrange on the bed of apples. Pour in the cider and add the seasoning. Mix together the breadcrumbs and cheese, cover each chop carefully and dot with butter. Bake at 400°F/ 200°C/Gas Mark 6 for forty-five minutes, and serve with jacket potatoes.

Serves 4

Pork in beer

1¼ lb (600 g) shoulder
  pork
1 oz (25 g) lard
2 leeks
1 garlic clove, crushed
2 oz (50 g) plain flour
Salt and pepper
½ pint (300 ml) brown ale
Thyme, parsley and bay
  leaf
Dash of Tabasco sauce
Piece of lemon peel
3 oz (75 g) small button
  mushrooms

Cut the pork into cubes and slice the leeks finely. Melt the lard and fry the leeks and crushed garlic for one minute. Toss the pork in the flour seasoned with salt and pepper, and add to the leeks. Fry for five minutes. Add the beer, herbs, sauce, lemon peel and mushrooms. Bring to the boil, cover and simmer for 1½ hours.

Serves 4

Boiled pork and red cabbage

A hand of pork
2 onions
1 small red cabbage

Serves 4

Score the joint, but not so finely as for roasting. Put in a casserole with onions, cover with water and bring to boil. Skim, season with salt and pepper, cover and simmer (or cook at 300°F/150°C/Gas Mark 2) for three hours. Remove pork and keep hot, then boil sliced cabbage in stock. Strain and serve.

The same recipe can be used for a piece of bacon, cooking quarters of firm white cabbage in the stock. Both are very good with pease pudding.

Roast pork with beer gravy

Loin of pork
2 oz (50 g) plain flour
½ teaspoon ground ginger
1 pint (600 ml) beer

Serves 4–6

Rub the pork with a mixture of flour and ginger. Put into an oven set at 425°F/220°C/Gas Mark 7 for 10 minutes, and then reduce heat to 375°F/190°C/Gas Mark 5. Pour on the beer and baste every twenty minutes until done. Use the juices in the pan to make gravy. Serve with apple sauce and a green vegetable.

Pork and apples

4 lean pork chops
4 eating apples
1 teaspoon chopped sage
Salt and pepper
½ pint (300 ml) apple juice
2 teaspoons olive oil

Brown chops in oil, then add peeled sliced apples, sage, apple juice and seasoning. Cover and simmer for twenty minutes, turning chops once. Serve in pan juices with mashed potatoes.

Serves 4

Beautiful Bangers

For a long time, the British sausage has been treated with contempt. It seems like a hangover from wartime when the ersatz sausage was reputedly made of sawdust, and the comedian told his audience 'never judge a sausage by its overcoat'. But the keen sausage-watcher will know that at last the banger is making a comeback, and all over the country butchers are making individually flavoured sausages – a superb meal at any time of the day. Sage sausages seem to be a favourite at the moment, and we have a butcher who has introduced a whiff of garlic which really brings out the pork flavour. We introduced a French friend to these last year and he couldn't stop eating them, and even packed a briefcase full to take back to Paris.

Of course these delicious sausages can be served plainly for any meal. I always like to grill them so the excess fat runs out and drains away, and there is nothing better to make a filling breakfast with bacon, eggs, tomatoes and mushrooms. They are great at midday, too, served my mother-in-law's way, making a pyramid of creamy mashed potatoes and arranging the sausages along the sides, with a big bowl of bread sauce.

One of my favourite convenience meals is a hot sausage sandwich which I first discovered in a cab-drivers' shelter when I was a student. This is just a sandwich of fairly thick new bread, liberally spread with butter and filled with hot grilled sausages split in half. You don't really need chutney or onions, but they make a tasty addition. This one makes a good picnic meal in the winter if you put the sausages into a vacuum flask just before leaving and fill the sandwiches when you need them.

When your butcher fails to offer tasty sausages, try making your own, particularly if you have a freezer so that a worthwhile quantity can be made. A mincer attachment for an electric mixer is the best tool to mince large quantities of meat quickly, either finely or coarsely ground. A skin-filling attachment is also available for an electric mincer and speeds up the job considerably.

Sausage mixtures are traditionally 'cased', which means stuffing them into a skin or casing, but if skins are not easily obtainable, the sausages may be wrapped in thin sheets of caul fat from the butcher, or the meat may be formed into cylinders or flat patties and used without skins. Caul fat can be obtained in small quantities from specialist pork butchers, but any butcher can order a large supply for you. The fat should be soaked in tepid water, allowing 1 tablespoon vinegar to 2 pints (1 l) water. When the fat is soft, it can be cut into any shape and size and the meat rolled in it, overlapping the edges well. This gives a firm casing for the meat and an attractive veining of fat.

Sausage casings may be obtained from a friendly butcher in family-sized quantities from his own stock, as commercial supplies are too big for household use. Synthetic casings are easier to handle than natural ones, which come processed and salted and must be rinsed thoroughly in fresh lukewarm water, then rinsed in cold. When the casings have been rinsed, they must be opened under a jet of water, and the easiest way to do this is to turn on the cold water tap, and with the water running, push each length of casing in turn on the end of the tap. Each length can then be fitted on the sausage filler ready for the meat mixture.

Press out any air which accumulates in the skins as the meat goes into them. For using synthetic casings have dry hands free from grease when you are handling them, or the skins will not fill evenly and be under-stuffed. Skins should not be filled too tightly or they will burst when cooked. When the sausage skins are filled, they should be moistened to make it easier to twist them into lengths.

In place of an electric mincer and filler, a small hand filler may be used, similar to a cake icing gun, but it is hard work to force the sausage meat into the casings. It is almost impossible to fill skins without either an electric or hand machine, and the filling will be uneven and rather messy, so it is then better to use caul fat instead.

A particular advantage of making sausages at home is that the meat and flavouring can be varied to suit family taste. The meat may be either coarse or fine, and the sausages may be all-meat or carry an addition of a small amount of cereal or breadcrumbs. Fresh or dried herbs such as parsley, sage, garlic, rosemary and pennyroyal may be used.

To make a spicy sausage, try adding a little ground ginger, cloves, coriander or paprika. Whatever you choose to make as your family sausage, start by making a basic sausagemeat recipe and practising filling the skins or wrapping them in caul fat, and then experiment to find the sausages you like best. Serve them plainly grilled, fried or cooked in the oven, or in a special dish for a splendid and inexpensive family meal.

Simple pork sausages

1 lb (450 g) lean pork
8 oz (225 g) pork fat
1 teaspoon salt
½ teaspoon ground allspice
Black pepper
Pinch of dried marjoram
1 oz (25 g) dried white
   breadcrumbs

Mince the lean pork and pork fat twice. Mix well and season, using freshly ground pepper. Stir in the breadcrumbs. Form into shapes or fill skins.

Spiced pork sausages

1½ lb (750 g) dried white
  bread
4 lb (2 kg) lean pork
1½ lb (750 g) pork fat
1½ oz (40 g) salt
½ oz (15 g) pepper
¼ oz (8 g) ground ginger
½ oz (15 g) ground mace

Soak the bread in cold water and wring it out with the hands to get rid of excess moisture. Put the meat and fat through a coarse mincer. Mix in the bread and seasonings and put the mixture through a fine mincer. Form into shapes or fill skins.

Sage sausages

3 lb (1.5 kg) pork
1 tablespoon salt
2 tablespoons sage
2 teaspoons marjoram
¼ teaspoon ground cloves
¼ teaspoon black pepper
Pinch of cayenne pepper

Use loin or shoulder pork if possible, making sure there is a good mixture of fat and lean for these special sausages. Mince the meat finely and spread it thinly on a board. Sprinkle on salt, finely chopped herbs and other seasonings. Work in thoroughly with the hands and then mince twice more. Chill for twenty-four hours, then shape or put into skins.

Toad-in-the-hole

This old favourite consists of cooked sausages inside a crisp puffy Yorkshire pudding batter. The best puddings are made with strong plain bread flour which is now sold by most grocers. I like to put some thinly sliced onions and a sprinkling of sage in the batter too.

8 oz (225 g) plain flour
Pinch of salt
2 eggs
1 pint (600 ml) milk
1 oz (25 g) lard
1 lb (450 g) pork sausages

Make the batter with flour, salt, eggs and milk and leave to stand while you cook the sausages. Grill these until just browned all over. Put the lard in a roasting tin and set the oven at 425°F/ 220°C/Gas Mark 7. Heat the lard until smoking and pour in a thin layer of batter.

Put into the oven for five minutes until it sets. Arrange the sausages on top and pour on the rest of the batter. Bake for 30–35 minutes until the batter is puffy and brown and serve straight away, with plenty of vegetables and some jacket or roast potatoes and rich brown gravy.

Serves 4

Dublin coddle

Sliced potatoes may be added to the dish, but they are not authentic for this traditional Saturday night supper dish. The Irish have eaten it since the eighteenth century, accompanied by fresh soda bread and glasses of stout, and it was a favourite of Dean Swift, who wrote *Gulliver's Travels*.

1 lb (450 g) onions
6 bacon rashers
1 lb (450 g) pork sausages
Pepper
½ pint (300 ml) water

Serves 4

Slice the onions thinly and put them into a saucepan. Put in the sausages and the bacon cut into large pieces. Use thick-cut rashers when you can. Season with pepper, but don't add salt as there is usually enough in the bacon. Add boiling water and put a piece of greaseproof paper on top. Cover with a tight lid and simmer gently for one hour until the onions are soft. (The dish can be put in the oven at 325°F/170°C/Gas Mark 3 for an hour instead.)

Sausages in beer

For best results, use stout with the sausages.

1 lb (450 g) pork sausages
½ pint (300 ml) beer
½ oz (15 g) butter
½ oz (15 g) plain flour

Serves 4

Grill the sausages until well browned. Put into a saucepan with the beer and simmer for fifteen minutes. Work the butter and flour into a ball and stir into the liquid. Simmer for five minutes longer, and serve with creamy mashed potatoes.

Sausages in cider

1 lb (450 g) small onions
2 lb (1 kg) pork sausages
2 oz (50 g) butter
1 pint (600 ml) cider
2 heaped teaspoons flour
Salt and pepper

Serves 4

Boil the onions until tender, drain well and toss them in melted butter, then put into a serving dish. Brown the sausages in the remaining butter, pour in cider, bring to boil, cover and simmer for fifteen minutes. Season to taste and thicken the sauce with the flour. Garnish with the onions, and serve with mashed potatoes.

Slow Cook, Good Cook

Some childhood memories stay with us all our lives, and I always remember the visits I paid to my mother's large family in the heart of England. There were always people in the house, and good simple food was prepared in abundance. My grandmother had only one cooking maxim: 'Slow cook, good cook'. She brought up ten children and knew that long slow cooking was the way to produce tasty meals from cheap meat, rabbit and game, with vegetables from the garden and those wonderful horse mushrooms. I often think of her as I put a brown earthenware stewpot in the cooker with an accompanying potato dish and a milk pudding to fill the corners of the oven.

There's nothing like a stew with some rib-hugging dumplings to keep the cold out in the winter, but even a simple stew needs a bit of care in the making. They are slow-cooking mixtures, made from economical cuts of meat or older poultry, and the flavour should be sealed in before simmering, or else it all goes out into the gravy and the meat becomes ragged. This 'sealing' is easily done by flouring the meat and cooking it for a minute or two in hot oil or fat until lightly golden. It's a good idea not to add the vegetables until about halfway through cooking, so they don't become soft and pulpy. To save fuel it is worth doubling a recipe and freezing half of it, but if you are doing this, don't add potatoes, rice or pasta to the stew to be frozen, or it will become soggy.

Dumplings are a traditional accompaniment, but even such an apparently simple subject as dumplings can be fraught with problems. Norfolk and Suffolk – the heart of the English cornlands – are the traditional home of dumplings. In the Fens, they're called 'swimmers', and I had always thought this was the universal name for Norfolk dumplings too, but my village authority tells me that 'floaters' are the traditional Norfolk yeast dumplings, which take twenty minutes to cook, while the suety variety are called 'sinkers'. According to a Norfolk museum's survey, however, suet was not used in Norfolk dumplings. They were made of plain flour and water, or of bread dough using yeast, which could be made at home or bought from the local bakehouse. The dough was shaped into balls (about the size of tennis balls when proved) and boiled for exactly twenty minutes, so they were often called 'twenty-minute swimmers'. It was important never to lift the lid from a pan before the time was up, or to keep a dumpling waiting, or to touch it with a knife: a dumpling had to be torn apart with two forks; any leftover dumpling could be sliced and toasted like bread. Norfolk dumplings could be eaten with gravy, or with treacle, or butter and sugar. With gravy, they were often served before the meat like Yorkshire pudding, to lessen hearty appetites.

Of course, there are all sorts of regional variations on the dumpling theme, either boiled or baked. There are Buckinghamshire dumplings with chopped liver, bacon and onions in suet pastry, flavoured with sage. There are kidney dumplings with a well-seasoned kidney inserted in an onion inside a suet crust, which is baked. There are Suffolk dumplings which are really suet puddings stuffed with pork and onions, and Sussex drip puddings, like a suet pudding cooked to serve with the joint instead of Yorkshire pudding, but boiled in a cloth as all Sussex puddings should be. Another favourite all over England was a savoury suet pudding highly flavoured with salt, pepper and herbs, and containing breadcrumbs, which was baked in the oven to eat with the joint. In Scotland, there were mealy puddings made from oatmeal, suet and onion boiled in a cloth.

Beef casserole with dumplings

1 lb (450 g) shin beef
1 tablespoon plain flour
Salt and pepper
2 oz (50 g) lean bacon
1 medium onion
6 oz (175 g) large mushrooms
1 oz (25 g) butter

Dumplings:
4 oz (100 g) self-raising flour
2 oz (50 g) shredded suet
Pinch of salt
1 tablespoon chopped parsley

Serves 4

Cut the beef into cubes and coat with the flour seasoned with salt and pepper. Cut the bacon into pieces and fry gently until the fat runs. Take out the bacon and brown the meat on all sides in the fat. Put the beef and bacon into a casserole. Chop the onion and cook until golden in the fat, then add to the meat.

Just cover with water, put on the lid and cook at 350°F/180°C/Gas Mark 4 for one hour. Slice the mushrooms and cook them for two minutes in the butter. Add to the casserole and continue cooking for thirty minutes. For the dumplings, mix the flour, suet, salt and parsley with a little cold water to make a firm dough. Form into small balls and add to the casserole, and cook for twenty minutes.

Braised bacon with parsley dumplings

3 lb (1.5 kg) collar bacon joint
2 carrots
1 leek
1 parsnip
1 oz (25 g) butter
½ pint (300 ml) water
5 oz (150 g) frozen peas

Dumplings:
4 oz (100 g) self-raising flour
1½ oz (40 g) shredded suet
½ teaspoon salt
1 tablespoon chopped parsley

Put the bacon into a pan and cover with cold water. Bring to the boil and simmer for fifteen minutes. Peel and slice the carrots. Cut the leek into slices and the parsnip into strips. Melt the butter in a pan and fry the vegetables for four minutes. Put them into a large deep casserole. Drain the bacon and put on top of the vegetables. Add bacon cooking liquid just to cover and put on a lid.

Cook at 350°F/180°C/Gas Mark 4 for thirty minutes. Take out the bacon and peel off the skin. Mark the fat in a diamond pattern and return to the casserole. Leave off the lid and return to the oven to brown the fat. Make the dumplings by mixing all the ingredients with enough cold water to make a soft dough and form into eight small balls. Add the peas to the casserole and put the dumplings round the bacon. Cook for twenty minutes in the oven until the dumplings are well risen, light and fluffy. Put on a serving dish, arranging vegetables and dumplings around the bacon joint.

Salt beef and dumplings

3 lb (1.5 kg) salt brisket
8 oz (225 g) carrots
8 oz (225 g) onions
4 celery sticks
2 bay leaves
6 peppercorns
1 firm-hearted cabbage (optional)

Potato dumplings:
8 oz (225 g) potatoes
¼ teaspoon salt
2½ oz (65 g) plain flour
1 tablespoon mixed herbs

Soak the beef in cold water overnight, and drain. Line the inside of a roasting tin with foil and put the joint in the centre. Cut the onions, carrots and celery in large pieces and put around the joint. Add the bay leaves and peppercorns and put ¼ pint (150 ml) water over the meat. Cover with a second piece of foil, tucking the edges well under the tin. Bake at 400°F/200°C/Gas Mark 6 for 1 hour 50 minutes.

Meanwhile, boil the potatoes for the dumplings, drain and mash well. Add the salt, flour and herbs and mix to a smooth dough. Shape into 1 in (2.5 cm) balls. Take the foil from the meat and put the dumplings on the vegetables around the joint. Cover with foil and bake for forty minutes. If the cabbage is used, cut it into eight wedges and put round the joint with the other vegetables. This is an old favourite, but cooked in the oven it can save fuel if a solid fuel cooker is on all the time, and there is no anxiety about boiling dry.

Lamb stew with dumplings

1 oz (25 g) dripping
2 lb (1 kg) neck of lamb,
   cubed
2 sliced onions
2 sliced carrots
2 sliced turnips
1 tablespoon plain flour
1 pint (600 ml) water
2 tablespoons
   Worcestershire sauce
Salt and pepper

Dumplings:
4 oz (100 g) self-raising
   flour
¼ teaspoon salt
2 oz (50 g) shredded suet
1 small onion
4 tablespoons cold water

Serves 4

Heat the dripping and fry the meat pieces until brown. Take out of the fat. Add the onions to the fat and cook for five minutes. Add the carrots and turnips and cook for three minutes. Stir in the flour and cook until golden. Add the water and bring to the boil, stirring well. Add the meat, Worcestershire sauce, salt and pepper, cover and simmer for 1½ hours. Make the dumplings by mixing the flour, salt, suet, grated onion and water. Shape into eight balls and add to the meat for the last twenty minutes' cooking time.

Beef casserole with mustard dumplings

3 oz (75 g) butter
1½ lb (750 g) chuck steak
4 oz (100 g) mushrooms
1 onion
1 oz (25 g) plain flour
1½ level teaspoons
   mustard powder
1 level teaspoon paprika
½ pint (300 ml) beef stock
Salt and pepper
2 tablespoons tomato
   ketchup

Dumplings:
6 oz (175 g) self-raising
   flour
1 teaspoon mustard
   powder
Pinch of salt
2 oz (50 g) butter
4 tablespoons milk

Serves 4

Melt butter. Cut meat in 1 in (2.5 cm) cubes and brown in butter. Drain and put into a casserole. Fry sliced mushrooms and onions for three minutes. Drain well and put on top of meat. Mix together flour, mustard and paprika and stir into remaining fat and cook for one minute. Remove from heat and gradually stir in stock. Return to heat and bring to the boil, stirring. Cook for a minute, remove from heat, add seasonings and tomato ketchup, and pour over meat. Cover and cook at 350°F/180°C/Gas Mark 4 for 1½ hours. Make the dumplings by mixing together flour, mustard and salt and rubbing in butter until mixture is like fine breadcrumbs. Add milk and mix to a soft but not wet dough. Divide mixture into eight and form into balls. Put on top of the meat in the casserole during the last fifteen minutes' cooking time.

Jugged beef

1½ lb (750 g) shin beef
2 oz (50 g) plain flour
Salt and pepper
4 oz (100 g) chopped
   streaky bacon
2 onions stuck with 4
   cloves
Grated rind ½ lemon
Bay leaf, thyme and
   parsley
6 small mushrooms
3 beef cubes in ¾ pint
   (450 ml) hot water

Serves 4

Cut meat in 2 in (5 cm) pieces and roll them in flour seasoned with salt and pepper. Fry bacon, and add the meat, browning lightly. Add onions, lemon rind, herbs, mushrooms and stock. Cover and cook slowly on top of the stove or in a slow oven (300°F/150°C/Gas Mark 2) for three hours. Remove onion and herbs before serving.

Hunter's beef

3 lb (1.5 kg) rolled ribs of
   beef
3 rashers streaky bacon
2 carrots
2 onions
1 celery stick
¼ pint (150 ml) dry red
   wine
½ pint (300 ml) stock
   made with a beef cube
Thyme, parsley and bay
   leaf

Cut up bacon and vegetables in small pieces and put into a heavy saucepan. Season with salt and pepper, cover and put over gentle heat to soften vegetables in the bacon fat. When just soft, add wine and hot stock, and put in meat and herbs. Cover and cook two hours at 325°F/170°C/Gas Mark 3. Cool. On the next day, remove any fat from the top, and heat in oven for forty-five minutes. Slice meat and arrange on vegetables on serving dish; reduce gravy by fast boiling and hand separately.

Beef in beer

3 lb (1.5 kg) beef topside
Seasoned flour
4 oz (100 g) butter
2 large onions
1 pint (600 ml) beer
¾ pint (450 ml) beef stock
1 crushed garlic clove
Sprig of thyme
Parsley and marjoram
1 bay leaf
2 teaspoons sugar
2 teaspoons lemon juice
   or vinegar

Cut the beef into thick slices and dust with flour. Cook in butter until lightly browned. Put into a casserole. Slice the onions and cook in the fat in the pan. Put the onions with the beef and add the beer, stock, garlic, herbs, sugar and lemon juice or vinegar. Cover and cook on top of the stove or at 325°F/170°C/Gas Mark 3 for 2½ hours. Thicken the gravy with a little butter and flour if liked. Serve with boiled potatoes and red cabbage.

Steak and mushroom casserole

1½ lb (750 g) chuck steak
2 oz (50 g) dripping
4 small onions
4 oz (100 g) button
   mushrooms
1 bay leaf
Parsley and thyme
½ pint (300 ml) stock
2 teaspoons cornflour

Cut the steak in cubes and lightly brown in melted dripping. Put into the casserole with onions cut in quarters, mushrooms, herbs and stock. Cover tightly and cook at 350°F/180°C/ Gas Mark 4 for two hours. Before serving, remove herbs and thicken with cornflour. Garnish with a little freshly chopped parsley.

Serves 4

Steak and kidney casserole

1 lb (450 g) stewing steak
4 oz (100 g) ox kidney
1 oz (25 g) plain flour
Salt and pepper
1 small onion
1 oz (25 g) lard or
   dripping
¾ pint (450 ml) water

Cube the steak and kidney and coat lightly in the flour seasoned with salt and pepper. Chop the onion finely. Brown the meat on all sides in the lard or dripping. Add the onion and cook until soft and golden. Stir in the water and bring to the boil. Cook at 325°F/170°C/ Gas Mark 3 for three hours.

Serves 4

Pork and apple casserole

4 spare rib pork chops
1 medium onion
1 cooking apple
4 oz (100 g) tomatoes
¾ pint (450 ml) stock
Pinch of sage or basil
Salt and pepper

Lightly brown the chops on both sides. Surround with sliced onion, cover with stock and season to taste, adding chosen herb. Cover tightly and cook at 325°F/170°C/Gas Mark 3 for an hour. Put sliced apple and tomatoes on top, and continue cooking for twenty minutes. Remove lid and allow meat to brown for fifteen minutes.

Serves 4

Lamb and apple casserole

2 lb (1 kg) middle neck of
   lamb chops
1 oz (25 g) plain flour
Salt and pepper
2 tablespoons oil
2 medium onions
2 medium carrots
1 celery stick
1 cooking apple
1 pint (600 ml) stock

Coat the chops with the flour seasoned with the salt and pepper, and brown them lightly in the oil. Chop the onions, carrots, celery and apple in small pieces. Add to the meat and fry for five minutes. Add the stock and bring to the boil. Put into a casserole and cook at 325°F/ 170°C/Gas Mark 3 for two hours.

Serves 4

Liver and bacon hot pot

1 lb (450 g) liver
Seasoned flour
4 rashers streaky bacon
1 large onion
2 lb (1 kg) potatoes

Serves 4

Cut liver into thin strips about 1 in (2.5 cm) long and dust lightly with flour seasoned with salt and pepper. Cut bacon into strips, and slice onion thinly. Fry liver, bacon and onion slowly in very little fat for five minutes then gradually add ½ pint (300 ml) water and bring to the boil, stirring well. You may need a little extra flour to thicken this gravy. Put into an ovenproof dish, and cover with thinly sliced potatoes, well seasoned with salt and pepper. Dot with a little dripping or bacon fat and bake at 350°F/180°C/Gas Mark 4 for 1½ hours.

Savoury hearts

1½ lb (750 g) hearts
1 teaspoon chopped sage
1 finely chopped onion
1 oz (25 g) bacon
2 oz (50 g) breadcrumbs
Salt and pepper
1 egg, beaten
1 oz (25 g) butter or lard
1½ lb (750 g) mixed
  vegetables (carrot,
  turnip or swede,
  parsnip, celery)
1 pint (600 ml) stout
¼ pint (150 ml) water

Serves 4

Use calf, pig or lamb hearts, washing well and soaking in salted water for an hour. Drain the hearts well. Cut off the lobes, gristle and membrane. Mix the sage, onion, finely chopped bacon and breadcrumbs. Season with salt and pepper and bind with the egg. Stuff the hearts with the mixture and secure with fine skewers. Brown both sides in melted butter or lard. Cut the mixed vegetables in cubes, and brown them lightly in the fat when the hearts have been removed. Put the vegetables into a saucepan or casserole. Put the hearts on top and cover with the stout and water. Cover and simmer or cook at 325°F/170°C/Gas Mark 3 for 1¾ hours, turning the hearts once. If stuffing is not liked, cut the hearts in half and put them on the vegetables with a teaspoon of mixed herbs, add the stout and water and cook as before.

Oxtail stew

1 oxtail
1 onion
4 whole cloves
Blade of mace
1 lemon
3 tablespoons flour
Salt and pepper
Parsley

Serves 4

Joint the oxtail and brown pieces in butter. Put into a pan with 2 pints (1 l) water, an onion stuck with the cloves, a blade of mace, the peel of the lemon (take it off with a sharp knife in one long piece), the juice of half the lemon, and a good sprig of parsley. Simmer for three hours, then remove meat from the bones. Work the flour into a little of the stock and add to the gravy. Remove peel and mace and cloves, season to taste with salt and pepper, and continue simmering meat for an hour. Serve sprinkled with chopped parsley.

Liver in stout

Serve hot with a garnish of chopped parsley – and do not overcook the liver.

12 oz (350 g) liver
Seasoned flour
2 oz (50 g) butter
2 teaspoons grated onion
1 teaspoon lemon juice
2 tablespoons stout or
   sweet stout
Chopped parsley

Cut calf, pig or lamb's liver into strips about $2\frac{1}{2} \times \frac{1}{2}$ in (6.25 × 1.25 cm) and roll in seasoned flour. Melt the butter and add the onion. Add the liver and stir it lightly in the butter until brown, with lemon juice and stout.

Serves 4

The Best of Bacon

For most of us, boiling bacon is a fairly everyday affair, but careful choice and cooking of the original joint can make all the difference between a stringy, salty piece of meat, and a succulent tender and sweet joint. Forehock *is one of the cheap boiling cuts, which can be boned and rolled to save time and trouble; one end is fatter than the other, so carving should be from alternate ends.* End of collar *is another cheap piece which can be boiled and pressed lightly; two pieces may be pressed together. Another cut which is good for boiling and pressing is* flank, *rather fattier, which is very good served with rabbit or chicken. These three joints are particularly useful if you like to use up the end pieces in pies or puddings.* Prime collar *is a middle price cut which is very good if long slits are cut in the meat and a stuffing of chopped herbs inserted.* Slipper *is a small lean joint which is good as a hot joint with spinach or broad beans. The three* gammon joints, middle, corner and hock, *are all choice cuts which respond particularly well to the treatment of boiling, then finishing in the oven with a glaze.*

The usual complaint about bacon is that it is too salty. Always allow time for the joint to be soaked for at least twelve hours. If you still have doubts, cook a potato in the water, which will take up the salt. Simmer the joint very gently, allowing twenty minutes a lb (450 g). If you want to glaze and decorate the bacon, strip off the rind while the meat is still warm, then put the joint on a rack in a roasting tin before the glaze is used. Try one of these for good flavour and stunning effect.

Treacle glaze

Mix two tablespoons plain flour and two table-spoons demerara sugar with two tablespoons golden syrup and three tablespoons warm liquid from bacon. Spread over bacon, put in a hot oven (400°F/200°C/Gas Mark 6) for twenty minutes.

Honey glaze

Spread two tablespoons clear honey over the bacon and sprinkle with one tablespoon fine breadcrumbs. Mix ¼ pint (150 ml) pineapple juice and ¼ pint (150 ml) vinegar and pour over joint. Bake for twenty minutes at 400°F/200°C/Gas Mark 6, basting occasionally.

Mustard glaze

Mix two teaspoons French mustard, two table-spoons wine vinegar and two tablespoons cook-ing liquor, and pour over bacon. Mix together two tablespoons fine breadcrumbs and one tablespoon demerara sugar, and sprinkle over the joint. Bake at 400°F/200°C/Gas Mark 6 for twenty minutes.

Clove and sugar glaze

Score the fat surface of the joint criss-cross and stud with cloves. Mix one teaspoon powdered cloves with 2 tablespoons soft brown sugar, and make a smooth paste with six tablespoons ginger ale. Spread on the bacon and bake at 400°F/200°C/Gas Mark 6 for twenty minutes.

One of the best things about a joint of bacon or a ham is that there is never a scrap of waste. Use the remains to stuff large firm tomatoes, mixed with a few breadcrumbs and herbs, and a little chopped onion. Or bind the same mixture with an egg, fry and put between buttered baps as 'baconburgers'. Scotch eggs can be covered with minced cooked bacon instead of sausage meat, or apples can be stuffed with minced bacon well seasoned with herbs, and baked in the oven. Most of us know how delicious bacon and egg pie is, but bacon also goes well with onions in a creamy sauce for a suppertime flan (sprinkle the top with grated cheese and give it a golden finish in the oven or under the grill). An old-fashioned bacon roly-poly pudding is usually made with chopped uncooked bacon pieces, but minced cooked bacon is equally good with a little sweet pickle, chopped onion and mixed herbs, rolled up in suet pastry and steamed for two hours, then served with hot tomato sauce. If you have a lot of sandwiches to prepare, make your own sandwich spread with minced cold bacon mixed with a little sweet pickle and onion, mayonnaise to bind and a spoonful of fine white breadcrumbs to stiffen the mixture. This is especially good for brown bread sandwiches with a few slices of tomato or cucumber.

Stuffed Ayrshire roll

This makes a really substantial hot meal, with plenty of slices over to eat cold.

4 lb (2 kg) middle-cut bacon
2 oz (50 g) butter
4 oz (100 g) mushrooms
3 oz (75 g) fresh white breadcrumbs
1 beaten egg
2 tablespoons chopped parsley
Salt and pepper

Soak the bacon overnight in cold water. Wrap it round a jam jar and tie firmly with string. Put in a large saucepan with fresh cold water and simmer gently for an hour. Take out of the water, cool slightly and remove the skin. Melt half the butter and fry chopped mushrooms gently for five minutes. Take off the heat and stir in the breadcrumbs, egg, parsley, salt and pepper. Take out the jam jar and fill the cavity in the bacon with the stuffing. Put into a roasting tin and make cuts in the fat about $\frac{1}{4}$ in (65 mm) apart. Brush with remaining melted butter and roast at 375°F/190°C/Gas Mark 5 for an hour. As a variation on this idea, use sage and onion stuffing with a spot of apple chopped into it, and put a couple of hard-boiled eggs in the centre of the stuffing before roasting.

Bacon galantine

8 oz (225 g) cooked bacon
4 oz (100 g) stewing steak
4 oz (100 g) fresh white breadcrumbs
1 large egg
$\frac{1}{2}$ teaspoon ground nutmeg
Pinch of ground mixed spice
1 teaspoon Worcestershire sauce
Pepper
Stock or water
1 level teaspoon gelatine

Mince bacon and stewing steak together and mix with breadcrumbs, spices, sauce and egg, using just enough water or stock to bind. Shape in a rectangle, wrap in greased greaseproof paper, then in a cloth, leaving a little room for expansion. Steam for $1\frac{1}{2}$ hours in a steamer, keeping water beneath boiling steadily. Lift out galantine, take off cloth and paper, and leave to cool. When cold, glaze the galantine with $2\frac{1}{2}$ fl oz (65 ml) stock flavoured with a little meat extract and thickened with the gelatine, using the glaze when it is just on the point of setting.

Serves 4

Liver and bacon pâté

6 rashers streaky bacon
8 oz (225 g) pig's liver
8 oz (225 g) fat bacon
1 garlic clove
1 large onion
2 oz (50 g) butter
Salt and pepper
3 bay leaves

Foundation sauce:
½ pint (300 ml) milk
2 blades mace
1 bay leaf
2 peppercorns
1 oz (25 g) butter
1 oz (25 g) plain flour

Take the rinds from the streaky bacon and stretch the rashers on a board with the back of a knife. Put rashers of bacon at the bottom and round the sides of a greased terrine or straight-sided dish. Fry the liver, chopped fat bacon, chopped garlic and onion in butter for ten minutes and mince finely. Make the sauce by heating the milk with the mace, bay leaf and peppercorns. Bring to the boil, leave to stand for ten minutes and then strain. Melt the butter, add the flour and cook for a minute. Take off the heat and gradually stir in the milk. Return to the heat and bring to the boil, stirring all the time until sauce thickens. Add to the liver mixture and blend well, seasoning to taste. Turn into the prepared dish and top with bay leaves. Cover with a piece of foil and a lid. Put into a roasting tin of water and bake at 350°F/180°C/Gas Mark 4 for one hour. Cool for twenty-four hours before serving.

Bacon and apple roll

8 oz (225 g) puff pastry
12 oz (350 g) minced
   cooked bacon
1 large cooking apple
1 small onion
2 tablespoons water
1 egg, beaten

Serves 4

Roll the pastry into a rectangle. Mix together bacon, peeled and chopped apple, chopped onion and water. Spread bacon mixture on dough and form into a roll, putting on baking sheet so that the join is underneath. Brush roll with beaten egg, cut slits in surface to allow steam to escape, and bake for twenty minutes at 425°F/220°C/Gas Mark 7 until the pastry is beginning to colour. Reduce heat to 350°F/180°C/Gas Mark 4 and continue cooking until pastry is golden and crisp (about an hour in all). Serve hot or cold.

Bacon Scotch eggs

10 oz (300 g) boiled bacon
Eggs
Salt and pepper

Mince the bacon and pack about two table-spoons of this mince over the bottom and sides of well-greased patty pans. Add a little chutney or mustard if liked. Break an egg into each and season with salt and pepper. Cover with a piece of foil and bake at 400°F/200°C/Gas Mark 6 for fifteen minutes.

Hot bacon loaf

Serve hot with beans or peas and new potatoes or jacket potatoes.

1½ oz (40 g) butter
1½ oz (40 g) browned
    breadcrumbs
1 large onion
12 oz (350 g) cooked
    bacon from a joint
½ teaspoon mixed herbs
½ teaspoon ground
    nutmeg
2 oz (50 g) fresh white
    breadcrumbs
1 egg
¼ pint (150 ml) bacon
    stock
Pepper

Grease 1 lb (450 g) loaf tin with ½ oz (15 g) butter and press 1 oz (25 g) browned breadcrumbs round the bottom and sides of the tin. Chop the onion finely and fry until golden in the remaining butter. Mince the bacon and add all the remaining ingredients. Taste the mixture to ensure that it is sufficiently salted. Then press the mixture into the loaf tin. Cover with foil and bake at 350°F/180°C/Gas Mark 4 for one hour. Turn out and sprinkle with the remaining browned breadcrumbs.

Serves 4

Bacon bake

6 rashers middle cut
    bacon
2 lambs' kidneys
4 oz (100 g) mushrooms
1 oz (25 g) butter
1½ lb (750 g) peeled sliced
    potatoes
4 oz (100 g) grated cheese
½ pint (300 ml) stock
Pepper and salt

Serves 4

Cut two of the rashers into pieces. Skin, core and quarter kidneys, and cut mushrooms in quarters. Fry together for two minutes in butter. In shallow casserole, put a layer of sliced potato, then cheese, kidneys, mushrooms and chopped bacon, then top with potato slices. Arrange remaining rashers of bacon on top. Add seasoned stock. Cover and bake at 375°F/190°C/Gas Mark 5 for one hour. Remove lid and continue cooking until top is brown.

Bacon suet roll

12 oz (350 g) plain flour
1½ teaspoons baking
    powder
8 oz (225 g) suet
1½ lb (750 g) bacon pieces
1 large onion
Sage

Serves 4

Sift flour with baking powder and a pinch of salt, rub in suet and add enough water to make pastry. Roll out on a floured board. On top, spread bacon pieces cut in dice and mixed with chopped onion. Season with pepper and chopped sage, and roll up like a sausage. Wrap in buttered paper, tie in a cloth and boil in water for two hours. Good with a brown gravy or hot tomato sauce.

Bacon pâté

12 oz (350 g) unsmoked
long back rashers
1 lb (450 g) minced pork
or veal
1 small onion
6 oz (175 g) fresh white
breadcrumbs
2 hard-boiled eggs
2 beaten eggs
Salt, pepper and mace

Line a loaf tin with four rashers. Keep six rashers, and mince the rest with the pork or veal. Add finely chopped onion, breadcrumbs, chopped hardboiled eggs, beaten eggs and seasoning. Press a layer of mixture into the tin, then put on three bacon rashers. Put in another layer of meat, then bacon, then finish with meat mixture. Cover with foil or double grease-proof paper; put loaf tin into tin of hot water, and cook at 325°F/170°C/Gas Mark 3 for 1½ hours. Remove from oven, and press lightly until cold. Turn out and serve in slices.

Bacon and beer casserole

This is very good with
baked parsnips.

2½ lb (1.25 kg) bacon
collar
1 carrot
1 onion
Pepper
1 tablespoon black treacle
1 bay leaf
1 pint (600 ml) ale
1 oz (25 g) butter
1 oz (25 g) flour

Serves 4

Soak bacon. Put in casserole, and add sliced carrot and onion, a shake of freshly ground black pepper, treacle, bay leaf and beer. Bring to the boil, skim, and simmer for one hour (or cook at 350°F/180°C/Gas Mark 4). Remove bacon, take off skin, and keep joint hot. Blend butter with flour and thicken the strained liquid.

Savoury
Pies
and
Puddings

Pies and Pasties

All farming families love pastry, and every farm wife knows that a lid or case of melting pastry can transform the dullest meat or the plainest fruit into a luxury dish which is also filling.

For shortcrust pastry, half as much fat as flour is needed, and the flour rubbed in with the fingertips. For the richer types, rough puff and flaky, the fat is rolled in, and lemon juice is added (for rough puff, use 4–6 oz (100–175 g) fat to 8 oz (225 g) flour and 2 teaspoons lemon juice; for flaky pastry, use 6 oz (175 g) fat to the same amount of flour and juice).

Basically, a good quality plain flour should be used, and everything kept as cool as possible. Rich pastry needs 'resting' in a cold place between rollings, or before use. Dry ingredients should be sieved to incorporate air and lighten the mixture. Water should be added all at once to make the mixture bind without being sticky. Pastry should be rolled lightly, but firmly, rolling on one side only. A hot oven is necessary, the richer the pastry the hotter the oven being a good general rule; the temperature can be decreased as soon as the pastry is firm and brown.

Fillings can be varied endlessly to suit the family taste and purse. Small pies for the lunchbox can be filled with leftover meat, egg, cheese or fish mixtures; a thick white sauce or good gravy should be used for binding the mixtures.

For supper time, the favourite bacon and egg pie can be improved with the addition of a few mushrooms or with slices of pork sausage. Or cooked bacon and hard-boiled egg may be combined in a creamy sauce.

For more formal occasions, the traditional steak pie can appear in many disguises. Pieces of pigeon or game can be included, hard-boiled eggs, diced vegetables, mushrooms, forcemeat balls, kidneys, or even a few canned oysters. This type of pie is delicious if the meat is rolled round a forcemeat filling and packed firmly into the piedish with some onions and a quantity of strong beef stock.

Chicken pies are a useful way of using the odd old boiler, or of eking out the remains of a roast bird. One mixture can be a combination of chopped cooked chicken and ham, onion and hard-boiled eggs and small forcemeat balls, with plenty of herbs and good chicken stock, and a topping of flaky pastry. This use of good stock and plenty of herbs is always important in a chicken pie; my favourite version is an American one combining equal quantities of cooked chicken and potatoes in a rich gravy of half-and-half chicken stock and evaporated milk, well seasoned with herbs and finished with flaky pastry.

Curried fish pies

8 oz (225 g) flaky pastry
1 small onion
1 small apple
2 teaspoons curry powder
2 teaspoons plain flour
1 teaspoon chutney
½ teaspoon lemon juice
½ oz (15 g) sultanas
Salt and pepper
4 oz (100 g) cooked
  haddock
1 hard-boiled egg
¼ pint (150 ml) fish stock

Serves 4

Make flaky pastry using a proportion of 6 oz (175 g) fat to 8 oz (225 g) flour, and a squeeze of lemon juice, and put in cold place. To make filling, soften chopped apple, curry powder and flour and cook for three minutes. Add chutney, lemon juice, sultanas, salt and pepper, then add fish stock (saved from cooking haddock), and simmer for twenty minutes. Mix with flaked haddock and sliced egg. Roll pastry into a large square, and divide into four squares. Cool the filling, then divide mixture between the four pieces of pastry. Wet pastry edges and bring together to form an envelope shape. Brush with beaten egg, and bake at 425°F / 220°C / Gas Mark 7 for twenty-five minutes.

Individual chicken pies

8 oz (225 g) puff pastry
1 small chicken
4 oz (100 g) mushrooms
4 hard-boiled egg yolks
1 medium onion
1 tablespoon vinegar
1 teaspoon parsley
½ teaspoon salt
½ teaspoon Worcestershire
  sauce
4 rashers streaky bacon
Stock made from chicken
  carcass

Remove flesh in neat pieces from an uncooked chicken, and simmer carcass in water for an hour to make stock. In a bowl mix pieces of light and dark flesh, sliced mushrooms, mashed egg yolks, finely chopped onion, vinegar, parsley, salt, sauce and chopped bacon, and divide mixture between four individual pie dishes. Half-fill each dish with stock, and cover with pastry. Brush tops with beaten egg, make an air vent in each, and cook at 375°F/190°C/ Gas Mark 4 for an hour.

Cottage cheese pie

8 oz (225 g) plain flour
6 oz (175 g) lard
Squeeze of lemon juice
3 eggs
8 oz (225 g) cottage cheese
2 tablespoons cooked peas
2 tablespoons chopped
  parsley
¼ teaspoon salt
Pepper
½ teaspoon mixed herbs

Serves 4

Make rough puff pastry by sieving flour with a pinch of salt and adding lard cut in walnut-sized pieces. Mix with lemon juice and enough iced water to make a stiff dough, using a knife to avoid breaking the fat. Shape into an oblong and roll lightly into a long strip. Fold into three, enclosing as much air as possible, close and seal ends; give pastry a half turn and repeat rolling and folding twice more. Leave in a cold place for twenty minutes, then line a 6 in (15 cm) flan ring with half the pastry.

  Whisk eggs and mix with sieved cheese, and stir in peas, parsley, salt, pepper to taste and herbs (if you have fresh marjoram, this is the ideal flavouring). Fill flan ring, and cover with remaining pastry, making a slit on the top, and brushing well with beaten egg. Bake high in oven set at 425°F/220°C/Gas Mark 7 and reduce heat at once to 350°F/180°C/Gas Mark 4. Bake for twenty minutes, then move pie to lower shelf for thirty minutes. Serve hot or cold.

Barbecue pie

8 oz (225 g) plain flour
4 oz (100 g) lard
Lard for frying
4 oz (100 g) onion
8 oz (225 g) tin tomatoes
Small tin tomato purée
2 teaspoons paprika
Few drops Tabasco
Salt
Squeeze of lemon juice
2 teaspoons horseradish
   sauce
1 tablespoon brown sugar
A little stock
1 lb (450 g) cooked
   poultry

Serves 4

Make shortcrust pastry by sieving flour with a pinch of salt and rubbing in lard until mixture looks like fine breadcrumbs; mix to a firm dough with cold water and chill before rolling. Melt lard for frying and cook chopped onion until transparent; drain off any excess fat. Add tomatoes, purée and other ingredients except meat, tasting for seasoning. These proportions give a slightly hot, slightly sweet and slightly savoury sauce. Cook gently until ingredients are well blended. Cut meat into large pieces and put into a piedish, pouring over enough sauce to moisten well (a little stock may be necessary). Roll out pastry to cover, glaze with beaten egg, and bake in the middle of the oven at 400°F/200°C/Gas Mark 6 until golden.

Autumn chicken pie

This is a good evening meal to follow soup, but is also excellent for a packed lunch with whole tomatoes.

8 oz (225 g) plain flour
1 teaspoon salt
2 oz (50 g) lard
2 oz (50 g) margarine
2 eggs
$\frac{1}{4}$ pint (150 ml) milk
1 teaspoon tarragon or
   parsley
Grated rind $\frac{1}{2}$ lemon
Salt and pepper
1 lb (450 g) cold cooked
   chicken

Sift together flour and salt, rub in lard and margarine, and add about six teaspoons cold water to make a stiff dough. Leave to rest for ten minutes, then roll out and line a 7 in (17.5 cm) flan ring or sponge tin with two-thirds of the pastry. Blend eggs and milk, add tarragon or chopped parsley, lemon rind, salt and pepper, and chicken cut in $\frac{1}{2}$ in (1.25 cm) strips. Put mixture into pastry case, cover with remaining pastry, seal and flute edges. Cut slits in the top, and bake at 425°F/220°C/Gas Mark 7 for twenty minutes. Remove flan ring and continue baking at 350°F/180°C/Gas Mark 4 for forty minutes. Serve cold with salad.

Serves 4

Beef and bacon pie

1 onion
8 oz (225 g) bacon pieces
8 oz (225 g) minced raw
  beef
1 tablespoon plain flour
¼ pint (150 ml) water
Pinch of fresh mixed herbs
Salt and pepper
8 oz (225 g) short pastry

Serves 4

Chop the onion and bacon in small pieces, put in a heavy pan, and cook gently until the fat runs from the bacon, and the onion and bacon are soft and golden. Add the mince and cook until mince browns. Stir in flour mixed with a little water, add the rest of the water, herbs and seasonings and cook until mixture is thick and well blended. Roll pastry into two rounds and line an 8 in (20 cm) pie plate. Put in filling, and cover with second round of pastry. Bake at 400°F/200°C/Gas Mark 6 for thirty minutes.

Fish envelope

This filling can be varied by adding a few mushrooms or shrimps to the mixture.

8 oz (225 g) cooked cod
  or haddock fillet
1 hard-boiled egg
1 tablespoon capers
¼ pint (150 ml) white
  sauce
Salt and pepper
8 oz (225 g) shortcrust
  pastry

Flake fish and chop egg, and add fish, egg and capers to sauce, seasoning with salt and pepper. Roll out pastry thinly to form a square, put fish filling in the centre, brush edges of pastry with beaten egg or milk and draw sides up over the centre to form an envelope. Seal edges well, decorate with trimmings and brush with beaten egg or milk. Bake at 400°F/200°C/Gas Mark 6 for thirty minutes, and serve hot or cold.

Serves 4

Curried lamb pies

Excellent for the lunch-box.

8 oz (225 g) flaky pastry
2 teaspoons lard
1 teaspoon minced onion
2 teaspoons plain flour
½ pint (300 ml) stock
1 teaspoon curry powder
Salt and pepper
8 oz (225 g) cubed cooked
  lamb
1 diced apple
2 tablespoons coconut
2 tablespoons sultanas

Line individual patty cases with pastry. Melt lard and brown onion lightly. Stir in flour, then stock, curry powder, salt and pepper to taste, and stir until the mixture thickens and boils. Add meat, apple, coconut and sultanas, heat through and leave to cool. Put a spoonful of the mixture into each patty case, top with rounds of pastry and seal edges; make a small hole with a skewer in the top of each, and bake at 450°F/230°C/Gas Mark 8 for twenty minutes. Serve hot or cold.

Serves 4

Fried meat pies

These pies make a very pleasant change when served really hot with a crisp salad. The filling may be varied by using corned beef flavoured with a little tomato purée or table sauce; a little chopped green pepper is also good cooked with the onion.

8 oz (225 g) shortcrust pastry
1 medium onion
1 tablespoon lard
1 lb (450 g) minced raw beef
½ pint (300 ml) stock
2 teaspoons chopped parsley
Salt and pepper
2 tablespoons plain flour
2 chopped hard-boiled eggs

Chop onion finely and soften in melted lard. Add minced beef, stock, parsley, salt and pepper to taste, and simmer with a lid on for thirty minutes. Stir in flour, heat and stir until thick, then add egg and leave to cool. Roll out pastry thinly and cut in circles the size of a saucer; this quantity should make six circles. Put three tablespoons of meat mixture on one side of each circle, fold over the other side, damp and pinch edges to seal them. Fry in hot deep fat for about three minutes until golden. If there is any meat mixture over, add a little water and simmer until the mixture is like a sauce, then use to pour over the pies at serving time.

Serves 4

Shetland pasties

12 oz (350 g) shortcrust pastry
3 medium herrings
4 oz (100 g) streaky bacon
1 large potato, grated
Grated rind of ½ lemon
Salt and pepper
Milk for glazing

Serves 4

Divide the pastry into four and roll out each piece into a 6 in (15 cm) square. Remove heads from the fish, split, clean and bone them. Grill the herrings, skin side uppermost, for about seven minutes until cooked. Remove the skin and flake the fish coarsely into a mixing bowl. Fry the chopped bacon for two minutes and add to the fish. Stir in grated potato and lemon rind and season to taste. Divide the filling between the pastry squares, placing it in the centre. Damp the edges of the pastry and bring four corners to the centre to form envelopes. Seal and flute the edges. Put on baking sheet and brush with milk to glaze. Bake at 425°F/220°C/Gas Mark 7 for ten minutes, and then bake at 375°F/190°C/Gas Mark 5 for twenty-five minutes until golden brown. Serve hot or cold.

Sausage and egg roll

1 lb (450 g) pork
  sausagemeat
2 hard-boiled eggs
1 small onion
Sage, salt and pepper
8 oz (225 g) shortcrust
  pastry
1 oz (25 g) grated cheese

Serves 4

Press the sausagemeat flat on a floured surface. Cover with chopped hard-boiled egg and finely chopped onion. Sprinkle with some dried or fresh sage and seasoning to taste. Roll up like a Swiss roll. Roll out the pastry and put the sausage in the middle. Fold over the edges and seal with a little water. Brush with a little milk and sprinkle with grated cheese. Bake at 400°F/200°C/Gas Mark 6 for forty-five minutes.

Bacon pasties

12 oz (350 g) shortcrust
  pastry
8 oz (225 g) minced raw
  steak
6 oz (175 g) streaky bacon
4 oz (100 g) lambs'
  kidneys
1 large onion
Salt and pepper
½ teaspoon Worcestershire
  sauce
Egg for glazing

Serves 4

Roll out the pastry and cut out six 7 in (17.5 cm) rounds. Chop the bacon, kidneys and onion and mix with the minced meat. Add the seasoning and sauce. Put the mixture on half of each round and fold over pastry. Pinch edges together. Put on a wet baking sheet, brush with beaten egg and bake at 425°F/220°C/Gas Mark 7 for fifteen minutes, then at 350°F/180°C/ Gas Mark 4 for forty-five minutes. Eat hot or cold.

Pork pasties

1 lb (450 g) shortcrust
  pastry
2 hard-boiled eggs
8 oz (225 g) cold cooked
  pork
3 crisp eating apples
6 spring onions
Sage, salt and pepper
Egg for glazing

Serves 4

Roll out the pastry and cut into seven or eight 7 in (17.5 cm) rounds. Mix together chopped hard-boiled eggs, chopped pork, apples and onions. Season with sage, salt and pepper. Brush edges with egg and bring them up to meet on top. Pinch together like a Cornish pasty and put on a baking sheet. Brush with beaten egg and bake at 400°F/200°C/Gas Mark 6 for thirty minutes.

All-Weather Flans

Flans can be delicious or disastrous. If they are made with pastry suitable to the ingredients, and these are beautifully fresh and carefully seasoned, what can be a nicer hot or cold meal, or a more perfect picnic dish? But a dry pastry case, perhaps with a heavy soggy bottom, filled with leftovers in a glutinous sauce, can be very nasty. Aim at a simple flan, without elaborate ingredients or heavy garnishing, and you have a splendid meal for all kinds of weather, and all times of day.

I like a creamy filling, well seasoned with sea-salt and freshly ground pepper, a pinch of fresh herbs, and perhaps a grating of fresh nutmeg, but I loathe seeing a flan decorated with bits of tomato, twists of cucumber and aimless pieces of parsley. Let a good savoury filling speak for itself.

Opinions vary on the best type of pastry case. Most flans can be made with flaky or shortcrust pastry, but unless the flaky pastry is well made and correctly baked it can be a bit heavy and greasy with the rich filling. If the pastry is lightly cooked before the filling is added, there is little danger of a soggy bottom under the filling. The pastry and filling can be prepared in advance, but should not be put together until just before cooking.

This basic shortcrust pastry is useful for flans, and the recipe makes up 10 oz (300 g) pastry, which will be enough for an 8–9 in (20–22.5 cm) flan ring or tin, to hold about 1 pint (600 ml) of filling. An 11 in (27.5 cm) flan will need 1½ pints (900 ml) filling.

Basic flan pastry.

6 oz (175 g) plain flour
Pinch of salt
2½ oz (65 g) butter
¾ oz (20 g) lard
3½ tablespoons cold water
Pinch of pepper

Sift the flour and salt, then rub in the butter and lard. Add pepper, if used, and mix to a firm dough with water. Leave in a cool place before rolling out.

Farmhouse flan

Basic flan pastry
6 oz (175 g) minced ham
4 oz (100 g) cottage cheese
3 eggs
¼ pint (150 ml) soured cream
Salt and pepper

Line an 8 in (20 cm) pie plate with the pastry. Mix the ham and cottage cheese. Beat the eggs into the cream, and add all the remaining ingredients. Season well and pour into the pastry case. Bake at 350°F/180°C/Gas Mark 4 for fifteen minutes, and then at 400°F/200°C/Gas Mark 6 for thirty minutes until set.

Serves 4

Bacon and egg flan

Basic flan pastry
½ oz (15 g) butter
1 small onion
1 oz (25 g) streaky bacon
1 egg and 1 egg yolk
2 oz (50 g) grated cheese
¼ pint (150 ml) creamy milk
Pepper

Serves 4

Roll out the pastry and line an 8 in (20 cm) flan ring. Bake blind, using tin foil and dried peas or beans, at 400°F/200°C/Gas Mark 6 for ten minutes. Chop the onion finely and soften it in the butter. Add the chopped bacon and cook until the onion is golden. Remove the pastry case from the oven and spread the bacon and onion mixture on the bottom. Lightly beat the egg, egg yolk, cheese, milk and a little pepper. Add some salt if the bacon is not salty. Pour into the flan case and bake at 375°F/190°C/Gas Mark 5 for thirty minutes.

Kipper flan

This flan should be served hot.

Basic flan pastry
6 oz (175 g) kipper fillets
2 hard-boiled eggs
8 oz (225 g) cottage cheese
Juice and grated rind of 1 lemon
1 tablespoon chopped parsley
Salt and pepper
2 eggs

Line an 8 in (20 cm) flan ring with the pastry and bake blind at 400°F/200°C/Gas Mark 6 for fifteen minutes. Take out lining foil and baking beans from the flan and continue baking for ten minutes. Poach the kipper fillets in a little water. Drain, skin and flake the fish. Mix the fish, chopped hard-boiled eggs, cottage cheese, lemon juice and rind, and parsley. Season to taste. Stir in beaten eggs and pour into flan case. Bake at 350°F/180°C/Gas Mark 4 for twenty-five minutes.

Serves 4

Country sausage flan

Basic flan pastry
2 leeks
1 medium onion
3 bacon rashers
4 oz (100 g) mushrooms
1 lb (450 g) pork sausagemeat
1 teaspoon made mustard
1 tablespoon finely chopped parsley
2 eggs

Line an 8 in (20 cm) pie plate with the pastry. Chop the leeks and onion. Remove the rind from the bacon and cut the rashers into strips. Chop the mushrooms. Melt a little fat and fry the leeks, onion, bacon and mushrooms until the onion is golden. Add the sausagemeat and cook for fifteen minutes, stirring frequently. Add the parsley and mustard and mix well together. Season to taste and spread over the pastry case. Beat the eggs together and pour over the top. Bake at 375°F/190°C/Gas Mark 5 for forty-five minutes.
190°C/Gas Mark 5 for forty-five minutes.

Serves 4

Egg rarebit flan

Basic flan pastry
2 oz (50 g) butter
1 large onion
1½ oz (40 g) plain flour
¾ pint (450 ml) milk
6 oz (175 g) strong
    Cheddar cheese
1 tablespoon
    Worcestershire sauce
Salt and pepper
4 hard-boiled eggs

Serves 4

Line an 8 in (225 g) flan ring with the pastry and bake blind at 400°F/200°C/Gas Mark 6 for fifteen minutes. Take out the lining foil and baking beans from the flan and continue cooking for ten minutes. Make the filling while the pastry is cooking. Melt the butter, add the chopped onion and cook for five minutes. Stir in the flour and stir over heat for two minutes. Take off the heat and gradually stir in the milk. Return to the heat and bring to the boil, stirring all the time. Add 5 oz (150 g) of the grated cheese, together with the sauce. Cut the eggs in half and reserve four halves for garnish. Chop the remainder add to the cheese sauce, and season to taste. Spoon into the cooked flan case and sprinkle with remaining cheese. Put under a moderate grill for five minutes until golden brown, and top with the remaining eggs. Serve at once.

Meat Puddings

Meat for roasting or grilling is so expensive it sometimes seems the only alternative must be an endless succession of stews, or the sort of made-up dishes which most men distrust on sight. But how many will turn down a nice old-fashioned suet pudding, made with meat, poultry, game or bacon, in which the crust has taken up some of the rich gravy created by long, slow cooking? If you have never thought further than steak-and-kidney, why not try minced beef, rabbit, hare or chicken, old partridge, pheasant or grouse, pork or sausagemeat and apple, bacon and onion?

In some of the recipes there are individual measurements for the suet pastry. If you want to make up your own recipe to suit the amount of filling you have available, allow 1 oz (25 g) flour to ½ oz (15 g) shredded suet for one helping of pudding. For a four- or five- person family, a suet crust of 8 oz (225 g) flour and 4 oz (100 g) suet will give enough for a good-sized pudding which will allow for some second helpings.

Flour can be self-raising, or plain with the addition of baking powder (one teaspoon to 8 oz (225 g) flour). Black treacle (about one teaspoon to 8 oz (225 g) flour) gives a rich-tasting and well-coloured crust. Six tablespoons of cold water will be enough to mix this proportion of suet pastry. Some people prefer to line the basin before putting in the filling, but others say this takes up too much of the meat juices and prefer all the crust on top. Some 'dry' puddings are better cooked as savoury roly-polys, to be served with gravy or a knob of butter, and this is a good method for the various types of bacon and onion pudding.

To cover a pudding, use kitchen foil or double greaseproof paper, brushed with melted fat, or use a pudding cloth. Make sure the water is at boiling point when the basin is put into the steamer or saucepan. Half-a-pint (300 ml) water will evaporate in thirty minutes when boiled, so puddings which are to be left to steam on their own for two or three hours should be put in a pan containing not less than 3 pints (1.5 l) boiling water. 'Topping up' should always be with boiling water.

Steak and kidney pudding

1 lb (450 g) stewing steak
3 lambs' kidneys *or* 4 oz
  (100 g) ox kidney
8 oz (225 g) self-raising
  flour
4 oz (100 g) shredded
  suet
Salt and pepper
6 tablespoons water

Serves 4

Cut steak into thin pieces and chop kidney in small pieces. If liked, wrap a piece of meat round each piece of kidney, but otherwise just mix the two meats. Mix flour, suet, salt and pepper to a firm paste with water. Line a greased basin with two-thirds of the pastry. Put in the meat, and season well with salt and pepper and add a sprinkling of flour. Add water or stock almost to the top of the basin. Cover with remaining pastry and seal edges. Cover and steam for four hours.

Variations: Either add 1 small chopped onion or substitute 3 sliced onions for kidney. 2 oz (50 g) chopped mushrooms may be added and/ or 8 oysters for a special occasion (tinned ones can be used). 1 lb (450 g) minced steak mixed with 4 oz (100 g) mushrooms and a small chopped onion also make a good pudding, with a pinch of thyme mixed with the seasoning.

Rabbit pudding

8 oz (225 g) self-raising
    flour
4 oz (100 g) shredded
    suet
Salt and pepper
6 tablespoons water
1 small rabbit
½ teaspoon sage
2 sliced onions
2 sliced tomatoes
2 oz (50 g) chopped
    mushrooms

Make in the same way as for steak-and-kidney,
using rabbit joints and stock or water.

Serves 4

Hare pudding

1½ lb (700 g) meat cut
    from hare
2 sliced onions
1 sliced apple
1 tablespoon red wine or
    redcurrant jelly

Make as for steak-and-kidney, adding red wine
or redcurrant jelly to stock or water, and using
plenty of seasoning. As hare joints are so large
it is better to strip the meat from them before
using.

Serves 4

Kentish pork and apple pudding

8 oz (225 g) self-raising
    flour
4 oz (100 g) shredded suet
8 oz (225 g) fresh lean
    pork
Medium-sized cooking
    apple
Salt and pepper
Sage
Stock or water

Prepare pastry with flour and suet and enough
water to make a firm paste. Line basin with
pastry, and put in pork cut in squares,
chopped apple, salt and pepper, a good pinch
of chopped sage and stock to cover. Put on
pastry lid, cover and boil for four hours.

Serves 4

Northamptonshire bacon roll

8 oz (225 g) self-raising
    flour
3 oz (75 g) suet
Salt and pepper
6 oz (175 g) chopped
    mixed bacon and onion

Make suet pastry, using just enough water to
make a firm dough. Roll into a rectangle and
put on bacon and onion, and plenty of seasoning. A little chopped sage may be added. Roll
in a floured cloth and boil for 1½ hours. Serve
with gravy.

Serves 4

Essex pork plugga

This is made in the same way, but using diced streaky pork instead of bacon.

Sussex bacon pudding

The bacon, onion and some chopped herbs are added to the suet mixture, together with a beaten egg and a little milk (instead of the usual water to make the pastry). The mixture is steamed in a basin for 1½ hours and served with gravy.

Suffolk layer pudding

6 oz (175 g) self-raising
  flour
6 oz (175 g) plain flour
¼ teaspoon salt
4 oz (100 g) suet
1 lb (450 g) cooked
  minced meat
1 medium onion
Salt and pepper

Serves 4

Mix suet pastry with the two kinds of flour, salt, suet and milk to moisten. Line a pudding basin with half the mixture. Use meat left from the joint, or fresh mince which has been cooked, and use a little stock or gravy to moisten. Mix meat with chopped onion and seasoning. Put a layer of meat mixture into basin, then a thin layer of suet pastry, then more meat and pastry until basin is full, ending with pastry layer. Cover and steam for two hours. Serve with gravy or parsley sauce.

Suffolk onion pudding

This is very good with boiled bacon or a piece of beef.

4 oz (100 g) plain flour
2 oz (50 g) suet
8 oz (225 g) onions
Salt and pepper

Serves 4

Mix flour and suet with water to a stiff dough – and roll out. Cut up onions, salt and pepper them, and put on to dough. Roll up into a cloth. Boil for 1¼ hours. Serve with a slice of butter.

Game

Fair Game

A lot of families might find it very odd that others can actually get tired of game. But those with menfolk whose lives revolve round magic dates like 'The Twelfth' or 1st October will know the increasing strain as the winter months continue. Men, and small boys, have a passionate interest in the ultimate eating of any fish, flesh, fowl or good red herring which they have actually done to death themselves – a heritage from the cavemen, perhaps. Their women-folk, sickened by mounting piles of feathers, gory pelts, or undisposable fish-scales, would sometimes more cheerfully settle for an hygienically wrapped and utterly tasteless chicken trapped in the supermarket.

Nothing can truly beat plainly roasted game with all its delicious accompaniments of crumbs and chips, currant jelly, rich gravy, chestnuts, cabbage or celery, but there is often a moment when even perfection palls and some variety is called for. Additionally, birds may be old or badly shot (or may have lurked in the freezer a long time) and they are not fit for the simple treatment. In the case of partridges, now becoming rare, it may also be necessary to eke out helpings in a way which isn't possible with roast birds.

If a simple casserole is liked, it can be improved if the game is left in a marinade for any period up to fourteen days, and the meat cooked in the liquid. A good marinade is a mixture of $\frac{1}{2}$ breakfastcup vinegar with 1 breakfastcup red wine, a bay leaf, a pinch each of pepper, salt and nutmeg, a sprig of thyme, and 4 chopped onions. This is good for hare, pigeon and venison as well as old tough birds (the tough tissues are broken down by the liquid and cooking time is shortened).

A good game soup can be very comforting on a winter evening. If you haven't old birds to spare, use the trimmings and carcasses of pheasants or partridges, and include onions, carrots, celery, a little lean bacon, a good bunch of herbs, and plenty of seasoning including a clove. The soup will taste best if the bacon is crisped before adding to the stock and if the sliced vegetables are cooked in a little butter until golden. A real family soup can have the vegetables left in; for a more elegant version the stock should be strained off and reheated with a little diced game taken from the breast of the bird.

If you like game pie, it can be made with a mixture of game, even with the addition of rabbit, and perhaps a little pork or veal. A little savoury forcemeat can be added for extra flavour. Hot water pastry is best used, and will be easy to handle if put into the refrigerator for just thirty minutes after making before

*moulding into shape. Stock for the jelly should be made
from the game trimmings with a pig's trotter or calf's
foot added.*

*Nothing is so tasty as a plainly roasted pheasant or
partridge unless it's the almost equally delicious
cold bird – but the trimmings are very important. One
of the nicest things about pheasant and partridge is
that they are so delicious with the other traditional
autumn foods such as apples, celery, chestnuts, red
cabbage and mushrooms, and this does, of course, help
to keep down the price of what may seem exotic dishes.
Watercress, a plain green salad, a crunchy winter
salad or freshly cooked spinach are also perfect vegetable accompaniments.*

*Game chips are essential and so are fried crumbs or
squares of fried bread to take up the juices. Bread sauce
is another favourite – I like to leave little bits of
soft onion in mine – and chestnut purée if you have
the energy to peel and skin them. It's also worth making
a few small pots of redcurrant or rowanberry jelly and
cranberry sauce to keep ready for the game season.*

Game pudding

If pigeons are used, only the breasts go into the pudding, and the rest can be simmered for stock. If partridges are used, they can be split in half. I like the addition of a little bacon and a chopped onion, and sometimes a few mushrooms to this pudding, but they are optional. If appetites are very hearty, the quantity of suet pastry may be increased so that the bowl can be lined as well.

8 oz (225 g) suet pastry
4 pigeons or 2 partridges
8 oz (225 g) stewing steak
Yolks of 3 hard-boiled
    eggs
Salt, pepper and nutmeg
Stock made from game
    trimmings

Line the bowl with ½ in (1.25 cm) thick pastry if liked. Put in pigeon breasts or halved partridges, chopped steak, egg yolks, seasoning, and gravy to come half way up the bowl. Put on pastry lid and cover with cloth. Cook in a pan of boiling water for three hours.

Serves 4

Poacher's pot

1 small bird per person
Seasoned flour
1 oz (25 g) butter
1 teaspoon mixed herbs

Any bird, or a mixture of birds, can be used for this. Prepare them as for roasting, and dip in well-seasoned flour. Heat the butter and brown the birds. Add the herbs, put on a close-fitting lid, and cook slowly for about 1½ hours at 325°F/170°C/Gas Mark 3. Serve with the liquid in the pan slightly thickened as gravy, bread sauce and game chips.

Game pie

This pie must be made the day before using. The same method can be used for a pork pie, allowing 1 lb (450 g) meat to the same amount of pastry. Both can be given a beautiful glaze if carefully brushed with a beaten egg and pinch of salt before baking.

10 oz (300 g) plain flour
½ level teaspoon salt
1 egg yolk
3 oz (75 g) lard
¼ pint (150 ml) water
1 pheasant, partridge or
   grouse
12 oz (350 g) veal and
   pork minced together
Salt and pepper
Nutmeg
Stock

Sieve flour and salt into a bowl, make a well in the flour, and drop in the egg yolk. Heat lard and water until fat has dissolved, then bring to the boil and pour quickly into flour mixture. Mix thoroughly until pastry is cool enough to handle, then shape into a ball, cover and leave to rest in a warm place for thirty minutes.

Meanwhile, strip flesh from game bird and cut in neat pieces, and cook bones and trimmings in water to make stock. Using a game pie mould or a round cake tin with removable base, mould the pastry into shape. Season the minced veal and pork with salt, pepper and nutmeg and put a layer all round the inside of the case. Fill the centre cavity with the game meat and cover the top with more minced meat. Put on pastry lid, cutting out a small hole to let steam escape. Bake at 400°F/200°C/Gas Mark 6 for thirty minutes, then lower heat to 350°F/180°C/Gas Mark 4 for 1¼ hours, covering the pie with paper if it browns too quickly. Remove mould and allow to cool. Make a jelly with stock and gelatine and when the pie is cool, carefully pour jelly through a funnel into the hole in the lid. Allow to set before serving.

Grouse

In season: 12th August to 10th December.

Young birds have pointed wings and rounded spurs. One younger bird will feed two people, and an older one will do for three. Grouse is best roasted unless very old, or badly shot. Roast for 20–25 minutes at 400°F/200°C/Gas Mark 6 with bacon over the breast; serve on pieces of toast spread with the cooked liver mashed in a little stock. Accompany with gravy, bread sauce, buttered crumbs and wafer potatoes, with a garnish of watercress; rowanberry jelly is delicious with grouse.

Grouse pudding

8 oz (225 g) plain flour
1 teaspoon baking powder
½ teaspoon salt
4 oz (100 g) suet
1 old grouse
1 lb (450 g) stewing steak
1 onion
1 oz (25 g) butter
Salt, pepper, nutmeg

Sift together flour, baking powder and salt, and add the grated or chopped suet. Stir in enough cold water to make a pliable dough, and line a pudding basin with two-thirds of the pastry. Cut the flesh of the grouse into neat chunks, stewing the bones and trimmings in water to make a good stock. Brown the grouse and cubes of steak in the butter and put into the basin with salt, pepper and a pinch of nutmeg, chopped onion, and enough stock or water to half fill the basin. Cover with top crust, put on paper and a cloth, and steam for three hours, adding boiling water to the saucepan to keep it almost to the top of the basin. Make a hole in the top crust before serving and pour in hot stock or gravy.

Potted grouse

A small glass of port improves this dish. Serve with hot fresh toast.

2 old grouse
1 carrot
1 onion
2 oz (50 g) streaky bacon
Butter
Bunch of mixed herbs
Salt and pepper

Slice the carrots and onions, and cut the bacon in neat pieces and fry in butter until golden. Put into a casserole with the herbs and plenty of salt and pepper, and put the grouse on top. Cover with stock and cook at 300°F/150°C/Gas Mark 2 for 2½ hours. Remove the carrot. Take meat from the bones of the grouse, and put the mixture through a mincer, then pound, sieve or put in a liquidizer. Press into a shallow dish and cover with melted butter.

Pheasant

In season: 1st October to 1st February.

A young cock bird has round spurs in the first year, short pointed ones in the second year, sharp long ones when older. A young hen bird has soft feet and dark feathers. Hen birds are smaller, but less dry and more tender with good flavour. One good bird should feed four pople. The pheasant is best hung for about a week in normal temperatures; if badly shot or mauled it is better to use the bird more quickly.

Roast pheasant is best cooked at 400°F/200°C/Gas Mark 6 for about forty-five minutes, according to the size of the bird. Bacon should be tied on the breast, and the bird seasoned inside and out with salt and pepper. The bird is better for basting with butter, and better still if a little red wine is added to the roasting pan at half time. Serve with clear gravy, bread sauce, fried crumbs, wafer potatoes. Mushrooms are a delicious accompaniment, also chestnuts and braised celery.

Pheasant terrine

This is a rather expensive recipe but makes a large quantity of a very superior pâté – an excellent beginning for a shooting picnic and well worth while for a special occasion. The recipe may be used for other game birds, hare, duck or chicken, and the mincemeat layers can consist of chopped up poultry or game, pork, liver or tinned liver pâté.

1 pheasant
1 lb (450 g) fat pork
8 oz (225 g) thin-cut
    streaky bacon rashers
1 wineglass white wine
½ wineglass Madeira
½ wineglass brandy
Salt and pepper
Mixed herbs (parsley,
    chives, basil, tarragon,
    garlic)

Take the breast and thighs from a plump pheasant, cut the meat in slices and leave for twenty-four hours in the wine, Madeira, brandy and herbs. Mince the pheasant trimmings and liver with pork and season well with salt and pepper. Line a terrine (if you haven't the correct dish, use a deep pie dish or an earthenware casserole) with rashers of bacon. Put in a layer of the mincemeat, then the pheasant slices, and continue in layers, finishing with a layer of mincemeat and using the alcohol, mixed with herbs, to moisten the meat. Cover with bacon rashers and put on a lid. Stand the dish in a tin of water and cook at 325°F/170°C/Gas Mark 3 for 1½ hours. Leave until cold with a weight on top.

Pheasant pâté

8 oz (225 g) calves liver
4 oz (100 g) bacon
1 small onion
Salt and pepper
1 cooked pheasant
Powdered cloves and
   allspice

Serves 4

Lightly fry the liver and bacon and put through the mincer with the onion. Season well with salt and pepper. Cut meat from pheasant in neat pieces and season well with powdered cloves and allspice. Put a layer of the liver mixture into dish, then a layer of pheasant and continue in layers finishing with the liver mixture. Cover and steam for two hours. Cool with heavy weights on top and run clarified butter over top.

Pheasant with chestnuts

1 pheasant
1 oz (25 g) butter
8 oz (225 g) peeled and
   skinned chestnuts
8 oz (225 g) small onions
1 heaped tablespoon flour
1 pint (600 ml) stock
Grated rind and juice of
   ½ orange
2 teaspoons redcurrant
   jelly
1 teaspoon red wine
   vinegar
Parsley, thyme and bay
   leaf
Salt and pepper

Serves 4

Brown the pheasant all over in hot butter. Remove from fire and put into casserole. Toss the chestnuts and onions quickly in the fat until they turn colour, and remove from fat, putting round the pheasant. Blend the pan juices with flour, then work in the rest of the ingredients. Bring to the boil and pour over pheasant. Cover tightly and cook at 325°F/170°C/Gas Mark 3 for two hours. Remove the pheasant and cut in pieces. Put on serving dish with chestnuts and onions. Remove parsley, thyme and bay leaf, skim the liquid and reduce if necessary. Pour over pheasant and scatter with finely chopped parsley.

Pheasant in cider

1 old pheasant
1 lb (450 g) cooking apples
8 oz (225 g) onions
2 oz (50 g) butter
½ pint (300 ml) cider
1 garlic clove
Bunch of mixed herbs
Salt and pepper

Serves 4

Wipe pheasant thoroughly inside and out. Cut the apples in quarters after peeling, and put into a casserole. Slice the onions and cook in butter until soft and transparent. Put the pheasant on top of the apples and cover with onions. Pour in the cider, and put in herbs, crushed garlic and seasoning. Cover tightly and cook at 325°F/170°C/Gas Mark 3 for 2½ hours. Serve immediately, or sieve the onions and apples in the sauce, reheat and pour over the bird.

Pheasant with celery sauce

The stock for cooking the pheasant should include a carrot and onion, and a couple of cloves, salt and pepper and a good sprig of parsley. If money is short, use a little top of milk instead of cream for the sauce. The same recipe may be used for partridges, and this quantity of sauce will be enough for two birds.

1 large old pheasant
1 pint (600 ml) stock
1 head celery
2 oz (50 g) butter
1 onion
Parsley, thyme and bay
    leaf
1 clove
Salt and pepper
1 oz (25 g) butter with
    1 oz (25 g) flour
¼ pint (150 ml) cream

Serves 4

Poach the pheasant in the stock until tender (this will depend on the age of the bird). Cut the bird into neat pieces for serving with the celery sauce. Make this by cooking the chopped celery in butter with the onion, herbs, clove, salt and pepper until tender, then simmering in ½ pint (300 ml) stock until really soft (use some of the pheasant stock). Put the celery through a sieve and thicken with the butter and flour worked together. Finally, stir in the cream and pour over the pheasant. The sauce should be rather thick. If time is short and the celery young and without strings, the pieces may be left whole without sieving.

Pheasant with apples

A wineglass of Calvados (apple brandy) is a delicious addition.

1 pheasant
4 oz (100 g) butter
1½ lb (700 g) apples
4 tablespoons cream
Salt and pepper

Serves 4

Season the bird with salt and pepper and cook in butter until golden. Peel and slice the apples and line a casserole with half of them. Pour in some of the butter, put in the bird and surround with remaining apples. Pour in the rest of the butter and the cream, cover tightly and cook at 350°F/180°C/Gas Mark 4 for forty-five minutes, though the time may be a little longer if the bird is old.

Partridge

In season: 1st September to 1st February.

First-year birds have the first flight feather pointed at the tip, not rounded. The grey partridge is most delicious after only three to four days' hanging, but the red-legged variety needs six to seven days. One bird will serve two people. Roast at 350°F/180°C/Gas Mark 4 for twenty-five minutes, with bacon on the breast, basting with butter. Serve split in two with clear gravy, watercress, wafer potatoes. A crisp apple and celery salad is a good side dish.

Potted partridge

2 partridges
8 oz (225 g) butter
½ pint (300 ml) stock

Season the birds inside and out and put a lump of butter in each. Put into a casserole with some good stock and the rest of the butter, cover with double cooking foil and a lid and cook at 325°F/170°C/Gas Mark 3 for 1½ hours. Leave until cold, when the butter will form a seal on top. Do not uncover until they are to be eaten; they will keep several days. Serve garnished with parsley, and with redcurrant jelly.

Partridge casserole

2 old partridges
2 onions
2 carrots
1 savoy cabbage
4 oz (100 g) streaky bacon
½ pint (300 ml) stock
Thyme and parsley
Salt and pepper
8 oz (225 g) chipolata
    sausages

Serves 4

Cut the vegetables into neat pieces and brown them in a little butter, together with the partridges. Cut the cabbage into quarters and cook in boiling water with the bacon for five minutes. Drain well. Cut bacon and cabbage into small pieces. Put half the cabbage into a casserole, season with salt and pepper, and put on the partridges. Cover with bacon and vegetables, chopped herbs, and the rest of the cabbage. Pour in stock, cover with a lid and cook at 300°F/150°C/Gas Mark 2 for three hours. Grill the sausages lightly and add thirty minutes before serving time.

The addition of a glass of dry cider, and a little less stock, makes a good variation to dish.

Partridge pie

2 partridges
8 oz (225 g) lean veal
8 oz (225 g) boiled bacon
  or ham
1 oz (25 g) butter
1 tablespoon chopped
  parsley
4 oz (100 g) mushrooms
Salt and pepper
Pinch of nutmeg
¼ pint (150 ml) onion
  sauce
2 hard-boiled eggs, sliced
Puff pastry
Rich stock or gravy

Cut the birds in halves and cook them lightly with butter until just coloured. In a pie-dish put a layer of mixed chopped veal and bacon. Put in partridges. Add parsley, mushrooms and seasoning, and put on a second layer of veal and bacon. Pour on the onion sauce and cover with slices of egg. Cover with pastry, glaze with beaten egg and bake at 400°F/200°C/ Gas Mark 6 for an hour. When the pie is removed from the oven, pour in a little rich hot stock or gravy. Serve hot or cold.

Serves 4

October partridge

2 partridges
Juice of ½ lemon
Salt and pepper
2 rashers bacon
1 small onion
1 small red cabbage
¼ pint (150 ml) cider
1 teaspoon vinegar
6 chestnuts
1 oz (25 g) butter

Serves 4

Wipe the partridges inside and out, dust with salt and pepper and sprinkle with lemon juice. Melt butter in a pan and brown the birds slowly all over. Cool slightly, then wrap each bird in a slice of bacon. Slice the onion and red cabbage very finely, season with salt and pepper and put into a saucepan with the cider and vinegar. Bring to the boil and simmer for twenty minutes. Put birds on top and put on lid, then simmer for 1½ hours. Peel the chestnuts, toss in butter and add to the dish ten minutes before cooking is finished.

Venison

In season: late June to January.

The meat should be hung eight to ten days, and is best larded or put into a marinade of wine and herbs before roasting, as there is little fat (a larding needle is used to thread the meat with strips of fat bacon or pork). Large joints are best roasted; smaller and unidentifiable pieces are best stewed. Chops and fillet may be grilled, and cutlets can be jugged. Cold venison makes excellent cottage pie, or a good galantine if pressed in a mould with plenty of seasoning. Traditional accompaniments are redcurrant, rowan or cranberry jelly.

Roast venison

1 joint of venison
½ pint (300 ml) red wine
½ pint (300 ml) vinegar
1 sliced onion
Parsley, thyme and bay
 leaf
Sour cream or yogurt
 (optional)

Mix together the wine, vinegar, onion and herbs and put the venison in it to soak for two days, turning the meat from time to time. When ready to cook the meat, put the joint on a rack in a baking tin, with the marinade in the tin. Cook at 375°F/190°C/Gas Mark 5 until meat is tender, basting frequently. Strain the pan juices through a sieve, thicken with a little flour, and if liked ¼ pint (150 ml) of sour cream or yogurt.

Venison roll

This can also be made with hare or a mixture of game.

2 lb (1 kg) venison
8 oz (225 g) fat bacon
Salt and pepper
1 small onion
6 oz (175 g) breadcrumbs
1 tablespoon chopped
 parsley
2 eggs
Stock to mix

Mince the venison and bacon. Add finely chopped onion, salt and pepper, breadcrumbs and parsley. Beat the eggs and add to the mixture, putting in just enough stock to bind to a firm mixture. Put into a pudding cloth, tie in a long roll and boil for 2½ hours.

Hare

In season: early autumn to end of February.
 Young hare can generally be recognized by white pointed teeth and fresh-looking fur; the older animals will have cracked brown teeth and be scruffy-looking. A hare will feed ten people easily. The saddle can be roasted (best for a young animal), while other parts are good in casserole, as soup or pâté.

Hare jugged in beer

1 hare (with blood)
Seasoned flour
Beef dripping
1 onion stuck with cloves
1 pint (600 ml) beer
1 good wineglass port or
 sherry

Serves 8–10

This is somewhat easier to tackle than the usual jugged hare. Flour portions of hare and brown in dripping. Put into a large casserole with the drippings from the pan and the blood. Add the onion and beer, cover and cook in a slow oven for five hours until the meat leaves the bones easily. Just before serving, take out the onion and pour in the port or sherry. Serve with redcurrant jelly.

Hare pâté

This pâté will keep for several weeks in a refrigerator.

1 lb (450 g) cooked hare, removed from bones
2 oz (50 g) mushrooms
1 thick slice bread soaked in milk
Rich gravy
2 oz (50 g) butter
2 egg yolks
6 tablespoons brandy or Madeira
Pepper and salt
1 bay leaf

Strip the hare from the bones and cut up meat in small pieces. Mix with sliced mushrooms cooked in butter and the soaked bread. Mince and pound until smooth. Moisten with a little gravy and mix with butter, egg yolks, brandy or Madeira and seasoning. Put the bayleaf in the bottom of a dish, put in the meat mixture, cover and steam for two hours (the dish may be placed in a tin of water and cooked at 325°F/170°C/Gas Mark 3 for two hours). Leave until very cold under a weight.

Pigeon Pair

Great houses bred pigeons for useful food, and the many different species of domesticated pigeons were not only for food but also for ornament, sport or messengers. They rejoice in such names as pouters, carriers, homers, fantails, jacobins, nuns, turbits, tumblers and trumpeters. The Star Chamber Accounts constantly carry the price of pigeons, making a difference between the tame or 'house' pigeons and the wild ones. From 1519 to 1535, the usual charge was a penny each or 10d a dozen. By 1590, the price had risen to 2½d each for wild birds and 6d for house birds. In 1602 and 1605 they cost 8d each, and by 1635 were 13s and 14s a dozen. Two-and-a-half centuries later, when they were a favourite on Victorian and Edwardian tables, the price remained at about 1s each. Cassell's Dictionary of Cookery, *popular at the beginning of the century, lists no less than forty-three recipes for them, including such delicacies as Pigeon Cutlets and Pigeons Stewed with Asparagus.*

It is a pity that pigeons are now classed as vermin. Like so many other good things to eat, we often reject or despise them just because they're plentiful and homely. Make them scarce, put up the price to £1 apiece, and we might queue for them. Pigeon flesh is tasty and lean – and for weight-watchers, the calorie content is equivalent to lean steak of the same weight. Hanging isn't essential or even desirable, because pigeons are best cooked fresh. If they are hung head downwards for an hour immediately after killing, though, they will bleed freely and the flesh will be paler.

When you have access to a lot of pigeons, it is

simplest to use the breasts only, and these should be removed complete with the breast bone. Put the bird on its back, part the breast feathers, and cut through the skin down the centre of the breast bone with a sharp knife. The skin may then be easily turned back and the breast bone can be lifted upwards from the tail. Cut through the shoulder joints with a pair of kitchen scissors, and lift the breast off complete.

When it comes to plucking, disregard the wings which have little or no meat on them. Cut them off at the first joint. Remove the guts and the contents of the crop. When fully plucked, the breast can still be used alone for dishes, and the bones and trimmings cooked up to make a rich stock.

Fat young pigeons can be roasted, but older birds are lean and dry. They will need cooking longer. When roasting, cover the breast with bacon or with cooking foil for part of the time to prevent drying out. Don't put hot fat on pigeons as the flesh is delicate, and overheated fat will toughen them and destroy the flavour. Put a slice of crustless toast under plainly roasted birds for ten minutes before serving to absorb gravy and fat and provide a delicious titbit.

Old-fashioned pigeon pie

Don't be alarmed by the omission of pastry from this 'pie'. Originally, game pies were made in thick earthenware casseroles without a pastry case. Even when pastry was used it was merely a box for the contents, and was discarded and given to the servants or animals. Making the 'pie' this way will produce a delicious jellied meat mixture to serve cold with a salad of lettuce, watercress and sliced oranges.

Take the meat from the raw birds and put aside. Boil the carcasses for five hours to give a good rich stock which will turn to jelly when cold. Put layers of pigeon meat in a casserole, alternating with sliced egg and raw sausage-meat with a little chopped bacon. Sprinkle layers with a little parsley and with seasoning. I like to add a little grated nutmeg to this kind of cold meat dish. Continue until the dish is three-quarters full. Pour over enough strained stock just to cover and simmer at 325°F/ 170°C/Gas Mark 3 for two hours. Leave until cold, remove fat, and top up with any remaining stock in which has been mixed plenty of finely chopped parsley and chervil. Leave in a cold place until set.

3 pigeons
4 hard-boiled eggs
12 oz (350 g) sausagemeat
2 oz (50 g) fat bacon
Salt and pepper

Fresh parsley
Fresh chervil
Grated nutmeg (optional)
Stock
Serves 4

Pigeon and potato pie

2 pigeon breasts
4 oz (100 g) stewing steak
12 oz (350 g) potatoes
4 oz (100 g) mushrooms
1 large onion
Seasoned flour
Salt and pepper
Stock
8 oz (225 g) puff or short-
    crust pastry
Beaten egg

Serves 4

Cut right through the bones to divide the breasts into four pieces. Cut the steak into small pieces. Dip breasts and steak in seasoned flour. Peel and slice potatoes, mushrooms and onion. Put the ingredients into a pie dish and season with salt and pepper. Fill the dish three-quarters full with hot stock. Cover with pastry and glaze with a little beaten egg. Bake at 425°F/220°C/Gas Mark 6 for twenty minutes, then reduce heat to 350°F/170°C/Gas Mark 4 for 1½ hours. Cover the pastry if necessary to prevent browning. Before serving, fill up with a little more hot stock.

Pigeon pudding

8 oz (225 g) suet pastry
Meat from breasts of 3
    pigeons
8 oz (225 g) stewing steak
Seasoned flour
1 medium onion
Mixed herbs
Stock or water
Red wine (optional)

Serves 4

Grease a pudding basin and line with three-quarters of the pastry. Cut the pigeons and steak into neat pieces and coat in a little seasoned flour. Fill the basin with the meat, sliced onion, herbs, and about four tablespoons of stock. Add a little red wine to give a good flavour. Put on a pastry lid, cover the whole basin with foil or a cloth and steam for four hours. Keep some extra stock to serve with the pudding.

Pigeons with cabbage

This is a good cold-day dish using a firm-hearted cabbage and old birds. A Victorian version suggests thickening the gravy before serving with a knob of butter and flour and two tablespoons of thick cream.

1 large firm cabbage
8 rashers fat bacon
Butter
2 pigeons
Parsley, thyme and bay
    leaf

Blanch a large firm cabbage in boiling water for ten minutes, drain very well and chop finely. Mix with four rashers of chopped bacon and put into a greased fireproof dish. Season with salt and pepper, and put in a sprig each of parsley and thyme, and a bay leaf. Brown pigeons in a little butter and put them into the dish, covering with the remaining rashers of bacon. Add some stock just to cover, cover tightly and simmer for two hours. Split the birds in half and serve on a bed of cabbage.

Serves 4

Cider pigeons

2 pigeons
2 oz (50 g) butter
1 small apple
1 small onion
1 oz (25 g) flour
$\frac{3}{4}$ pint (450 ml) stock
$\frac{1}{4}$ pint (150 ml) cider
Fried apple rings } for
Bacon rolls   } garnish
Parsley, thyme and bay
   leaf, tied in a muslin
   bag

Brown the pigeons in butter and split them in half. Slice the apple and onion and brown them in the same fat. Sprinkle on the flour and cook until golden. Add the stock and cider and bring to the boil. Season with salt and pepper, add the herbs and the pigeon halves. Cover tightly and simmer on top of the stove or in a low oven for $2\frac{1}{2}$ hours. Remove the herbs and serve the pigeons in their gravy with a garnish of fried apple rings and bacon rolls.

Serves 4

Jellied pigeons

This is a very good way of dealing with old birds.

3 or 4 pigeons
Salt and pepper
Mixed herbs
1 oz (25 g) gelatine

Simmer the birds in just enough water to cover with plenty of seasoning and herbs for about $1\frac{1}{2}$ hours until the meat leaves the bones easily. Remove the meat from the bones, taste the gravy for seasoning, and dissolve the gelatine (which has been softened in a little cold water) in the hot liquid. Pack the meat into a wetted mould and pour the stock over it. Leave to set before turning out to serve with salad.

A Day on the Marsh

It's difficult for a woman to appreciate the pleasures of wild-fowling, when the male addict is twitching his way through the winter months waiting for the right horrid combination of chill and damp to lure him out to the soggy windswept marshes. This is a rare sport, though, for few of the men are particularly concerned with the size and type of bag, but far more with their study of the birds, the weather and flight patterns, and the sheer beauty of the lonely marsh. Ask a wildfowler to describe the flight of the geese and you'll discover that you are talking to a poet.

In the kitchen, one awaits the bag with trepidation. The birds come in an extraordinary assortment of varieties and sizes, and they're often pretty wet and soggy. Duck and goose should be hung depending on personal taste, age and the weather, to tenderize the flesh. Be sure the air circulates freely round the bird, and allow at least three days for hanging. In very cold weather, this time can be lengthened. Conventionally, wildfowl are hung by the neck or beak, but wet birds can be hung by a wing or leg instead. Normally birds are hung in the feather and undrawn, but WAGBI (Wildfowlers' Association of Great Britain and Ireland) suggests gutting widgeon and even duck as soon as they are brought into the kitchen.

Plucking is a messy business, best done out of doors. When most of the feathers are off, remove the down by rubbing the skin firmly with the ball of the thumb, and then singe the skin. Remove the head and neck and cut off the legs, then cut through the skin from the lower end of the breast bone to the vent, removing the latter. Discard the intestines, lungs and windpipe, but use the giblets for stock.

Wipe outside and inside the bird with a cloth wrung out after being dipped in very hot water containing a little vinegar. Some people like to skin rather than pluck a bird, which is less messy, but the finished dish doesn't look so good, and many people enjoy meat skins. When wildfowl is to be frozen, it must be plucked and drawn first (and hung before plucking). It's important to label carefully as the birds are unidentifiable after a month or two in the freezer.

There are many different ways of cooking the different birds, but carefully roasted wildfowl is probably the most delicious. It should be served underdone showing slightly pink flesh on the breast.

A rotating spit on your cooker is perfect for cooking any of the duck family. Salt the birds and paint them with oil, and start roasting at maximum temperature, reducing to medium heat after ten minutes. Teal is delicious spit-roasted, and needs about thirty minutes. Allow an hour for mallard. Bacon rashers can be trussed round a dry duck to improve the flavour, but should be removed in time to crisp the skin.

For oven-roasting, put the birds breast down in a shallow roasting tin just large enough to hold them. Roast at 425°F–450°F/220°C–230°C/Gas Mark 7–8, and baste with butter, cooking oil or dripping. Turn the birds on their backs ten minutes before the end of cooking time.

For a crisp skin, sprinkle on salt after the final basting, or froth by sprinkling lightly with flour. When a bird is likely to be tough, rub it well with fat and wrap in foil, then roast at 450°F/230°C/Gas Mark 4 for the rest of cooking time. Young teal, my favourite wildfowl, can be split in half, seasoned and grilled under medium heat until tender.

If you like roast birds stuffed, try putting in a little shallot or onion; a few sections of orange or tangerine; the traditional sage and onion; a mixture of raw apple slices and soaked prunes; some lightly fried sausage meat with chopped apple and a pinch of cinnamon; a mixture of raw apples, raisins, suet, breadcrumbs and egg; or some chopped parsnips or Jerusalem artichokes with plenty of butter. I prefer plainly roasted birds with a delicious accompaniment.

Try adding the juice of an orange or a few spoon-fuls of red wine, sherry or port to the pan juices. A few pieces of chopped onion, mushroom or some almonds are also good additions. Some people like a rather strongly flavoured sauce, which can be based on a brown gravy enriched by some chopped onion softened in butter, some red wine or port, orange rind and juice, and redcurrant jelly. Cherries are sometimes added to this sauce, and there are many other popular fruit and salad accompaniments.

Watercress is both decorative and good to eat, but a winter salad of celery, apple, raw carrot and nuts is delicious with wildfowl. Try apple sauce, or cranberry sauce or jelly, and experiment with oranges, which have an odd affinity with rich duck and goose flesh. A simple salad can be made with peeled sliced oranges served in French dressing; the rind and juice of orange can be added to dark rich gravy; or the orange slices can be lightly fried in butter, dusted with castor sugar and served hot. Other fruits which 'cut' the fatness of the meat and enhance its flavour are apricots and pineapple; green olives are a more sophisticated accompaniment.

As a change, try braising or pot-roasting the birds. Wild duck is good in a bacon-lined pan with plenty of sliced onions, carrots and chopped fresh herbs. Pour off the fat at half-time and add some brown gravy sharpened with lemon juice and a glass of wine.

To make a bird tender, try putting it in a casserole with butter, shallots or small onions and a little garlic, and cook it in the oven in its own juices and steam. Another variation can be made with apples and potatoes in the casserole, and a drop of cider for moisture.

Incidentally, many wildfowl are all the better for a little wine in the cooking, but dry cider is a splendid substitute. If you think a bird may be tough, leave it for a day or two before cooking in a dish of dry white wine or cider with some sliced onions.

Wild duck with ginger

2 wild ducks
Salt and pepper
¾ teaspoon ground ginger
Mixed herbs
1½ wineglasses port
Juice of large orange

Serves 4

Season the duck with salt, pepper, ginger and herbs and roast with a liberal dressing of butter for one hour. To make the sauce, add port and orange juice to the pan juices and cook gently for a minute, adding a little salt if needed. A pleasant accompaniment is a baked apple each, stuffed with raisins, cloves and redcurrant jelly.

Wildfowlers' pie

1 lb (450 g) cooked
  wildfowl
8 oz (225 g) sausagemeat
2 cooked onions
2 ripe tomatoes
6 bacon rashers
2 hard-boiled eggs
2 teaspoons horseradish
  sauce
Fresh mixed herbs
Salt and pepper
1 lb (450 g) shortcrust
  pastry
Beaten egg

Serves 4

Line a large piedish with pastry. Cook the sausagemeat until the fat runs out, and then add the chopped cooked onions. Cook gently until golden and then drain off the fat. Skin the tomatoes and slice them thinly, and slice the eggs. Carve the game in thin slices (other game such as hare and venison may be added if liked). Put slices of game into the pastry case. Top with a layer of sausage and onion, a layer of chopped bacon, tomato and egg slices. Sprinkle layers well with herbs, salt and pepper. Follow with a layer of game, a layer of bacon and dabs of horseradish and continue filling the dish in layers. Cover with a pastry lid, glaze with beaten egg, and bake at 425°F/220°C/Gas Mark 7 for forty minutes, covering the pastry if it begins to get too brown. Serve very hot with vegetables, or cold with salad.

Victorian salmi

1 mallard (teal or other
  duck can be used)
4 oz (100 g) bacon
1 onion
Parsley and thyme
2 bay leaves
1 oz (25 g) lard
1 oz (25 g) butter
1 oz (25 g) plain flour
½ pint (300 ml) stock
Large wineglass red wine
Few black olives

Serves 4

Dice the bacon and fry lightly. Add the herbs and bay leaves. Put half the mixture into a fireproof serving dish, and the rest into a baking tin. Put the bird in the tin on the bacon and add the onion, cut in slices. Add some lard, putting it on the bird's breast. Roast at 350°F/180°C/Gas Mark 4 for twenty minutes. Slice off all the meat and put it on the bacon in the fireproof dish. Melt the butter, work in the flour, and add the stock and wine. Simmer for five minutes, and pour over the meat, adding the stoned olives. Cover and cook at 325°F/170°C/Gas Mark 3 for thirty minutes. Serve from the dish with plain boiled potatoes, and vegetables.

Wild duck pâté

This pâté freezes well –
but do not put on the
final topping of butter.

1 or 2 ducks
Ox liver
Fat bacon
1 small onion
1 garlic clove
A little sherry (optional)

Use only raw meat cut from wild duck, or use
meat from other birds to make up a suitable
amount. Allow the same weight of liver and
bacon. Mince all the ingredients twice through
a fine mincer. Season well and add a little
sherry if liked. Press into an ovenware dish,
cover, and stand the dish in an oven tin of
water. Cook at 325°F/170°C/Gas Mark 3 for
one hour. Cool and press under weights for
twenty-four hours. Pour over a little melted
butter to seal the pâté.

Return of
the Rabbit

*There was a time when rabbit meat was cheap, and
many country families seldom ate 'butcher's meat':
they relied on this plentiful wild food, eked out with
the occasional chicken which had stopped laying or a
piece of pork bartered with a neighbour. A friend who
grew up in Lincolnshire describes with relish her
mother's traditional roast rabbit stuffed to bursting
with fresh parsley while her husband reminisces about
Essex rabbit pies. His mother's rabbit pies were pies
with a difference, served regularly for Monday morning
breakfast, and during the month of May (and May
only) containing a mixture of rook and rabbit. At
other times, the mixture was moorhen and rabbit.*

    *Pieces of boned rabbit are delicious if flattened
like veal, dipped in egg and breadcrumbs, fried until
golden, and served with wedges of lemon. Rabbit used
to be called 'poor man's chicken' and this recipe really
does taste like chicken. Rabbit will always taste better
if the pieces are soaked for half an hour before
cooking in a pint (600 ml) water with two tablespoons
vinegar.*

Irish roast rabbit

1 rabbit
1 tablespoon plain flour
Pepper
2 oz (50 g) butter
4 rashers bacon
2 medium onions
2 teaspoons chopped
  parsley
½ pint (300 ml) scalded
  milk

Cut up rabbit and soak in vinegar and water.
Dry pieces well and coat in flour seasoned
with pepper. Brown in the butter and put into a
casserole. Add chopped bacon, onions and
parsley and pour over milk. Cover and bake at
375°F/190°C/Gas Mark 5 for one hour. Serve
with plenty of floury potatoes. Parsley sauce is
also good with this.

Serves 4

Little rabbit pies

Delicious for a packed meal.

1 rabbit, jointed
½ pint (300 ml) thick white sauce
8 oz (225 g) cooked ham or corned beef
4 tablespoons breadcrumbs
½ teaspoon grated lemon rind
1 teaspoon chopped parsley
Pepper and salt
Shortcrust or puff pastry

Simmer the rabbit pieces gently until tender, cook, and mince the flesh with the ham or corned beef. Add breadcrumbs, lemon rind, parsley and seasoning and bind with white sauce. Roll out pastry thinly and cut into 4 in (10 cm) rounds. Cover half the rounds with rabbit mixture and top with the other half, pressing edges together. Brush tops with milk and bake at 450°F/230°C/Gas Mark 8 for twenty minutes.

Rabbit brawn

A little cooked ham, bacon or stewing beef is a good addition.

1 rabbit
2 carrots
2 onions
Salt and pepper
Pinch of nutmeg
Pinch of ground cloves
Sprig of thyme
2 hard-boiled eggs
2 oz (50 g) gelatine

Cut up rabbit and simmer until tender in 3 pints (1.5 l) water with sliced carrots and onions, seasoning, spices and thyme. Rinse a mould with cold water and decorate the bottom with slices of hard-boiled egg. Cool the cooked rabbit and cut meat into small pieces. Dissolve the gelatine in a little water, then add it to the rabbit stock and boil. Strain over the rabbit meat and leave in a cold place to set.

Rabbit with onion sauce

Rabbit and onions have an affinity for each other. This dish goes very well with jacket potatoes.

1 rabbit
3 lb (1.5 kg) onions
3 oz (75 g) butter
Some thick cream

Serves 4

Joint and soak rabbit, then put in cold water with salt and pepper. Bring to the boil, reduce to simmering heat and cook for about 1¼ hours until tender, depending on the age of the rabbit. Cut rabbit in pieces and serve covered with onion sauce, made by cutting onions very finely and stewing gently in butter until they are very soft but not brown, keeping lid on the pan and stirring frequently. Add ¾ pint (450 ml) rabbit stock, season again to taste, and stir in some thick hot cream before pouring over rabbit.

Hunter's rabbit

1 rabbit
1 small hard cabbage
1 lb (450 g) chipolata
   sausages
1 small onion
4 bacon rashers
Thyme, parsley and bay
   leaf
Salt and pepper
¼ pint (150 ml) stock (can
   be made with a beef
   cube)
½ pint (300 ml) dry cider

Cut rabbit in pieces and soak, then dry thoroughly. Cut cabbage lengthways into six or eight pieces, and boil in very little water for five minutes, draining well. Fry sausages and sliced onion. Put cabbage in a casserole, then put in rabbit pieces, followed by sausages and onion, and the chopped uncooked bacon. Add herbs and seasoning, pour in stock and cider and cover tightly. Cook at 325°F/170°C/Gas Mark 3 for 2½ hours.

Serves 4

Jugged rabbit

Serve with forcemeat
balls and redcurrant jelly.

1 rabbit
1 onion
1 bay leaf
Salt and pepper
Pinch of nutmeg
Dripping or bacon fat
1 teaspoon sugar
½ pint (300 ml) dry cider
Flour or cornflour

Soak rabbit joints overnight in 1 pint (600 ml) water with two tablespoons vinegar, together with chopped onion, bay leaf, salt and pepper and nutmeg. Drain joints, keeping the liquid, and dry joints well. Fry rabbit in dripping or bacon fat until golden, then cover with liquid and simmer very gently until tender (about one hour). Add sugar and cider to pan and continue cooking for fifteen minutes. Thicken gravy with a little flour or cornflour.

Serves 4

Rabbit in ale

1 rabbit
1 tablespoon vinegar
6 streaky bacon rashers
8 oz (225 g) onions
Salt and pepper
1 tablespoon mixed
   mustard
2 × 1 in (2.5 cm) bread
   slices
¾ pint (450 ml) ale
1 teaspoon sugar
Chopped parsley

Serves 4

Cut the rabbit into joints and soak in water with the vinegar for an hour. Drain and dry thoroughly. Cut the bacon in pieces and cook gently in a thick pan until the fat runs. Keep three tablespoons fat and use it to brown the sliced onions. Transfer bacon and onions to a casserole and use the fat to brown the pieces of rabbit. Put rabbit on top of onions and season well with salt and pepper. Toss the mustard and the bread cut in cubes together and add to the casserole with the ale and the sugar. Cover tightly and cook at 325°F/170°C/Gas Mark 3 for two hours. Serve sprinkled with plenty of chopped parsley.

Rabbit in cider

1 rabbit
1 tablespoon lemon juice
1 oz (25 g) bacon fat
4 large onions
1 bay leaf
Sprig of thyme
2 bacon rashers
8 oz (225 g) tomatoes
¼ pint (150 ml) dry cider
Salt and pepper

Serves 4

Joint the rabbit and soak it in water with the lemon juice for one hour. Dry well and fry the joints in bacon fat until golden. Add the onions, cut in slices, and cook until they are soft. Add the bay leaf, thyme, chopped bacon and peeled sliced tomatoes. Simmer for ten minutes, then pour in the cider. Cover and cook at 325°F/170°C/Gas Mark 3 for 1½ hours. Adjust seasoning before serving. If fresh tomatoes are not available, use canned or frozen ones.

Rabbit pie

The pie can also be made with boned rabbit meat (the bones should be used for the stock). Ham or bacon, hard-boiled eggs or forcemeat balls can also be added for extra richness.

1 rabbit
1 onion
Salt and pepper
1 oz (25 g) plain flour
¼ pint (150 ml) water or
  stock
1 teaspoon chopped
  parsley
12 oz (350 g) fat bacon
12 oz (350 g) puff pastry

Joint the rabbit and soak the pieces in cold water for an hour. Dry them and toss in flour seasoned with salt and pepper. Put a layer into a pie dish and sprinkle with pieces of bacon, onion and parsley. Continue in alternate layers, seasoning well, until the dish is full. Add the water or stock and cover with pastry. Bake at 400°F/200°C/Gas Mark 6 for 1½ hours, and serve hot or cold.

Serves 4

Potted rabbit

Hare, or a mixture of hare and venison, can be prepared in the same way.

1 young rabbit
Salt and pepper
Mace
Allspice
Cayenne pepper
Butter

Cut the meat from the bones. Discard the head but use the liver. Pack the meat closely into a small covered dish, seasoning it well with salt and pepper, powdered mace and allspice and a pinch of cayenne pepper. Cover liberally with butter and bake at 300°F/150°C/Gas Mark 2 for 2½ hours. Cool, then pack the meat into small pots. When completely cold, cover with clarified butter.

Outdoor
Eating

Picnics with Pleasure

Long bright days turn our thoughts to outdoor eating. For some, food out of doors suggests family picnics and expeditions to the sea or river. For others it refers to a box of midday nourishment to be eaten between spells of work in the fields where every minute is precious. Sandwiches are boring for such meals, though baps filled with cooked hamburgers and onions, crispy bacon and scrambled egg, or with salad spiked with salmon or sardines, can make a pleasant and easily prepared meal. Tomatoes, chunks of cucumber, pieces of cheese, apples, bananas and chocolate all give a contrast of texture and flavour which is welcome, and they need no preparation.

The best kind of packed meal, however, is that which is wrapped in pastry, easy to handle, crisp outside and soft inside. The variety of fillings is endless. Traditional pies – pork, veal and ham, chicken and ham, bacon and egg – are all popular. And what can beat a wedge of cold steak-and-kidney pie, with the filling softly set in its own juices?

From the sandwich-and-apple for the solitary gun to a full-scale luncheon party for the race meeting, it's surprising how often winter picnics have to be prepared. The first essential to outdoor winter meals is a really strongly flavoured meat dish. Even if the meal has to be of the sandwich-and-flask variety, the meat can take the form of a sausage mould, pressed beef in baps or individual pies rather than slices of bread. Something crisp and refreshing like celery, chicory or apples would offset the richness.

Take along something really sweet to restore energy quickly. This can be a rich fruit cake or sticky gingerbread, a wedge of apple pie to eat with cheese, or even that great favourite, treacle tart. Finally, a flask of scalding coffee is imperative, a bottle of wine a reviving thought, and a nip of cherry brandy a distinct comfort. If you like to serve a drink before your meal, take along a bottle of madeira or marsala, to stimulate healthy appetites.

Use equipment wisely to keep meals steaming hot. Casserole dishes can be carried safely in a simple hay-box, and taste all the better for reheating. If a hay-box is not a practical proposition, invest in a large vacuum flask to hold stew alone, or one of the large three-container varieties which take potatoes and other vegetables as well. Potatoes baked in their jackets in aluminium foil can be thickly wrapped in newspaper, then in flannel or towels and will keep hot for an hour or two.

If you want to serve a simple meal with a cold roast joint or bird, the technique of cooking the meat *must be carefully considered. The best method is to seal the surface first by putting the meat or poultry into a hot oven, 450°F/230°C/Gas Mark 8 for five minutes, then reduce the heat to 350°F/180°C/Gas Mark 4 for the remainder of the cooking time, basting with the pan juices. If a joint is brushed with salad oil, liberally rubbed with dry mustard and sprinkled with pepper, salt and flour, it will have a delicious brown and tender crust.*

Savoury butters

These are delicious used alone for sandwiches, and they give a lift to heartier sandwiches or rolls filled with salad, or hard-boiled eggs.

Sardine butter: mash 2 oz (50 g) sardines and blend with 2 oz (50 g) softened butter and a squeeze of lemon juice, pepper and salt to taste.

Kipper butter: grill or poach 4 kipper fillets, cool and remove bones. Mash flesh with 2 oz (50 g) butter, pepper and salt and a dash of Worcestershire sauce. Eat with plenty of crisp lettuce.

Curry butter: cream 3 oz (75 g) butter and work in 1 oz (25 g) chopped mango chutney, 1 teaspoon made mustard, ½ teaspoon curry powder, a squeeze of lemon juice, pepper and salt. Useful with cold meat or poultry sandwiches.

Shooter's beef

Good with salad and jacket potatoes.

8 lb (4 kg) boned and
   rolled topside beef
4 cloves
1 tablespoon whole
   allspice
1 tablespoon peppercorns
½ teaspoon powdered
   mace
1 sprig each parsley,
   thyme and rosemary
1 bay leaf
2 small onions
1 teaspoon salt
2 teaspoons brown sugar

Tie the joint in muslin and put into a large saucepan with all the other ingredients and enough water to cover. Cover, bring to the boil, then simmer for five hours. Leave to cool in the cooking liquid, then drain, put on a board, cover and put under a heavy weight. Leave overnight, remove weight and muslin, and coat with glaze.

Serves 20

Shooter's sandwich

1 large thick rump steak
1 sandwich loaf
4 oz (100 g) mushrooms
Butter
Salt and pepper

Serves 4–6

Grill the steak medium rare, and fry the chopped mushrooms in butter. Cut off the end of the sandwich loaf, remove some of the crumbs, and put in the well-seasoned steak and mushrooms. Put back the crust, wrap the loaf in blotting paper, then greaseproof paper, and tie into a neat parcel with string. Put under heavy weights for six hours, and do not slice until needed.

Sausage shape

This can be used for sandwiches, or glazed when cold and served with salad.

1 lb (450 g) beef
    sausagemeat
1 lb (450 g) pork
    sausagemeat
1 lb (450 g) cooked ham
    or tongue
2 teaspoons chopped
    pickles
1 teaspoon mixed spice
Pinch of freshly ground
    black pepper
1 tablespoon sweet stout
1 tablespoon
    Worcestershire sauce
Pinch of rosemary
Salt

Mix together the sausagemeats and finely chopped ham or tongue. Add pickles, spice, pepper, stout, Worcestershire sauce, rosemary and salt to taste. Tie in a cloth, and cook very slowly in stock for two hours. Lift out and press between two dishes under heavy weights until cold.

Serves 8–10

Sausage pies

12 oz (350 g) shortcrust
    pastry
8 oz (225 g) pork
    sausagemeat
4 oz (100 g) cooked ham
1 small onion
2 tablespoons parsley
Sage and thyme
Salt and pepper
2 tablespoons gravy
Beaten egg

Roll out pastry and line twelve patty tins. Mix sausagemeat with finely chopped ham, onion and parsley and mix with a pinch of sage and thyme, salt and pepper, and the gravy. Put a spoonful of mixture in each patty tin. Cover with pastry and seal edges. Cut a slit in each, and brush with beaten egg. Bake at 400°F/200°C/Gas Mark 6 for ten minutes, then at 350°F/180°C/Gas Mark 4 for thirty minutes.

Pressed beef

2 lb (1 kg) boned and
   rolled salt brisket
1 pint (600 ml) beef stock
1 chopped onion
Dash of pepper

Soak beef in cold water for two hours. Drain and cover with stock, onion and pepper. Simmer gently for 1½ hours. Cool in cold water, press into cake tin, fill up with liquid, and top with weights. Leave until next day.

Serves 4

Pork loaf

1 lb (450 g) sausagemeat
1 tablespoon tomato sauce
1 grated onion
Salt and pepper
Pinch of sage
2 slices bread
1 beaten egg

Mix together sausagemeat, sauce, onion, seasoning, crumbled bread and egg. Press into a greased loaf tin and bake at 400°F/200°C/ Gas Mark 6 for forty minutes. Leave until cold, then wrap in foil for carrying. Eat with buttered baps.

Serves 4

Pâté in a loaf

Particularly good for older children and parents.

1 white plait loaf
4 oz (100 g) streaky bacon
1 large onion
12 oz (350 g) pigs' liver
1 tablespoon oil
1 egg
1 crushed garlic clove
½ teaspoon fine herbs
1 teaspoon salt
Pepper
2 hard-boiled eggs

Cut a horizontal slice across top of loaf and scoop out inside, leaving a firm shell, and use 4 oz (100 g) of the scooped-out bread to make breadcrumbs. Cut bacon in small pieces and fry gently until crisp. Remove and cook finely chopped onion in the fat for four minutes. Remove and add to bacon. Chop liver finely and cook quickly, using oil, for four minutes, stirring continuously. Add to bacon, onions, breadcrumbs, beaten egg, garlic and herbs and mix well together. Put half the mixture into bottom of loaf. Put whole hard-boiled eggs in a line down the centre and cover with remaining mixture. Cover with top of loaf and wrap tightly in foil. Bake at 350°F/180°C/Gas Mark 4 for 1¼ hours. Remove foil, brush bread with oil and bake for fifteen minutes. Leave to cool and cut into slices.

Serves 4–6

Devilled chicken

1 large roasting chicken
¼ pint (150 ml) whipped
   cream
1 tablespoon
   Worcestershire sauce
1 dessertspoon French
   mustard
1 teaspoon curry powder
Salt and pepper

Roast the chicken and cut into joints (or cook chicken pieces). Whip the cream with all other ingredients. Spread the mixture on the chicken and put under grill to brown. Wrap in foil to carry.

Serves 6

Picnic pie

8 eggs
1 medium onion
1½ lb (700 g) sausagemeat
1 tablespoon chopped
  parsley
1 lb (450 g) puff pastry
Beaten egg or milk

Serves 6

Hard-boil eggs, and shell them. Chop onion and mix with sausagemeat and parsley (depending on the seasoning of the sausagemeat, you may like to add some mixed herbs, and additional salt and pepper). Roll out pastry in an oblong and put half sausagemeat down the centre of the pastry. Put the eggs on top and cover with remaining sausagemeat. Fold pastry over, damping edges, and put on baking sheet, folded side down. Make diagonal cuts in top of pastry, brush with milk or beaten egg, and bake at 450°F/230°C/Gas Mark 8 for thirty minutes. Wrap in foil for a picnic with salad or pickles, or serve hot with vegetables.

Bacon and egg saucerpies

6 oz (175 g) shortcrust
  pastry
6 oz (175 g) cooked bacon
4 eggs
1 tablespoon chopped
  parsley
Salt and pepper

Serves 4

Use half the pastry to line four old saucers. Cover each with chopped bacon and break an egg in each. Sprinkle with salt and pepper and parsley. Cover with remaining pastry. Cut a cross on each one and bake at 425°F/220°C/Gas Mark 7 for twenty minutes.

Fish puff

A little finely chopped
chutney can be included
in this pie.

8 oz (225 g) puff pastry
8 oz (225 g) cooked cod,
  haddock or smoked
  haddock
2 oz (50 g) grated cheese
2 large eggs, beaten
Salt and pepper
Pinch of thyme

Serves 4

Roll pastry into an oblong about 12 × 8 in (30 × 20 cm). Put half on a wet baking sheet. Mix flaked fish with cheese and beaten eggs and save a spoonful of egg for glazing. Add salt and pepper and a pinch of thyme. Put mixture on pastry, and cover with second piece of pastry. Brush with beaten egg and bake at 425°F/220°C/Gas Mark 7 for twenty-five minutes.

Cornish treacle tart

8 oz (225 g) puff pastry
4 oz (100 g) golden syrup
3 oz (75 g) breadcrumbs
½ lemon
Beaten egg
Caster sugar

Serves 4

Line a tin with half the pastry. Mix together golden syrup, breadcrumbs, juice and grated rind of ½ lemon. Spread over the pastry, cover with the other piece of pastry and seal the edges. Bake at 425°F/220°C/Gas Mark 7 for thirty-five minutes. Just before finishing, remove from oven, brush with beaten egg white, dust with caster sugar and return to the oven for two or three minutes.

Burnt house cake

8 oz (225 g) butter
8 oz (225 g) granulated
  sugar
10 oz (300 g) plain flour
8 oz (225 g) seedless
  raisins
8 oz (225 g) sultanas
1 teaspoon mixed spice
¼ pint (150 ml) milk
1 teaspoon bicarbonate of
  soda
6 oz (175 g) ground rice

Cream together butter and sugar, and work in flour, spice and dried fruit. Bring milk to the boil, add soda and pour at once on to other ingredients. Beat well and put into 10 in (25 cm) diameter cake tin. Bake at 350°F/180°C/Gas Mark 4 for 1½ hours.

Plum cake

Best stored for a week
before use.

8 oz (225 g) butter or
  dripping
1 lb (450 g) plain flour
12 oz (350 g) soft brown
  sugar
8 oz (225 g) currants
4 oz (100 g) candied peel
Grated rind of 1 lemon
8 oz (225 g) raisins or
  sultanas
1 teaspoon mixed spice
½ pint (300 ml) stout
4 eggs
1 teaspoon bicarbonate
  of soda

Rub fat into flour and add sugar, currants, peel, lemon rind, raisins or sultanas and spice. Whisk stout, add beaten eggs and soda and mix thoroughly with dry ingredients. Turn into 10 in (25 cm) cake tin and bake at 350°F/180°C/Gas Mark 4 for two hours. Store for a week before use.

Ginger cake

8 oz (225 g) plain flour
4 oz (100 g) soft brown
  sugar
2 teaspoons ground ginger
1 teaspoon mixed spice
¾ teaspoon bicarbonate of
  soda
¼ pint (150 ml) milk
8 oz (225 g) golden syrup
4 oz (100 g) butter
2 eggs

Mix together flour, spices, sugar and soda. Warm milk and melt in it the syrup and butter. Add to dry ingredients together with the beaten eggs and mix well together. Put into 7 in (17.5 cm) square or round tin and bake at 325°F/170°C/Gas Mark 3 for one hour.

Date and walnut cake

4 oz (100 g) soft brown
  sugar
4 oz (100 g) golden syrup
8 oz (225 g) chopped
  dates
3 tablespoons water
6 oz (175 g) vegetable oil
  or fat
3 eggs
11 oz (325 g) wholewheat
  flour
6 tablespoons milk
1½ oz (40 g) chopped
  walnuts
2 level teaspoons baking
  powder
Pinch of salt

This recipe makes a batch of 'loaf' cakes, which keep well in a tin or can be frozen. Grease and line three 1 lb (450 g) loaf tins. Mix sugar, syrup, dates and water, keeping a few dates for decoration. Add fat and eggs and half the flour and beat to a smooth batter. Add milk, some of the walnuts, and the remaining flour sifted with baking powder and salt. Mix well and divide between prepared tins. Scatter with reserved dates and walnuts. Bake at 375°F/190°C/Gas Mark 5 for 1 hour 20 minutes, and cool on wire rack.

Food from the Fields

It seems instinctive to gather 'spoils' on a country walk; a few nuts, an interesting twig, a bird's broken egg, or a mixed bunch of wild flowers held in a hot little hand. If the same spoils can be eaten, so much the better. Don't we all remember the grubby handkerchief cradling a few mushrooms, and those first hard, slightly pink blackberries which create visions of blackberry pie, and jam, and jelly, and all the other delights of a chilly autumn day?

In a spirit of experiment almost anything that grows in a field can be eaten without harm, but so many things are hardly worth the trouble or they would have been cultivated long ago. Nettles may taste reasonably like any other green vegetable, and purify the blood, but gathering them can hardly be an enjoyable pastime. Field sorrel can be used but is very sour-tasting, and those who truly enjoy the flavour are better off cultivating a garden variety. Those gardeners' enemies, ground elder and mallow, can be cooked and eaten, but one's pleasure would be vindictive only!

Here's a guide to the field harvest which may be found in reasonable quantities in various parts of the country, which are worth finding and are delicious.

Beechnuts

(October and November)
Remove kernels and place on baking sheet. Sprinkle with olive oil and bake at 350°F/180°C/Gas Mark 4 until golden. Drain on crumpled kitchen paper, toss in salt, and eat as salted almonds.

Blackberries

(September and October)
While the flavour of wild blackberries is delicious, they are often rather small and pippy, so it is best to use the juice or pulp in recipes, rather than the whole berries. The flavour of blackberries is greatly enhanced by a few drops of rosewater (from any chemist) or a couple of rose geranium leaves used in the cooking. These two recipes are particularly good with the wild fruit.

Blackberry flummery

Simmer 1 lb (450 g) well-washed blackberries with 8 oz (225 g) sugar until soft. Sieve, and thicken with two tablespoons cornflour. Add a pinch of salt, and simmer for five minutes, stirring well. Add one teaspoon lemon juice, and cool. Serve with sugar and cream.

Blackberry and apple cheese

This is a smooth version of the jam, which can be cut with a knife, and is useful for all sorts of puddings. Peel, core and quarter 2 lb (1 kg) cooking apples and cook in ¼ pint (150 ml) water until tender. Add 2 lb (1 kg) blackberries and simmer until soft. Strain through a fine sieve, and measure the pulp. Add 1 lb (450 g) sugar to each pint (600 ml) juice, stir until dissolved, and boil the mixture until it sets when tested on a cold plate. It should be very firm. Put into warm pots and cover. This 'cheese' may be turned out, cut in slices and served with cream. If warmed, it makes a good sauce for steamed puddings or milk puddings.

Blueberries

(August and September)
These appear in various parts of the country as bilberries, blueberries, whortleberries, whorts, hurts. They can be used for any recipe which specifies elderberries. Good specimens freeze well in sugar syrup. The fruit is a good source of Vitamin C, and popular in mining areas where it is thought the fruit offsets the effects of the toxic fumes of the mines. The fruit is at its most delicious in pies or steamed puddings, and since this is a popular international fruit, here's an American version of our Summer Pudding.

American blueberry pudding

Sprinkle six slices of buttered bread very lightly with cinnamon. Cook 1½ lb (700 g) blueberries with 6 oz (175 g) sugar and ¼ pint (150 ml) water for ten minutes. Arrange bread and fruit in alternate layers in a bowl. Chill overnight in refrigerator. Turn out and cut in slices and serve with thin cream.

Cranberries

(August and September)
These are best turned into sauce and jelly ready for Christmas (recipe p. 230). A few plump raisins and chopped walnuts in cranberry sauce make this a delicious relish to serve with cold turkey.

Elderberries

(September and October)
The fruit is good stewed with a pinch of cinnamon, and excellent cooked with apples. Also good in pies, and mixed with apples or with sloe juice for jam. Elderberry wine is, of course, well known and the best is like port, but elderberry syrup is quicker and easier to make, and is excellent mulled on winter evenings with brandy and a pinch of spice.

Elderberry syrup

Free berries from stalks, cover liberally with water and boil for ten minutes. Strain and add 1 lb (450 g) sugar to each pint (500 ml) juice. Boil for ten minutes, skim and bottle.

Hazelnuts

(September and October)

These have a high food value and are delicious in many cake recipes. Their flavour is particularly delicious made into a paste which can be added to the filling for Eccles cakes, mincepies, and for making thin brown bread sandwiches.

Hazelnut paste

Put 4 oz (100 g) caster sugar and two tablespoons water in a pan, bring to the boil and add one tablespoon finely chopped candied peel. Boil for three minutes, then stir in 7 oz (200 g) ground hazelnuts. Leave until cold before using.

Mushrooms

(Summer and Autumn)

For the last fifty years or so, the British have mainly confined themselves to eating field mushrooms, probably because they travel well and can be cultivated on a large scale. We have a strong distrust of other fungi, though anyone who has lived in Europe will know that some of the more highly coloured and weirdly shaped specimens such as the Chanterells are delicious, and that our own choice of mushrooms is considered positively effete. Sadly, the one lethal fungus in this country, the Death Cap, looks extremely like our common field mushroom. The field mushroom should be picked with pink or light brown gills (Death Caps have white gills). Other local favourites are the rather coarse horse mushroom, which is good for making ketchup, and the Blewit, Morel and Beefsteak varieties which are best cooked slowly with butter. For all these specimens, it is best to refer to local knowledge for the right kind of fungus, and the right place to find it. If you have any qualms, remember, 'if in doubt, leave out'.

Rosehips

(September and October)

Wild rosehips are a valuable source of vitamins. Commercial syrups are so good it is hardly worth the trouble making one's own, but a delicious jam can be made when the fruit has been touched with frost.

Rosehip jam

To each lb (450 g) hips allow ½ pint (300 ml) water, boiling until the fruit is soft. Put through a sieve, and allow 1 lb (450 g) sugar to 1 lb (450 g) pulp. Boil until a little sets on a plate, and put into warm pots. A delicious flavour may be obtained by adding a few drops of rosewater just before the jam is potted.

Rowanberries

(August and September)
Rowan jelly is particularly liked with mutton, venison and hare, and is preferred by many to redcurrant jelly because of its slightly bitter taste. The berries are best soaked in hot water for five minutes, then strained before using for jelly. Use a proportion of ½ pint (300 ml) water to 1 lb (450 g) fruit for simmering, and allow 1 lb (450 g) sugar to a pint (500 ml) liquid for making the jelly. A little lemon juice can also be added and a few crabapples help set and colour.

Samphire

(Best in early summer)
Hardly a product of the fields, but very much part of our coastal scene and suitable for holiday harvesting. The variety which is common on rocks has fleshy leaflets, dull yellow flowers, and an aromatic, slightly resinous taste. It makes a good pickle. A somewhat different variety which grows on salt marshes is commonly called Poor Man's Asparagus and is often seen for sale on the East Anglian coast. This can also be made into pickle with the addition of spices. Boiled and eaten with butter, it makes a wholesome, though rather insipid vegetable dish.

Sloes

(October)
These are the fruit of the blackthorn, most popular in the form of sloe gin. Since this pre-supposes a supply of gin, there may be many who object to the waste of money and/or good gin in order to use up a 1 lb (450 g) or two of wild fruit. The flavour of cooked sloes is similar to that of damsons, but the fruit is very small, so it is best to strain off the cooking liquid, thicken with arrowroot or cornflour and chill to serve as a light pudding with cream. Sloes combined with apples or crabapples yield a delicious ruby-coloured jelly.

Fruit
and
Preserving

Fruit in Season

Rhubarb

Make the best of this first fruit of spring by cooking the delicious young stems very carefully. Use crisp fresh stalks, and don't bother to peel them; just wash the stems. If you like fresh rhubarb stewed, cut the stems into 1 in (2.5 cm) pieces and sprinkle with sugar (about 4 oz (100 g) to 1 lb (450 g) is enough). Add three tablespoons water, and a grating of orange or lemon rind, and simmer very gently with a lid on until soft but not mushy. Sometimes it's more convenient to use the oven, and all you need to do is add the same amount of sugar and water and cook in a covered casserole at 300°F/150°C/Gas Mark 1 until the rhubarb is tender. When the rhubarb gets a bit older and lacks flavour, leave out the water, and use four tablespoons raspberry jam or orange marmalade instead – the flavour will be delicious and the colour appetizing.

The first young rhubarb doesn't need much extra flavouring, but ginger, orange, lemon or cinnamon are all good for a change, while angelica and almonds make attractive garnishes. If you have someone in the family who complains that rhubarb causes acidity, serve milk, cream, custard or cheese at the same meal to counteract the effect.

Want some new ways to serve the old favourite? Try filling pancakes with stewed rhubarb and raisins; or fold chopped raw rhubarb and grated orange rind into plain steamed pudding mixture. If you're baking a custard tart put chopped uncooked rhubarb at the bottom on top of the pastry, sprinkle with sugar and pour over the custard before baking. A sponge flan case can be filled with stewed rhubarb and the top set with lemon jelly made with hot rhubarb juice and water, or a cooked pastry case can be filled with rhubarb, sugar and whipped cream.

If the family likes apple crumble, then try serving rhubarb crumble, sweetened with brown sugar, flavoured with orange, and with brown sugar in the topping. Rhubarb fool can be made just like all other fools, and is specially delicious if decorated with slices of ginger. In place of the usual cream, try mixing a carton of yogurt or ¼ pint (150 ml) dairy sour cream with the custard before folding in the sieved fruit – it's a sophisticated taste, but very good.

For a change from apple sauce, try using half-and-half rhubarb and apple, adding a few sultanas and serving with pork or ham.

On cold-meat days there's nothing like an old-fashioned suet pudding, so try making one with rhubarb. Butter the pudding basin thickly and sprinkle well with brown sugar before putting in the suet crust. Add a little chopped candied peel and some currants to the rhubarb filling, with a dusting of cinnamon and the juice and rind of half a lemon. Allow about 4 oz (100 g) sugar to 1½ lb (750 g) rhubarb, but only half a teacup of water. This pudding can be steamed or baked in a moderate oven (350°F/180°C/Gas Mark 4) for 1¼ hours. If there isn't much time to spare, put the rhubarb, sugar and water into a saucepan and make a dough of 4 oz (100 g) plain flour, one teaspoon baking powder, 2 oz (50 g) prepared suet, a pinch of salt and a little water. Flatten out the dough to fit the saucepan, cover with a lid, and simmer for twenty minutes.

Strawberries

The first strawberries are greeted with surprise and joy, but soon this turns to resignation, and finally despair as they keep on turning up as the easiest-ever pudding.

When the berries are less than perfect, they can be tossed in sugar to coat them, then sprinkled with a little orange juice and Grand Marnier or Curaçao (use 2 tablespoons orange juice and 1 tablespoon liqueur to 1½ lb (700 g) strawberries). Another idea is to leave the berries with stems attached, arranging each helping round a cone of icing sugar and serving with a glass of Bordeaux or Beaujolais. The berries can be dipped in wine and sugar, or the wine served separately.

For a delicious extra when there's a glut of berries, cream 8 oz (225 g) fresh butter and 1 lb (450 g) icing sugar and gradually work in 1 lb (450 g) sieved strawberries and a pinch of salt; add 2 oz (50 g) finely chopped almonds if liked. Press the mixture into a covered jar and store in a cold place to serve with toast, waffles or small pancakes.

On a cool summer evening, try a hot strawberry pudding. Hull 2 lb (1 kg) strawberries and put them in a fireproof dish with 1 lb (450 g) sugar and a pinch of cinnamon. Put in a very low oven until the sugar has melted, then drain off the syrup. Stir in two wineglasses of red wine, pour the liquid over the fruit and return to the oven until hot. Just before serving, add two teaspoons honey, two teaspoons lemon juice, and serve very hot with thick cream.

If you like a really fresh-tasting ice, dissolve 12 oz (350 g) sugar in $\frac{3}{4}$ pint (450 ml) water and boil to a light syrup. Cool and add 8 oz (225 g) crushed strawberries and the juice of an orange, then freeze in a refrigerator tray; when half-frozen add a stiffly whipped egg white and return to freezer. If you've been disappointed with the flavour of frozen strawberries, try pulping the fruit with an equal quantity of sugar and a squeeze of lemon juice and freeze this pulp to make ices in the winter.

Raspberries

Everyone thinks strawberries are the delectable symbol of summer until raspberries come along – and then some of us have doubts. Sieved fresh raspberries blended with caster sugar make an unusual sauce to serve with the late strawberries, or to pour over bananas, vanilla ice-cream or peaches. If you pour the sauce over peaches *and* ice-cream, you have the original peach melba. To reverse the procedure, a syrup of redcurrants and sugar is delicious over whole fresh raspberries. Sieved fresh raspberries make a better 'fool' than cooked ones, lightly sweetened and stirred into thick cream.

Use sugared raspberries to fill a fluffy omelette, and dust the surface with icing sugar; or layer raspberries and cream between rounds of shortbread or layers of meringue.

Stewed raspberries are dreary, but if you want to bottle them for winter puddings, try mixing equal quantities of raspberries, currants and gooseberries in the jars – the flavour is excellent. Raspberry syrup for winter drinks is made by squeezing fresh raspberries through double muslin, and adding to every pint (600 ml) juice a syrup made from 1 pint (600 ml) water and 1 lb (450 g) sugar. Boil the mixture, then simmer for an hour, and when cold bottle and cork down, or put into preserving jars, and sterilize; this makes a delicious drink with water or soda water, or can be used to flavour winter puddings, or on sponge puddings.

Gooseberries

Gooseberries are the cook's friend because they'll happily wait, all green and hard, lurking in their prickly bushes, until the softer fruits have been dealt with, and then be ready to form the basis of useful jams, chutneys and puddings.

The gooseberry is the summer equivalent of the apple for helping along other fruit, with its splendid setting qualities. Use gooseberry jelly as the basis of mint jelly, or try putting in rosemary, sage, marjoram or bay leaves to give different savoury jellies to use with meat or fish. Elderflowers have a peculiar affinity for gooseberries and flower at the fruiting period; trail an elderflower head in gooseberry jam or jelly to give a wonderful muscat flavour. Infuse a flower head in the syrup for winter use to give a refreshing flavour to fresh fruit compotes, water ices and drinks.

To make a good green gooseberry jelly, simmer 3 lb (1.5 kg) fruit in 2 pints (1 l) water (don't bother to top and tail them). Strain and boil quickly with 1 lb (450 g) sugar to each pint (600 ml) juice. Gooseberry jam tends to turn pink, and to keep it a good green colour it's important to keep boiling time to the minimum. Allow twenty minutes for cooking the fruit, and twenty fast-boiling minutes when the sugar has been added.

If you want a different chutney to serve with meat or fish, try spicing gooseberries. You'll need to cook together 2 lb (1 kg) gooseberries with 8 oz (225 g) brown sugar and 1 pint (600 ml) white wine vinegar. When the berries are tender, stir in one tablespoon dry mustard and two whole crushed garlic heads, 12 oz (350 g) raisins and ½ oz (15 g) cayenne pepper. Add another pint (600 ml) cold white wine vinegar, stir well and put into preserving jars, storing for at least six months before using.

Finally, if you're tired of gooseberry fool and bored with plainly stewed gooseberries, try cooking 2 lb (1 kg) fruit in a syrup of 8 oz (225 g) sugar, 1 pint (600 ml) water, one tablespoon apricot jam and one small wineglass Kirsch; don't let the gooseberries overcook and break, and serve them very cold in the syrup.

Currants

The first large and perfect currants are refreshing if stripped from their stalks (use a large fork to do the job quickly) and chilled in a bowl with sugar. Red, white and black currants can be mixed, and a few raspberries added. Don't try to stew redcurrants – they turn into a mass of pip and skin, but if you have a lot use the juice for setting other summer jams, such as raspberry.

Plain redcurrant jelly is useful to keep in the kitchen, to serve later with mutton, ham, pork and game: 6 lb (3 kg) redcurrants will give a good quantity of juice if heated until tender, then strained and added to sugar, allowing $1\frac{1}{4}$ lb (550 g) sugar to each pint (600 ml) juice. The jelly will reach setting point quickly and should not be left long in the pan once it is removed from the stove. Currant and raspberry jelly is good, allowing equal quantities of the fruit and using about $3\frac{1}{2}$ lb (1.75 kg) together. Allow two-thirds sugar to juice when boiling to set.

If you have the rare white currants, copy the French preserve Bar-le-Duc to eat with cream cheese or cottage cheese. Put fruit into a pan with 4 oz (100 g) sugar to each 1 lb (450 g) fruit. Stand overnight, then bring slowly to the boil and boil evenly for just three minutes. Stand preserve overnight, then put into very small jars and cover well.

Blackcurrant jam is easy and good to eat, and useful in the winter to dissolve in hot water as a soothing drink for sore throats and colds. Blackcurrant syrup can be bottled in preserving jars to use for puddings or winter drinks.

Cherries

Fresh cherries and plenty of space to get rid of the stones can be one of the pleasures of a summer's day, but cooked ones can be very dreary. If you do have Morello cherries, simmer them gently in a syrup of sugar and water and add a dash of cherry brandy or Kirsch, and there won't be any complaints. Better still, simmer the cherries in a little claret with sugar to taste, a pinch of cinnamon and a little redcurrant jelly, and serve very cold. Use this compôte over vanilla ice-cream for a special pudding. The cherries will be even better if stoned, and if you haven't a special gadget, use a large old-fashioned hairpin, or a pen-nib stuck into its holder the wrong way round.

To cheer up pieces of cold chicken, simmer good black cherries in very little water with a spoonful of brown sugar, pepper and salt and a pinch each of nutmeg, ginger and cinnamon, and heat the pieces of chicken in this sauce. Serve with mashed or new potatoes and green salad.

Cherry jam is a wonderful breakfast treat. To get a good colour and set, boil an equal weight of cherries and sugar for five minutes. Remove the fruit and cook the syrup for twelve minutes, adding $\frac{1}{4}$ pint (150 ml) blackcurrant syrup. Add fruit and boil for twelve minutes before potting. Once again, the fruit is much better for being stoned first.

Cherry chutney sounds unusual, but is very good with poultry. Use a breakfast cup to measure out five cups of cherries, then remove stones. Simmer cherries, quarter cup honey or syrup, half a cup vinegar, one cup raisins, two teaspoons mixed spice and four tablespoons brown sugar in a pan until sugar has dissolved, boil for five minutes, then simmer until thick, stirring well, and put into jars, covering tightly.

Cherry brandy? Well worth the trouble and expense. To each pound (450 g) of Morello cherries allow 4 oz (100 g) sugar-candy, $\frac{1}{4}$ oz (8 g) shredded bitter almonds and $\frac{1}{2}$ in (1.25 cm) cinnamon stick. Prick the cherries all over and pack into jars with other ingredients. Fill the jars to the top with brandy. After six months, or better still a year, drain off liquid – and eat the brandied cherries with cream for a superb pudding! Store the drink in bottles.

Apples

Apples are best left to sweeten and mature in an airy place before final storage. Second-best fruit can be pulped and put into preserving jars, or apple slices are good preserved in syrup (allow 1 pint (600 ml) water to 6 oz (175 g) sugar). Sweetened apple pulp can be frozen in tubs. Apple rings should be soaked in a solution of $\frac{1}{2}$ oz (15 g) salt to 2 pints (1 l) water for ten minutes before stringing on sticks or pieces of string and drying at 150°F/70°C/ Gas Mark ¼ in a slight draught (leave the oven door slightly ajar) until the apples are the consistency of dry chamois leather.

To keep the colour of fresh apple pieces, dip them in lemon juice before serving. If apples are stewed in cider instead of water, the flavour is better, or apple slices can be simmered in fresh butter to keep their shape for open apple tarts. Apple sauce is best made by baking rather than by boiling the fruit.

If apples are a bit short, make the best of them by serving fried apple slices with bacon and potato for breakfast. Or try the apples raw and hollowed-out, filling the centres with walnuts, raw cabbage and a grating of onion tossed in mayonnaise for a refreshing salad. Duckling is good stuffed with small apples lightly sifted with sugar, and apple slices simmered in a little redcurrant jelly are good with roast pork or chops. Another way of serving apples with pork is to stuff them with chopped boiled onion and sage, baking them round the joint.

For a quick pudding, whisk up well-chilled and slightly sweetened apple purée with a pinch of cinnamon, and serve with thin cream. Or fill cold baked apples with whipped cream and serve scattered with brown sugar. Baked apples are excellent served stuffed with fruit mincemeat, with a sprinkling of sugar, handed with a bowl of grated cheese.

Blackberries

A blackberrying expedition is always a good excuse for a family outing, and the results can be turned to good account with delicious puddings and unusual preserves. Serve the large cultivated blackberries with sugar and cream without cooking them, and use this kind for open tarts. The wild blackberry, which has such a good flavour for preserving, usually needs sieving, as the pips may irritate the very old and the very young. To enhance the flavour of both kinds, add a little rosewater (easily obtained from the chemist) or a couple of rose geranium leaves.

A good pudding, which can be eaten as a cake, is made with any simple plain cake mixture put into a buttered square tin, thickly scattered with well-wiped blackberries, then sprinkled with a mixture of 2 oz (50 g) butter, 4 oz (100 g) sugar, 2 oz (50 g) flour and ½ teaspoon cinnamon rubbed to crumble consistency. An hour in a moderate oven will produce a hot pudding to eat with cream or custard; as a cold cake it is excellent eaten fresh.

An excellent blackberry pie can be made with about 2 lb (1 kg) berries. Put the best berries in a deep piedish, dotted with butter and well sweetened, then cover them with the remaining blackberries simmered with sugar and put through a sieve. A short pastry crust covers the lot, and the pie is best served just warm with cream.

A nice variation of a fruit fool can be made with blackberries simmered with sugar until soft, then thickened with a little cornflour and spiked with lemon juice. Blackberries and apples simmered together are excellent if well sweetened and only just tender, served very cold. The best proportion of fruit to use is 1 lb (450 g) blackberries to 2 large apples and 8 oz (225 g) sugar with only four tablespoons water.

Plums

Stewed plums can be utterly dreary and plum jam just plain dull. Improve plain stewed plums with a dash of cinnamon, a little lemon or orange rind and juice, or a sprinkling of flaked almonds, or add a little cherry brandy or red wine to the liquid when cooking. The best way to cook all types of plums is to layer them in a casserole with caster sugar and a piece of cinnamon stick, half cover with water and cook in a slow oven until they are tender and the juice runs.

For an unusual salad to serve with chicken or roast beef, split fresh ripe plums, moisten them with French dressing (allow three parts oil to one part vinegar), and garnish with tarragon, serving well chilled.

To make a change from conventional plum jam, cook 5 lb (2.5 kg) plums with 2 lb (1 kg) seedless raisins and three oranges cut in thin crosswise slices. Simmer until the fruit is soft, then add 5 lb (2.5 kg) sugar and boil to the consistency of marmalade.

To eat with meat, try spiced plums, using large Victorias. Wipe and halve them, prick

well and put into preserving jars. Boil together
1 pint (600 ml) white vinegar, 1 oz (25 g)
cinnamon stick, $\frac{1}{4}$ oz (8 g) mixed pickling
spice, $\frac{1}{4}$ oz (8 g) allspice berries and 2 lb (1 kg)
sugar until thick. Pour cool syrup over fruit,
then next day strain off syrup, reboil, cool and
pour over fruit again. When cold, cover and
store for at least three months before using.

Quinces
mulberries
and
medlars

In an old farm garden, there's many an old-
fashioned fruit tree with a delicious crop.
Quinces, medlars and mulberries are rare and
precious these days, so make the best of them in
the kitchen.

Quinces are pear-shaped, hard and yellow
when ripe, and not attractive to eat raw. When
they are cooked, the flesh turns rich pink-
red and releases a wonderful flavour and
fragrance, which blends well with apples, pears,
oranges, lemon and cloves. A few pieces in an
apple pie make a world of difference. To serve
the quinces on their own, roast them in a very
hot oven until a skewer goes through easily.
Scrape the flesh from the skins and mix with
sugar, cream and a pinch of ginger.

To keep the flavour for winter, stew cut-up
quinces in a little water until pulpy, then put
through a sieve and mix with an equal
quantity of sugar. Cook very slowly until the
mixture dries and leaves the sides of the pan,
then cool and roll out $\frac{1}{2}$ in (1.25 cm) thick.
Stamp out rounds with a pastry cutter and
leave to dry, turning often until the pieces
are like leather, then store in tins well-dusted
with icing sugar – a lovely sweetmeat for cold
dark evenings. For an unusual marmalade,
simmer eight cup-up sweet oranges until tender, then add 5 lb (2.5 kg) sugar and the
liquid strained from cooking 5 lb (2.5 kg)
quinces in very little water. Thirty minutes'
hard boiling will produce a good set.

Mulberries are delicately flavoured, hang
heavily on the branch and fall quickly when
ripe, so spread hay, straw or paper under the
tree in the season to catch the ripe fruit (the
juice stains very badly indeed). Use the fruit for
any recipe which indicates raspberries or logan-
berries, or enjoy it fresh with sugar and cream.
Mulberry pie is excellent, or the fruit can be
heaped in a deep dish and heavily sugared,

put into a hot oven until the juice runs, then eaten with cream or milk pudding. If you want to make jam, use a proportion of 2 lb (1 kg) mulberries simmered in ½ pint (300 ml) water to 1½ lb (700 g) sugar and the grated juice and rind of a lemon.

Medlars look like large round rosehips the colour of unripe russet apples, and they are very hard. They should be gathered hard and kept some weeks until soft or 'bletted'. Remove the soft brown flesh to serve with thick cream and brown sugar, or bake medlars in the oven with butter and cloves and serve with cream and sugar. Medlar jelly should be made from 1 lb (450 g) medlars and ½ pint (300 ml) water, allowing 12 oz (350 g) sugar to every pint (600 ml) juice.

Pears

It's a good idea to pick pears before they are fully ripe, because they spoil in autumn frosts, and they can be ripened quickly in a warm place. Pears ripen more suddenly than apples, so inspect the store often. For preserving, pears are best bottled in syrup, and the finest varieties for bottling are good dessert pears which are fully ripe; they do not freeze well as they tend to discolour badly.

Pears are usually peeled, halved and cored for puddings, but hard winter pears can just be peeled and left whole complete with stalk for oven cooking (they taste best if cooked in a casserole with red wine and sugar until they are dark mahogany colour). For traditional stewing, pears taste better if cooked in butter rather than water; allow 2 oz (50 g) butter to each 1 lb (450 g) fruit.

Try stuffing ripe pear halves with cream cheese or cottage cheese, sprinkling with walnuts and serving on a bed of lettuce. A ripe pear is delicious eaten with Camembert cheese, while poached pear halves on vanilla ice-cream are excellent with a rich chocolate sauce.

Pears poached in a light syrup can be improved with a few slices of preserved ginger and served well chilled; or the addition of Grenadine to the syrup will give a lovely flavour. Rum is another good flavouring to use with them, or they can be spiced with cloves or cinnamon.

Sweet Preserves

There's no need to fill the store cupboard with rows of boring plum jam. Fruit preserves of all sorts are delicious, and it's nice to make small quantities of special ones which can be used as sauces or tart fillings as well as with bread or toast.

Potted raspberries

This is just like eating spoonfuls of fresh raspberries.

4 lb (2 kg) raspberries
1 oz (25 g) unsalted butter
4 lb (2 kg) caster sugar

Pick over the fruit and put in a preserving pan rubbed with the butter. Meanwhile warm the sugar in a bowl in a low oven. Heat the berries over a low heat and when they start to bubble, pour in the warm sugar. Beat with a wooden spoon for thirty minutes and put into pots.

Redcurrant conserve

Redcurrants
Loaf sugar

Stem the currants, and wash in running water. Put into preserving pan with loaf sugar, allowing 12 oz (350 g) to every 1 lb (450 g) currants weighed after stemming. Cover and leave to stand overnight. Bring very slowly to the boil, and boil steadily for only three minutes. Cover again, and leave overnight, then put into small jars. Serve with ice-cream or junket.

Strawberry conserve

This is not a jam, but whole fruit suspended in thick syrup, delicious served with puddings or on its own with thick cream.

Strawberries
Preserving sugar

Weigh out equal quantities of strawberries and sugar. Clean the fruit and put in alternate layers with the sugar in a bowl. Leave for twenty-four hours, then boil for five minutes. On the second day, boil for five minutes and on the third day for seven minutes. Put into warm jars and seal.

Raspberry and apple jelly

Early windfalls can be used for this jelly, and it is useful for glazing fruit flans.

4 lb (2 kg) raspberries
2 lb (1 kg) cooking apples
2 pints (1 l) water
Sugar

Cut up apples and put in pan with raspberries and water and cook until tender. Strain through jelly bag and add 1 lb (450 g) warm sugar to each pint (600 ml) juice. Bring to boiling point and boil for ten minutes. Test for setting, pot and cover.

Apricot marmalade

This is a thick preserve which is excellent for filling jam tarts or for spreading on slices of almond shortbread.

1 lb (450 g) dried apricots
12 oz (350 g) sugar
6 tablespoons lemon juice
1 tablespoon grated lemon
    rind
1 tablespoon grated
    orange rind

Soak the apricots overnight in just enough cold water to cover them. Cook them in the water, then sieve both fruit and juice. Add sugar, lemon juice and grated rinds, and cook over a good heat for fifteen minutes until thick. Put into hot jars.

Apricot and date marmalade

This makes an excellent filling used between two layers of flaky pastry, baked in a hot oven and sprinkled with caster sugar.

1 lb (450 g) dried apricots
2 pints (1 l) water
1½ lb (700 g) dates
8 oz (225 g) sugar
1 lemon
2 oz (50 g) blanched
    almonds

Soak the apricots overnight in 1 pint (500 ml) water. Add another pint (600 ml) water, chopped dates, sugar and the juice of a lemon. Cook slowly until the mixture is soft and thick, stir in chopped almonds and cook for five minutes. Pot at once in warm jars.

Tipsy apricots

Delicious as a sauce with steamed sponge puddings or with vanilla ice-cream, or as a filling for a crusty sponge cake.

8 oz (225 g) dried apricots
1 lb (450 g) granulated
    sugar
12 tablespoons gin or
    brandy

Soak fruit overnight in 1 pint (600 ml) boiling water, then drain, and chop fruit. Melt sugar in ¼ pint (150 ml) cold water, add apricots, boil, then simmer for fifteen minutes. Leave until cold for two hours. Stir in gin or brandy, and put in small screwtop jars.

Cherry marmalade

The juices are made by simmering fruit in water and sieving through a jelly bag.

3 lb (1.5 kg) black cherries
½ pint (300 ml) raspberry juice
½ pint (300 ml) redcurrant juice
2 lb (1 kg) sugar

Put cherries, juices and sugar into a preserving pan, and simmer gently until sugar has dissolved. Cook gently, until a firm, clear jelly mingles with the cherries. Remove from heat and press cherries gently with the back of a spoon. Cool, and pot when cold.

Three fruit jam

This makes an excellent tart filling, or a sauce for steamed pudding.

Apples
Pears
Plums
Sugar
Lemon rind
Root ginger

Weigh out equal quantities of apples, pears and plums. Peel, core and slice apples and pears and stone plums. Cook gently, allowing ¼ pint (150 ml) water to each lb (450 g) fruit until soft. Weigh the fruit and add warmed sugar in the proportion of 1 lb (450 g) to 1 pint (600 ml) fruit. Add the grated rind of a lemon to each lb (450 g) fruit, and suspend crushed root ginger in a muslin bag in the preserving pan. Dissolve sugar over a gentle heat, then bring to boiling point. Test for setting after ten minutes' boiling, pot and cover.

Pear ginger

Serve with cream as a pudding, or as a sauce for ice-cream.

8 lb (4 kg) pears
4 lb (2 kg) sugar
4 lemons
4 oz (100 g) preserved ginger

Do not peel pears, but quarter and core them, and cut into small pieces. Add sugar and chopped ginger and leave to stand overnight. Add lemons cut in very thin pieces and cook slowly for three hours, keeping pieces of pear whole. Pot and seal.

Rhubarb and ginger jam

4 lb (2 kg) rhubarb
2 teaspoons ground ginger
or 1 oz (25 g) bruised root ginger in muslin bag
3 lb (1.5 kg) sugar
½ teaspoon citric acid

Cut rhubarb into 1 in (2.5 cm) lengths, and put into a bowl with sugar in layers. Leave overnight, then put into preserving pan. Add ginger and acid, bring to the boil, and boil rapidly until the jam jells when tested (about fifteen minutes). Remove bag of root ginger, pot and cover at once.

Rhubarb and fig jam

2 lb (1 kg) rhubarb
8 oz (225 g) dried figs
3 lb (1.5 kg) sugar
Juice of 1 lemon

Cut rhubarb and figs finely, combine with sugar and lemon juice, and leave to stand for twenty-four hours. Bring to boil, and boil rapidly until a little sets when tested on a cool plate. Leave to stand for thirty minutes before filling jars.

Rhubarb and blackberry jam

This makes an inexpensive jam with a good blackberry flavour. It is very good used for tarts or jam slices with a meringue topping.

4 lb (2 kg) blackberries
2 lb (1 kg) prepared
   rhubarb
¾ pint (450 ml) water
Sugar

Use ripe blackberries for this, and simmer them in the water until tender, then put through a sieve. Cut rhubarb into 1 in (2.5 cm) pieces, add to blackberry pulp, and simmer until tender. Measure and add 1 lb (450 g) warm sugar to each 1 lb (450 g) pulp. Stir until dissolved and bring to boiling point. Boil for ten minutes and test for setting. Pot and cover.

Plum and apple cheese

This may be used as a spread, or if put into jars without shoulders, it can be turned out and served in slices with cream.

3 lb (1.5 kg) apples
1 lb (450 g) plums
Sugar

Cut up apples and plums without peeling or stoning. Add just enough water to prevent burning, and cook until tender, stirring often. Rub the fruit through a sieve and allow 12 oz (350 g) sugar to each pint (600 ml) purée. Cook until mixture thickens and clears. Pour into pots.

Plum conserve

This is good as a spread, makes a delicious tart filling, or is good with ice-cream.

3 lb (1.5 kg) stoned plums
3 lb (1.5 kg) sugar
6 oz (175 g) stoned raisins
4 oz (100 g) chopped
   blanched almonds

Put the plum stones into a muslin bag, and suspend in cooking pan. Put plums and raisins, and a little water if necessary, in pan, and simmer until soft. Add sugar, stir until dissolved, and boil rapidly to setting point. Remove bag, stir in almonds and pour into warm jars.

Everlasting rumpot

The fruit should be sound, whole and ripe. The rumpot should not be overloaded with fruit and it is best to preserve a little at a time, using only the choicest fruits. Citrus fruits, apples, bananas and pears should not be used.

1 bottle light or dark rum
Granulated sugar
Strawberries, cherries,
  apricots, raspberries,
  plums, redcurrants,
  peaches, grapes, melon

Gently wipe the fruit, and do not peel or stone (except for melon, which should be peeled, seeded and cut into large chunks). Put fruit into a large stone crock with its own weight of sugar, and cover with rum. For each addition of fruit, add the equivalent in sugar and cover with rum. Cover crock tightly with waxed paper and a lid and keep in a cool place. Continue adding fruit to the rumpot throughout the season. The fruit and syrup may be used in small quantities as required:

(a) eat fruit as it is, or with cream or yogurt;
(b) add to fresh fruit salad with oranges, apples, nuts;
(c) remove top of a melon, pierce flesh with a knitting needle, and fill case with fruit and syrup. Serve chilled;
(d) drain fruit, put into pastry case and top with whipped cream.

Rum raisins

Excellent with puddings or ice-cream, or to fill tartlet cases topped with a blob of thick cream.

8 oz (225 g) caster sugar
8 oz (225 g) seedless
  raisins
6 tablespoons rum

Melt sugar in $\frac{1}{4}$ pint (150 ml) water, bring to the boil, add raisins and simmer for fifteen minutes. Leave until cold, add rum, and put into small screwtop jars.

Grapes in spirit

Brandy can be used for this, and for preserving such fruit as peaches, apricots and greengages, but it tends to stain delicate fruits, and I find vodka more satisfactory.

White grapes
Caster sugar
Vodka
Angelica

Use large grapes for this. For perfection, peel them and remove pips with a needle, leaving fruit whole; this is not really necessary but the skins may toughen during keeping. Rinse grapes, dry thoroughly and pack in jars with a few pieces of angelica and 3 oz (75 g) sugar to each 1 lb (450 g) grapes. Top up jars with vodka, seal and leave for a month. Serve in small dishes with thick cream.

Mincemeat

1 lb (450 g) peeled and
    cored apples
1 lb (450 g) suet
1 lb (450 g) sultanas
1 lb (450 g) currants
1 lb (450 g) stoned raisins
1 lb (450 g) demerara
    sugar
1 lb (450 g) candied peel
    without sugar
2 lemons
1 teaspoon grated nutmeg
$\frac{1}{2}$ teaspoon ground
    cinnamon
$\frac{1}{2}$ teaspoon ground allspice
$\frac{1}{2}$ teaspoon salt
$\frac{1}{4}$ pint (150 ml) brandy

Put finely chopped or grated suet in bowl. Put apples, sultanas, currants and raisins through mincer and add to suet. Add finely chopped candied peel, grated rind and juice of lemons, spices and brandy. Mix well together, pack into clean dry jars, cover and store in a cool dry place. Leave at least three weeks before using.

Oranges and Lemons

Once upon a time, though not nearly so long ago as we might imagine, citrus fruits in Britain were rare and highly prized. In the earlier days of this century, a bun and an orange were the traditional Sunday school party gift on going home, while a tangerine in the toe of a stocking spelt Christmas delight. Today we have the pick of the crop from South Africa, America, Spain, Italy and Israel, their different seasons contributing to plenty all the year round. Even so, the winter remains a favourite time for using oranges, lemons and grapefruit, packed full of healthy vitamins, staving off winter colds, and giving a flavour lift to heavy food.

When the best fruit is in the shops, orange and grapefruit segments can be frozen for future use, and are invaluable revivers on a snowbound winter morning. They may be packed separately or as a mixture, lightly sugared, in waxed cartons.

For those without a freezer, economies can be effected by using those parts of the fruit more often thrown away. The rind can be peeled off very thinly, put on a tray in a warm place such as an airing cupboard or a cooling oven, then stored in tightly covered jars to use for flavouring soups, stock and sauces. Essence can be made by packing a small jar with finely peeled citrus fruit skin, covering with vodka and covering tightly. Shake the jar each day for six weeks, then remove peel, and cover jar tightly (about one teaspoon orange or lemon essence will flavour a large cake). Orange or lemon sugar is delicious for sprinkling on puddings or cakes, and for substituting for part of the sugar in a recipe. Make this by rubbing sugar cubes over the surface of oranges or lemons to absorb the zest and colour, then crushing them with a rolling pin, drying them slowly in a warm place, and putting the crystals in an airtight jar. Another method of doing this is to mix 4 oz (100 g) caster sugar with the powdered dry rind of three oranges, storing in the same way.

Candied peel is a useful addition to the store cupboard at Christmas time, and makes an excellent sweetmeat if cut in strips and dipped in melted plain chocolate. Use thick-skinned fruit for making peel. To the skins of three large oranges, allow 6 oz (175 g) granulated sugar, 4 fl oz (100 ml) water and one tablespoon golden syrup. Cover the skins with cold water and golden syrup, bring to the boil and drain; then repeat the process twice more. With a sharp spoon, scrape out the remains of any orange pulp, then cover with cold water, add a pinch of bicarbonate of soda, and boil until skins are tender, then drain.

Put the measured water, sugar and syrup into a pan, dissolve and bring to the boil. Add peel, simmer with the lid off the pan until the syrup has almost gone and the peel is clear. Put into a preserving jar and cover tightly. This will keep for about six weeks, and may be dried off on a wire rack in a cool oven before using for cakes. Lemon peel may be made the same way, but double quantities of ingredients are needed for three grapefruit.

Professional candying is a more complicated business and really needs the use of a sugar thermometer and involves a rather long process of basting with syrup and drying out. This is a good way of using peel left from making puddings or cakes, or curds.

Home-made fruit drinks are always popular, and useful during the snuffling season. To make lemonade syrup for diluting, put 3 lb (1.5 kg) loaf sugar, 1 oz (25 g) citric acid, ½ oz (15 g) tartaric acid in a basin, and pour over 6 pints (3.5 l) boiling water, stirring until sugar has melted. Add the juice of six lemons, and the peel of three of them cut in fine strips. Leave overnight, then strain and bottle.

For all recipes involving juice, fruit will yield the maximum if lightly warmed (over a stove or solid-fuel cooker) before using. Best results will be obtained obviously from the best fruit, so buy with care. The best lemons are smallish, thin-skinned and shiny; oranges cannot be judged by colour or thickness of skin, but should be heavy in the hand – a soft, light spongy orange with dull skin will not be good.

Marmalade-making is a routine kitchen chore in January and February when citrus fruit is at its best, and the bitter Seville oranges are available. It always seems a pity to knock yourself out with a vast batch of only one kind, though, and I like to spread out the work through the year, experimenting with smaller quantities of different citrus fruit preserves. The winter batch never lasts right through the year anyway, so I've had to try out a lot of recipes with sweet oranges, lemons and grapefruit. Many of these ideas don't perhaps conform to the traditional idea of a dark thick marmalade to eat with breakfast toast, but many people like a sweet light marmalade better. I've also found some of the experiments are just as good used for tart fillings, pudding toppings and ice-cream sauces, or served with buttered toast at teatime.

Whatever fruit is used, the rules are the same. The fruit must be sliced, simmered in water until tender, then boiled rapidly with sugar to setting point. If the peel is boiled too long with the sugar, a syrupy preserve is the result with hard chunks of peel. It is not essential to soak the fruit overnight, but the peel must be thoroughly soft between the fingers. The water in the first cooking must be evaporated, and usually the contents of the pan should be reduced by about half to ensure a good set.

Cutting up the fruit can be exhausting. If the fruit is very pithy, the skin must be peeled off, the pith removed, and then the peel sliced. Sweet oranges which are thin-skinned can be time-savers because their cutting is easy. Cut the oranges in quarters lengthways, put two quarters together flat side down on the chopping board, and cut fruit and peel together in thin or thick strips. Thin-skinned lemons can also be quickly cut this way, but grapefruit and thick-skinned lemons need the 'de-pithing' treatment. Even if you're aiming at a chunky marmalade, cut the peel on the thin side, because it does swell in cooking.

The pips and white pith contain pectin, which helps the set of the preserve, so suspend them in a muslin bag in the pan during cooking, and remove the bag before potting.

When the sugar is added, stir gently to dissolve it before boiling, then boil very quickly. Marmalade has reached setting point when a little poured on a cold plate will start to set and wrinkle when pushed with a finger. Cool the marmalade slightly before potting, and stir well to prevent the peel rising in the jars. Use clean warm jars, and fill them right to the top, then cover with a wax circle. Cover at once or when completely cold.

Spiced orange rings

6 large oranges
12 oz (350 g) sugar
3 in (7.5 cm) cinnamon
   stick
¾ pint (450 ml) vinegar
2 teaspoons whole cloves

Wipe oranges and cut them in ¼ in (65 mm) rounds across (keeping peel on). Put into pan with water to cover and simmer for forty-five minutes until fruit is tender. Put sugar, spices and vinegar into another pan and bring to the boil. Add drained orange rings a few at a time and cook gently until rind is tender and clear. Put fruit into hot preserving or honey jars, and boil syrup until it thickens. Pour on to the fruit in jars, add a few of the cloves, and cover at once. Serve this pickle with ham, pork or poultry.

Orange jam

This is a delicious preserve, which is best eaten in small saucers with thick cream as a pudding, or served with vanilla ice-cream as a sauce.

Use twelve good thin-skinned oranges and prick them all over with a fork. Cover with cold water and soak for three days, changing the water twice daily. On the third day, cook slowly in plenty of water until oranges are really tender. Put oranges into cold water and leave overnight to draw out bitterness. Cut each orange into six sections, remove pips, and weigh fruit. Put into preserving pan with equal weight of preserving sugar. Add the juice of six more oranges, and cook very gently over low heat until a little of the syrup sets on a saucer. Put into jars and cover.

Grapefruit jam

This again is an unusual conserve, quite different from marmalade which is not to everyone's taste. The apple juice may be the bottled variety or made by putting sliced cooking apples in a jar, covering with water and leaving in a slow oven until the juice runs.

Peel the rind thinly from six medium grapefruit. Take all the pith off the fruit, and cut out the skinned segments. In a pan put 1 pint (600 ml) apple juice, 1 pint (600 ml) strained orange juice and 2 lb (1 kg) sugar and dissolve without boiling until the syrup is clear. Bring to a slow rolling boil for ten minutes, add grapefruit sections and cook for twenty minutes. Put into pots and cover.

Lemon curd

1 lb (450 g) loaf sugar
4 oz (100 g) butter
6 egg yolks
4 egg whites
3 lemons

Put sugar, butter, egg yolks and whites, grated lemon rind and juice into the top of a double boiler and cook gently over hot water until smooth and creamy. Pour into warm jars and tie down.

Lemon marmalade

8 large lemons
8 pints (4.5 l) water
Sugar

Peel the lemons very thinly and cut the peel into very thin shreds. Put any pith and pips into a muslin bag or piece of clean linen. Cut up the flesh of the lemons. Put the fruit, peel and bag of pips into a pan with water and simmer for 1½ hours. Remove the bag of pips and squeeze out the liquid. Weigh the contents of the pan and add an equal weight of sugar. Stir in the sugar over gentle heat for twenty minutes. Cool slightly and stir well, then pour into warm jars.

Dark orange marmalade

3 lb (1.5 kg) Seville
   oranges
1 lemon
5 pints (2.75 l) water
6 lb (3 kg) sugar
1 tablespoon black treacle

Cut the oranges in half and squeeze out the juice. Put the pips into a muslin bag or piece of clean linen. Cut the fruit peel into thick shreds. Put the peel into a pan with the juice, the juice of the lemon, water and the bag of pips. Simmer for two hours, until the peel is tender. Take out the bag of pips and squeeze out the liquid. Stir in the sugar and black treacle over gentle heat until dissolved, then boil rapidly to setting point. Cool slightly, stir well, pour into warm jars and cover. If liked, four tablespoons rum or whisky may be added just before putting into jars.

Pineapple and orange marmalade

This is an unusual preserve which is delicious for breakfast and tea-time, and also makes a good cake or tart filling.

3 sweet oranges
1 lemon
2 lb (1 kg) tin pineapple
   chunks
4 lb (2 kg) sugar

Shred the oranges and lemon and put into enough water to cover. Add the pips tied in a muslin bag or piece of clean linen. Simmer for two hours until tender and remove the pips. Cut the pineapple into small pieces and add to the oranges, together with the syrup from the tin. Simmer for fifteen minutes, and then stir in the sugar until dissolved. Boil rapidly for thirty minutes. Cool slightly, stir well and pour into warm jars.

Blender chunky marmalade

This marmalade is made very quickly as the fruit does not need soaking, and only takes about five minutes to prepare.

2 lb (1 kg) Seville oranges
1 lemon
4 pints (2.25 l) water
4 lb (2 kg) sugar

Cut the fruit into quarters and take out the pips, tying them in a muslin bag or piece of clean linen. Blend the fruit with some of the water on high speed until well chopped (put about eight orange quarters into the machine at a time so that you can control how coarsely or finely they are chopped). Put into a preserving pan, using all the water, and hang the pip bag from the side of the pan. Boil for one hour and take out the pips. Stir in the sugar over gentle heat until it has dissolved, then boil rapidly to setting point. Cool slightly, stir well, and pour into warm jars.

Ginger marmalade

5 Seville oranges
5 pints (2.75 l) water
3 lb (1.5 kg) cooking
apples
6 lb (3 kg) sugar
8 oz (225 g) crystallized
ginger
½ oz (15 g) ground ginger

Cut the oranges in half and squeeze out the juice. Shred the peel finely and cut up the flesh. Put the pips into a muslin bag or piece of clean linen. Put the peel, flesh, juice and water into a pan with the bag of pips and simmer for 1½ hours. Take out the pip bag, squeezing out any liquid. Peel and core the apples and cut them into slices. Simmer in four tablespoons water until pulped. Add the apples to the oranges and stir in the sugar until dissolved. Add the ginger cut in pieces and the ground ginger. Boil rapidly to setting point. Cool slightly, stir well and pour into warm jars.

Three fruit marmalade

2 large sweet oranges
2 large grapefruit
4 lemons
6 lb (3 kg) sugar
6 pints (3.25 l) water

Peel fruit and shred the rinds. Cut up the fruit. Put pith and pips in a muslin bag and put in pan with fruit, peel and water. Simmer for two hours until peel is soft. Remove pith and pips. Stir in sugar until dissolved and boil hard to setting point.

Grapefruit and lemon marmalade

2 large grapefruit
4 lemons
4 pints (2.25 l) water
3 lb (1.5 kg) sugar

Peel the fruit and squeeze out the juice into preserving pan. Put lemon pips into a muslin bag, but not the grapefruit pips – they would make the marmalade bitter. Cook the shredded peel in the water until the contents of the pan are reduced by half. Remove muslin bag, add sugar, and stir until dissolved. Boil rapidly for twenty minutes until setting point is reached.

Winter Relishes

There is nothing like a jar of home-made pickle or chutney to accompany a slice of cold meat or a chunk of cheese with crusty new bread and butter. For more elegant meals, old-fashioned spiced fruits are worth trying, to add a little variety to winter meals.

Pickles and chutneys can be made from quite small quantities of surplus fruit and vegetables, although a glut of apples, rhubarb, marrow or green tomatoes can usefully be converted into large batches of spicy fruity relish.

Be sure to cook chutney until it is really rich and brown – too often the home-made kind is unpleasantly khaki-coloured and the ingredients have not cooked enough to blend well. And be sure to cover vinegar-based preserves carefully to prevent evaporation, although you must not use metal covers without a lining or the vinegar will eat through the lid.

Military pickle

1 medium marrow
1 medium cauliflower
1 lb (450 g) runner beans
1 lb (450 g) onions
Cooking salt
1 lb (450 g) demerara
   sugar
4 pints (2.25 l) vinegar
7 chillies
1 oz (25 g) turmeric
   powder
1 oz (25 g) ground ginger
4 oz (100 g) plain flour

Cut the vegetables into small pieces and cover with salt. Leave to stand overnight, then drain. Put into a saucepan, add sugar, vinegar and chillies and boil for five minutes. Mix the dry ingredients to a smooth paste with a little cold water. Add to the pan, stirring. Boil for thirty minutes, stirring to prevent burning. Bottle when cold.

Apple chutney

5 lb (2.5 kg) apples
1 tablespoon salt
1 tablespoon ground
   ginger
6 chillies
1 lb (450 g) demerara
   sugar
½–1 pint (300–600 ml)
   vinegar
8 oz (225 g) onions
8 oz (225 g) stoned dates
8 oz (225 g) raisins or
   sultanas

Peel, core and slice the apples. Put the salt, ginger, chopped chillies and sugar into a pan with about a third of the vinegar. Add the apples and minced onions and bring to the boil. Add the chopped dates and whole raisins or sultanas and simmer until thick and brown, adding more vinegar as required. The apples make a lot of juice so don't allow the chutney to become runny. Put into warm jars and cover well.

Rhubarb chutney

2 lb (1 kg) rhubarb
8 oz (225 g) onions
1½ lb (700 g) brown sugar
8 oz (225 g) sultanas
½ oz (15 g) mustard seeds
1 teaspoon mixed spice
1 teaspoon pepper
1 teaspoon ground ginger
1 teaspoon salt
¼ teaspoon cayenne
   pepper
1 pint (600 ml) vinegar

Cut the rhubarb into 1 in (2.5 cm) lengths and chop the onions finely. Put all ingredients into a heavy pan and simmer gently, stirring frequently until the mixture is of the consistency of jam. Put into jars and cover tightly.

Ripe tomato chutney

I find the flavour and colour of this chutney preferable to that made with green tomatoes.

1 lb (450 g) ripe tomatoes
4 oz (100 g) apples
8 oz (225 g) onions
1 lb (450 g) stoned raisins
4 oz (100 g) soft brown
   sugar
¼ oz (8 g) ground ginger
Pinch of cayenne pepper
½ pint (300 ml) vinegar

Skin the tomatoes and peel and core the apples. Chop the tomatoes, onions, apples and raisins. Mix all the ingredients and simmer for an hour or more, until thick and brown. Pour into small jars and cover.

Hot Indian chutney

As its name suggests, this is particularly good with curry.

5 lb (2.5 kg) apples
2 lb (1 kg) onions
1 lb (450 g) raisins
1 lb (450 g) sultanas
1 lb (450 g) demerara
   sugar
1 teaspoon dry mustard
1 teaspoon ground ginger
1 teaspoon crushed
   allspice

Peel, core and slice apples, and put through a mincer with onions, raisins and sultanas. Put all the ingredients into a pan and bring to the boil. Simmer gently for several hours until the mixture thickens.

Grape and apple chutney

This is delicious made with the cheapest white grapes.

2 lb (1 kg) grapes
2 lb (1 kg) cooking apples
6 oz (175 g) raisins
½ pint (300 ml) cider
   vinegar
1½ lb (700 g) brown sugar
¼ pint (150 ml) lemon
   juice
Grated rind of lemon
½ teaspoon whole allspice
½ teaspoon whole cloves
¼ teaspoon ground ginger
1 in (2.5 cm) stick
   cinnamon
¼ teaspoon salt
¼ teaspoon paprika

Seed grapes, core and chop apples, and put in thick pan with raisins, vinegar, sugar, lemon juice and rind. Put spices and salt in a piece of muslin and hang it in the mixture. Bring to boil, reduce heat and simmer until thick. Take out spice bag, put in hot jars and seal.

Pear chutney

3½ lb (1.75 kg) winter
   pears
1½ lb (700 g) sugar
2 oranges
1 teaspoon ground
   cinnamon
1 teaspoon ground cloves
1 teaspoon ground allspice
12 oz (350 g) seeded
   raisins
½ pint (300 ml) vinegar

Peel, core and chop pears and put in pan with sugar. Grate orange rind and squeeze juice and add to pears. Add spices, raisins and vinegar, bring to the boil, reduce heat and simmer for two hours. Put into hot jars and seal.

Marrow and apple chutney

4 lb (2 kg) marrow flesh
3 oz (75 g) salt
2 lb (1 kg) cooking apples
1 lb (450 g) shallots
1 oz (25 g) mixed pickling
   spice
3 pints (1.5 l) vinegar
1 lb (450 g) brown sugar

Cut peeled marrow into pieces and put in a basin with salt sprinkled between the layers. Leave for twelve hours, then drain thoroughly. Chop peeled cooking apples and shallots and add to other ingredients. Simmer gently, stirring well until soft. Add vinegar and sugar and continue cooking to the consistency of jam. Remove spice bag and put into pots.

Orange and date chutney

1 lb (450 g) stoned dates
6 medium oranges
8 oz (225 g) onions
2 teaspoons salt
2 teaspoons ground
  ginger
1 pint (600 ml) vinegar

Chop the dates. Peel oranges, remove pips, and slice fruit thinly. Chop onions finely. Cook all ingredients together until mixture is thick (about 1½ hours).

Grapefruit chutney

Very good with poultry
or ham.

4 lb (2 kg) grapefruit
½ oz (15 g) ground cloves
1 pint (600 ml) vinegar
2 lb (1 kg) white sugar
2 oz (50 g) brazil nuts
8 oz (225 g) raisins

Peel the grapefruit, remove pith and pips, and cut up grapefruit roughly. Simmer this pulp with vinegar, cloves and sugar until soft (about one hour). Stir in finely chopped nuts and whole raisins. Stir mixture well and remove from heat.

Lemon chutney

This chutney is
particularly good with
poultry, and with curry.

4 large lemons
8 oz (225 g) onions
¾ pint (450 ml) vinegar
1 lb (450 g) white sugar
4 oz (100 g) raisins
1 oz (25 g) salt
1 oz (25 g) mustard seed
1 teaspoon ground ginger
½ teaspoon cayenne
  pepper

Slice lemons thinly and remove all pips. Peel and chop onions and put on a dish with sliced lemons. Sprinkle with salt and leave for twenty-four hours. Put all ingredients into preserving pan, crushing the mustard seed well before putting it in. Bring to the boil, then simmer until completely tender, and of the consistency of jam.

Tomato sauce

4 lb (2 kg) ripe tomatoes
4 large onions
1 lb (450 g) demerara
  sugar
1 oz (25 g) salt
2 oz (50 g) peppercorns
½ oz (15 g) cloves
2 teaspoons cayenne
  pepper
1 pint (600 ml) vinegar

Slice the tomatoes and onions and mix with the other ingredients. Simmer gently for two hours, stirring occasionally. Rub through a fine sieve, leaving nothing but seeds and skins in the strainer. Return pulp to the pan, bring to the boil and boil for five minutes. Bottle when cold. This sauce keeps well and improves with keeping.

Pickled pears

Serve with cold ham or
pork.

4 lb (2 kg) pears
Lemon juice
2 lb (1 kg) granulated
  sugar
1 pint (600 ml) malt
  vinegar
2 teaspoons whole cloves
2 teaspoons whole allspice
3 pieces stick cinnamon
1 piece root ginger
2 pieces lemon rind

Peel, quarter and core the pears and place in a
bowl of cold water with a little lemon juice to
prevent browning. Place the sugar and vinegar
in a large saucepan. Tie the remaining ingredients in a muslin bag and add to the pan.
Stir over a low heat to dissolve the sugar before
bringing to the boil and adding the pears.
Cover the pan and simmer gently until the
pears are tender. Remove the pears and pack
into clean, warm preserving jars. Remove the
spices from the syrup and boil rapidly until
the syrup is reduced by half. Cover the pears
with syrup and seal. Store for four months
before use.

Spiced plums

Particularly good with
cold poultry, pork and
ham.

1½ lb (700 g) black plums
1½ lb (700 g) sugar
1 pint (600 ml) malt
  vinegar
¼ oz (8 g) ground mace
¼ oz (8 g) ground allspice
¼ oz (8 g) ground
  cinnamon

Prick each plum several times with a needle.
Boil the sugar, vinegar and spices together
for ten minutes. Pour over the fruit and set
aside for twenty-four hours. Pour off the
vinegar and boil for another ten minutes. Pour
on to the fruit again and leave until the next
day. On the third day, boil all together gently
for five minutes. Pour into warmed preserving
jars and seal tightly. Keep for three months
before using.

Pineapple relish

1 medium-sized ripe
  pineapple
½ pint (300 ml) cider
  vinegar
8 oz (225 g) sugar
1 tablespoon bruised
  cinnamon stick
1 teaspoon whole cloves
1 teaspoon crushed
  ginger root
1 tablespoon curry
  powder

Peel and core pineapple and cut in small
chunks, reserving any juice. Combine juice,
vinegar and sugar and bring to rolling boil.
Add spices tied in muslin bag and simmer in
syrup for five minutes. Add pineapple pieces
and cook five minutes. Take out spice bag and
pour mixture into hot jars, sealing at once.

Spiced prunes

1 lb (450 g) prunes
Cold tea
¾ pint (450 ml) vinegar
8 oz (225 g) sugar
2 teaspoons whole mixed
  pickling spices

Wash prunes and soak overnight in cold tea. Boil together vinegar with sugar and spices in a muslin bag. Cook prunes in tea for fifteen minutes until soft. Drain, reserving juice. Add ½ pint (300 ml) juice to spiced vinegar and pour over prunes. Put into jars and cover. These may be used after twenty-four hours, but will keep as long as required.

Pickled melon

4 lb (2 kg) honeydew or
  cantaloup melon
1 lb (450 g) sugar
1 pint (600 ml) vinegar
  (white)
8 cloves
½ oz (15 g) stick cinnamon
Brine (2 oz (50 g) salt to
  1 pint (600 ml) water)

Peel melon, cut in ½ in (1.25 cm) cubes and soak overnight in brine. Remove from salt water, put in fresh water and bring to boil. Simmer until tender and clear. Dissolve sugar in vinegar with spices and boil for twenty minutes until syrup. Strain syrup and bring to boil. Add drained melon, boil for ten minutes and bottle at once.

Spiced apples

2 lb (1 kg) apples
½ oz (15 g) whole cloves
½ oz (15 g) stick cinnamon
½ oz (15 g) whole allspice
1 pint (600 ml) white
  vinegar
2 lb (1 kg) sugar
½ teaspoon salt

Put sugar, vinegar and salt into a saucepan, with the spices tied in a muslin bag. Bring to the boil and add the peeled, cored and sliced apples. Cook gently until the apples are tender, then take out the fruit, draining it carefully, and pack into warm jars. Boil the syrup until it thickens, take out the spice bag, pour over the apples and seal tightly.

Spiced apricots

Very good with ham.

1 lb (450 g) dried apricots
1½ pints (900 ml) white
  vinegar
½ oz (15 g) whole cloves
½ in (1.25 cm) cinnamon
  stick
½ oz (15 g) whole allspice
1¼ lb (600 g) sugar

Soak apricots overnight in cold water and drain. Tie spices in a muslin bag and put into a saucepan with the vinegar. Bring slowly to the boil, then add apricots and simmer for five minutes. Spoon apricots into warm jars. Add sugar to vinegar and bring to boil, then boil for five minutes. Remove spice bag, pour syrup over fruit and seal tightly.

Orange and apricot relish

This is a delicious relish to eat with poultry, ham or pork.

1 lb (450 g) dried apricots
½ pint (300 ml) white wine vinegar
1 lb (450 g) soft brown sugar
1 orange
2 chillies
2 cloves garlic
1 small onion
Pinch of ground ginger
1 teaspoon salt

Soak apricots overnight, and then simmer in the same water until soft. Cut in quarters. Put vinegar in a pan with sugar, grated rind and juice of the orange, and very finely chopped chillies (remove seeds), garlic and onion, and salt and ginger. Bring vinegar to boil, then add apricots and simmer for thirty minutes, stirring constantly. Put into small jars.

Spiced cranberries

Cranberries are traditional with turkey, and also very good with ham and pork.

1 lb (450 g) fresh cranberries
½ pint (300 ml) cider vinegar
8 oz (225 g) sugar
¼ oz (8 g) root ginger
¼ oz (8 g) stick cinnamon
¼ oz (8 g) allspice berries
4 cloves

Put cranberries in a pan with vinegar and the spices tied in a bag, and simmer until the skins start to pop and the cranberries are soft. Add sugar and simmer for thirty minutes. Remove spice bag, put into small warm jars, and cool before sealing.

Cherry relish

This relish is particularly good with cold chicken and duck.

2 lb (1 kg) cherries
8 oz (225 g) raisins
2 oz (50 g) honey
2 teaspoons mixed spice
8 tablespoons vinegar
4 tablespoons brown sugar

Stone the cherries, and put all ingredients in a thick pan. Simmer gently until sugar has dissolved. Boil for five minutes, then continue simmering until thick, stirring all the time. Put into small jars.

Sweet Puddings and Pies

Iced Delights

Most of us are used to buying ice-cream from the corner shop or the travelling van, but bought ices are sadly synthetic (try reading the wrapper before you eat the contents and you may go right off the idea) so it's worth trying to make your own.

Although it is perfection to have a sorbetière which beats the ice to creamy smoothness as it freezes, no special equipment is necessary except a refrigerator, and it is rather less trouble to make a superb ice-cream than the usual party pudding with all the trimmings.

You can make cream ices or fruit water ices or sorbets, and one of my favourites is a milk ice. Ice-cream can be thickened with pure cream, gelatine or egg yolks, or evaporated milk. If the latter is used, the unopened tin of milk should be boiled for ten minutes, cooled and left in a refrigerator overnight.

Ice-cream must be frozen quickly or it will be 'grainy' and rough, and it must also be beaten during freezing to make it smooth. Eggs, gelatine, cream or sugar syrup stop large ice crystals forming, and gelatine gives a particularly smooth ice. If whipped egg whites are introduced, they give extra lightness. Be careful not to over-sweeten ice-cream as sugar prevents freezing. The best temperature for ice-cream making is in the ice-making compartment of a refrigerator. If you want to make ice cream for freezer storage, make it in the fridge and, when it is completed, pack the ice-cream into a freezer container to keep it. It is not at all satisfactory just to make the mixture and put it straight into freezer storage.

The ice-cream mixture should be frozen in a metal ice-cube tray or a shallow cake tin. When it is frozen about $\frac{1}{2}$ in (1.25 cm) from the edge, the mixture should be beaten quickly in a chilled bowl, then frozen for a further hour. This freezing and beating technique should be repeated for up to three hours for perfect smoothness. If you have an electric beater, that can be used to break up and smooth the ice cream, or a powerful liquidizer can be used.

Strawberry water ice

12 oz (350 g) sugar
$\frac{3}{4}$ pint (450 ml) water
8 oz (225 g) strawberries
Juice of 1 orange
1 egg white

Serves 4

Dissolve the sugar in hot water for five minutes. Cool and add sieved strawberries and orange juice. Freeze in a tray. When half frozen, put into a chilled bowl, beat out the lumps and fold in the stiffly whipped egg white. Return to the fridge until frozen.

Custard ice

½ pint (300 ml) creamy
  milk
1 vanilla pod
2 large egg yolks
2 oz (50 g) sugar
Small pinch of salt
¼ pint (150 ml) double
  cream

Serves 4

It is best to use a vanilla pod for flavouring, as vanilla essence is often synthetic and the flavour is not pleasant when frozen. Scald the milk with the vanilla pod, remove the pod and pour the milk on the egg yolks, sugar and salt, whisking lightly until well blended.

Cook the mixture in a double boiler, or in a bowl over a pan of hot water until it coats the back of a spoon. Cool and strain and stir in the cream. Pour into a freezing tray and beat twice during a total freezing time of about three hours.

For a *coffee* ice, add a little instant coffee to the hot milk. For *chocolate* ice, melt 2 oz (50 g) plain chocolate in four tablespoons hot water and add to the hot milk.

Lemon water ice

8 oz (225 g) caster sugar
Rind and juice of 3 lemons
1 egg white

Serves 4

Dissolve the sugar in 1 pint (600 ml) water over a low heat. Add thinly peeled lemon rind and boil gently for ten minutes. Leave to cool. Add the lemon juice and pour into freezing tray. Leave until half frozen, then beat in a chilled bowl. Whisk the egg white stiffly. Fold the lemon mixture and continue freezing.

Gelatine ice

This recipe is particularly good for flavouring with coffee or chocolate.

½ pint (300 ml) creamy
  milk
1 vanilla pod
2 teaspoons gelatine
2 tablespoons cold water
3 oz (75 g) sugar
Pinch of salt

Heat half the milk with the vanilla pod to boiling point. Heat the soaked gelatine in a bowl standing in hot water until the gelatine is syrupy. Pour warm milk on to the gelatine, and stir in the sugar, salt and remaining milk. Take out the vanilla pod and freeze the mixture, beating twice during three hours total freezing time.

Serves 4

Café frappé

4 oz (100 g) sugar
¾ pint (450 ml) fresh,
  strong hot coffee

Serves 4

Add sugar to coffee, cool and freeze to a mush. Pile up in tall glasses and garnish with whipped cream. Serve this after a rich main course.

Frozen apple cream

½ pint (300 ml) strained
  apple sauce
Pinch of nutmeg
Pinch of cinnamon
1 teaspoon melted butter
2 teaspoons lemon juice
½ pint (300 ml) double
  cream

Whisk apple sauce until foamy, add nutmeg and cinnamon, then butter and lemon juice. Chill in refrigerator for one hour. Fold in whipped cream and put in freezing tray. Freeze until firm, and serve with freshly baked ginger-bread.

Serves 4

Blackcurrant sorbet

1 lb (450 g) blackcurrants
2 oz (50 g) icing sugar
½ pint (300 ml) natural
  yogurt
Juice of ½ lemon
½ oz (15 g) gelatine
4 tablespoons water
2 egg whites

Serves 4

Put the blackcurrants into a pan with ½ pint (300 ml) water, and simmer until the fruit is soft. Put through a sieve. Mix this purée with the icing sugar, yogurt and lemon juice in a bowl. Dissolve the gelatine in the water over a pan of hot water until it becomes syrupy. Stir the gelatine into the blackcurrant purée. When the mixture begins to set, fold in the stiffly whipped egg whites. Pour into an ice tray and freeze, without further beating.

Fruit milk ice

This is nicest made with a distinctively flavoured jelly like raspberry or orange. For a really special ice, fold in some appropriate fruit during the beating, such as fresh or drained canned raspberries, drained canned mandarin oranges or canned pineapple. This is a particularly good light ice for children, and the recipe makes a large quantity.

Put the jelly in a saucepan with the water and heat gently until the jelly has melted. Stir well and remove from the heat. Add the sugar, milk and lemon juice. The mixture may look lightly curdled. Freeze (you may need two trays), beating once when nearly firm.

Serves 4

1 packet fruit jelly
½ pint (300 ml) water
4 oz (100 g) sugar
1¼ pints (750 ml) creamy
  milk
Squeeze of lemon juice

Raspberry honey ice

1 lb (450 g) raspberries
¼ pint (150 ml) double
  cream
¼ pint (150 ml) natural
  yogurt
10 tablespoons clear
  honey
2 tablespoons lemon
  juice
Pinch of salt
4 egg whites

Sieve the raspberries and put the purée into a bowl with the cream, yogurt, honey, lemon juice and salt. Mix thoroughly and pour into freezing tray. Partially freeze and then put into a chilled bowl and beat until smooth. Whisk the egg whites until stiff and fold into the mixture. Return to the tray and continue freezing.

Serves 4

Iced mincemeat

Serves 4

Make up vanilla ice-cream and press a quarter of it into a freezing tray or mould. Spread on mincemeat (better still if spiked with a few toasted almonds and a spot of rum), then finish off with remaining ice cream. Freeze until solid, and serve in slices.

Easy to Make Cheesecake

Cheesecakes used to be the sort of thing that nice mothers made for their sons who had been tending the cows, and their daughters who had been working in the dairy. Now every supermarket, delicatessen and frozen food cabinet is full of them, although they're not always just like mother made.

The traditional cheesecake has a fairly solid topping of sweetened cream cheese on a pastry or biscuit crumb base baked in the oven and even slightly sunken in the middle. Popular taste favours the light fluffy uncooked cheesecake, chilled in the refrigerator. Both kinds are equally good, easy to make and pretty nourishing. They can be made well in advance of a meal, and the uncooked kinds freeze beautifully.

The uncooked cheesecake is usually made on a base of biscuit crumbs mixed with sweetening and fat, which can be varied according to the topping. Some are made with cottage cheese, others with cream cheese, and small packets of full fat soft cheese are available at most grocers these days. I find the cream cheese recipes quicker to prepare because no sieving is required, but they all taste just as good and the choice may have to depend on your shopping facilities.

Most of the cheesecakes have more than enough flavour to be eaten on their own, with perhaps a little cream, but the plainer ones are very special served with lightly sugared soft fruit.

Soft fruit cheesecake

2 oz (50 g) butter
2½ oz (65 g) caster sugar
2 oz (50 g) walnuts
4 oz (100 g) digestive
  biscuits
8 oz (225 g) packet full fat
  soft cheese
3 oz (75 g) caster sugar
2 eggs, separated
¼ pint (150 ml) natural
  yogurt
½ oz (15 g) gelatine
4 tablespoons water
8 oz (225 g) fresh or frozen
  raspberries or
  strawberries

If frozen fruit is used, allow it to thaw in a basin before beginning to make the cheesecake. Make the base by melting butter and stirring in sugar, finely chopped walnuts and finely crushed biscuits. Press into base of a greased 8 in (20.5 cm) cake tin with removable base. Cream the cheese and sugar, and then work in the egg yolks and yogurt. Add the gelatine mixed with the water and melted in a bowl over hot water. Sieve the fruit and any juice and stir into the mixture until creamy and smooth. Whisk the egg whites and fold in. Pour into the tin and chill until firm. This cheesecake may be finished off with a topping of lightly whipped cream and decorated with fresh fruit.

Chocolate cheesecake

1½ oz (40 g) butter
4 oz (100 g) chocolate
  digestive biscuits
8 oz (225 g) packet full
  fat soft cheese
4 oz (100 g) caster sugar
4 oz (100 g) plain
  chocolate
½ oz (15 g) gelatine
8 fl oz (225 ml) water
¼ pint (150 ml) double
  cream

Melt the butter and stir in the finely crushed biscuits. Press into the base of an 8 in (20.5 cm) cake tin with removable base. Bake at 350°F/180°C/Gas Mark 4 for ten minutes. Leave to cool. Cream the cheese until smooth, gradually working in the sugar. Melt the chocolate in a basin over a pan of hot water. Gradually add to the cheese mixture, beating well. Dissolve the gelatine in the water in a basin over hot water. Blend into the cheese mixture and then fold in the lightly whipped cream. Pour on top of the base and chill until firm. Decorate with some whipped cream and walnut kernels or curls of chocolate.

Baked country cheesecake

6 oz (175 g) shortcrust
  pastry
1¼ lb (550 g) cottage
  cheese
5 oz (150 g) caster sugar
2 oz (50 g) plain flour
3 eggs
1 oz (25 g) butter, melted
Grated rind of 1 lemon
1 teaspoon icing sugar

Roll out the pastry and line a 7 in (18 cm) square shallow cake tin. Cream together the sieved cottage cheese and sugar. Add the flour, beaten eggs, melted butter and lemon rind. Mix well together, pour into the pastry case, and bake at 375°F/190°C/Gas Mark 5 for one hour until firm. Sift icing sugar on top.

Fluffy lemon cheesecake

2 oz (50 g) butter
1 oz (25 g) soft brown
sugar
4 oz (100 g) digestive
biscuits, in crumbs
8 oz (225 g) packet full
fat soft cheese
3 oz (75 g) caster sugar
2 eggs
6 fl oz (75 ml) natural
yogurt
Juice and grated rind of 1
lemon
½ oz (15 g) gelatine
4 tablespoons water
¼ pint (150 ml) double
cream

Melt the butter and remove from heat. Stir in sugar and digestive biscuit crumbs. Press into base of a greased 8 in (20 cm) cake tin with removable base. Leave in a cool place to harden slightly while making the topping. Cream together the cheese and sugar until smooth. Separate the eggs and gradually beat the yolks into the cheese mixture. Work in the yogurt, lemon juice and rind. Dissolve the gelatine in the water in a basin placed over a saucepan of hot water. When the gelatine mixture is syrupy, cool slightly and then add to the cheese mixture, mixing very thoroughly until creamy and smooth. Whip the cream lightly and fold into the mixture, and then add the egg whites whisked until stiff. Pour into the tin on top of the biscuit base. Chill until firm. Gently ease from the tin and serve on the metal base.

Anytime is Pancake Time

For breakfast, make them small – the American way, and top with jam and cream, or golden syrup. For a traditional pudding at lunchtime, the usual English accompaniments of lemon and sugar are hard to beat. For a special meal, thin delicate pancakes in the French and Austrian manner are temptingly sweet with fruit, with liqueurs, and with jam or flavoured sauces.

First essential is to make a good basic batter. When it's time to start cooking, heat a little lard in the pan, use only a little batter to cover the base of the pan, and cook quickly until the first side is golden. Toss (or flick with a palette knife) and brown the other side. The first side cooked is always better-looking than the second, and should be folded outwards.

If the pancakes are not to be served straight away, stack them flat on a plate and put a pudding basin over them; they can be reheated in the oven or by steaming, without toughening. Those with a freezer can prepare pancakes months in advance, layering them with greaseproof paper for easy separation at a later date.

Pancakes can be stacked like a cake with a filling between and served in wedges and this is particularly good if a sauce is handed with them.

Basic batter

Sieve 2 oz (50 g) plain flour with a pinch of salt, and blend into a batter with one egg, ¼ oz (8 g) cooled melted butter and ¼ pint (150 ml) milk. Beat until smooth, cover and, if possible, leave in a cool place for about one hour. This mixture should make four to five thin pancakes about 8 in (20 cm) diameter.

Cream pancakes

Delicious for a very special party.

Basic pancake batter
¼ pint (150 ml) double cream
2 oz (50 g) toasted almonds or hazelnuts

Cook thin pancakes. Whip cream, sweeten to taste and fold in chopped toasted nuts. Put a spoonful of mixture on each pancake, roll up and serve at once sprinkled with sugar and any liqueur.

Spanish pancakes

Basic pancake batter
1 teaspoon grated orange rind
4 tablespoons orange marmalade
Chocolate sauce

Make a basic batter and add orange rind. Fry pancakes and fold each one round a spoonful of orange marmalade. Serve at once with hot chocolate sauce.

Apple pancakes

8 pancakes
½ pint (300 ml) sweet apple sauce purée
2 oz (50 g) sultanas
½ teaspoon ground cinnamon
Icing sugar
Whipped cream

Turn the cooked pancakes on to sugared greaseproof paper. Mix apples, sultanas and cinnamon, and put a spoonful of the mixture on each pancake. Roll up and put in a hot dish to keep warm. Sprinkle with icing sugar just before serving, and hand with whipped cream.

Viennese coffee pancakes

4 oz (100 g) plain flour
Pinch of salt
1 egg
¼ pint (150 ml) strong black coffee
¼ pint (150 ml) single cream

Make a batter with flour, salt, egg and coffee, and gradually add the cream to make a thick pouring consistency. Fry pancakes in the usual way, and serve them with icing sugar and whipped cream. (They are even better served with a rich chocolate sauce flavoured with coffee or rum.)

179

Cottage cheese pancakes

These are very light griddlecakes and are particularly good for people who don't want much starch in their diet, but sometimes feel they need a pudding or teatime delicacy.

8 oz (225 g) cottage cheese
3 well-beaten eggs
2 tablespoons soft butter
1 oz (25 g) plain flour
¼ teaspoon salt

Blend together all ingredients, and cook by tablespoons on a hot griddle or thick frying pan. Eat hot with butter, or with crabapple or redcurrant jelly.

Baked pancakes

This quantity makes about twelve pancakes, but the recipe is easy to prepare in smaller quantities if necessary. These pancakes can be served with a simple sprinkling of caster sugar, but we particularly enjoy them with warm syrup.

3 oz (75 g) butter
4 oz (100 g) caster sugar
Grated rind of 1 lemon
Grated rind of 1 orange
6 oz (175 g) plain flour
1 teaspoon baking powder
4 eggs
¾ pint (450 ml) milk

Beat the butter and sugar to a cream, and add the grated lemon and orange rinds. Sift the flour and baking powder and stir into the creamed mixture, together with the beaten eggs and then the milk. Butter some old strong saucers – and pour a little mixture into each. Bake at 375°F/190°C/Gas Mark 5 for twenty minutes. Serve at once, heaped on a dish and sprinkled with sugar. (Before tins, earthenware dishes and saucers were always used for baking pies and cakes.)

Basic griddlecake batter

These are the small American-style pancakes, which are known to us variously as griddle-cakes, drop scones, flapjacks, Scotch pancakes and many other regional names. For these use 8 oz (225 g) self-raising flour, a pinch of salt, 2 oz (50 g) caster sugar, 2 beaten eggs, 1 oz (25 g) cooled melted butter and ¼ pint (150 ml) milk. The batter should rest for fifteen minutes before using and this quantity should make about twenty small pancakes. Cook them on moderate heat until the underside is browned and the top bubbles, then turn and brown on the other side. Cool in a clean cloth to keep soft.

Winter Fruit Puddings

There's a joke in our family that I always ask 'Apple or rhubarb?' in the winter, and 'Rhubarb or apple?' in the spring. There always seem to be supplies of these two fruits, and somehow a fruit pudding seems healthier and not quite so filling as any other sort. With today's frozen fruit, as well as bottled and canned, and apples and pears from the attic, we always seem to have fruit available now, but it's nice not to serve the plainly stewed variety.

Apple batter

4 small cooking apples
2 tablespoons mincemeat
3 eggs, separated
1 oz (25 g) sugar
2 oz (50 g) plain flour
¼ pint (150 ml) milk
Pinch of salt

Serves 4

Peel and core the apples and put them into a buttered ovenware dish. Put a little mincemeat into the centre of each. Beat together the egg yolks, sugar, flour and milk with the salt. Whisk the egg whites until stiff, and fold into the batter. Pour over the apples and bake at 350°F/180°C/ Gas Mark 4 for one hour. Sprinkle with sugar and serve at once.

Bramble betty

Raspberries may be used instead of blackberries. If using canned fruit, drain well and thicken the liquid with a little arrowroot or cornflour to make a sauce for the pudding.

1 lb (450 g) cooking apples
8 oz (225 g) blackberries
2 oz (50 g) sugar
2 oz (50 g) butter
6 oz (175 g) fresh white breadcrumbs
2 oz (50 g) soft brown sugar

Peel, core and slice the apples. Put the apples, blackberries, sugar and one tablespoon water in a pan. Cover and cook gently until the fruit is tender. Leave to cool. Melt the butter and mix in the crumbs and brown sugar, stirring well so that the crumbs are coated. Layer the fruit and crumbs alternately in a bowl, ending with a layer of crumbs. Leave in the refrigerator overnight and serve with cream or custard.

Serves 4

Winter pears

For a party dish, red wine can be used instead of cider.

2 lb (1 kg) cooking or hard eating pears
4 oz (100 g) caster sugar
½ pint (300 ml) cider
½ pint (300 ml) water
Twist of lemon peel
Shredded almonds

Serves 4

Peel the pears, leaving stems on and keeping the fruit whole. Arrange them upright in a deep casserole. Sprinkle on sugar and pour over the cider and water. Add the lemon peel. Cover and cook at 300°F/150°C/Gas Mark 2, until the pears are tender and can be pierced with a fork. (They can be left in the low oven of an Aga cooker overnight.) Leave to cool in the juice. Remove the pears and simmer the juice until it becomes thick and syrupy. Put almonds here and there in the pears, and pour over the syrup. Serve with cream.

Plum gingerbread pudding

1½ lb (700 g) plums
6 oz (175 g) caster sugar
2 oz (50 g) butter
3 oz (75 g) black treacle
1 oz (25 g) golden syrup
5 tablespoons milk
1 egg
4 oz (100 g) plain flour
1 oz (25 g) granulated sugar
1 teaspoon ground mixed spice
1 teaspoon ground ginger
½ teaspoon bicarbonate of soda

Plums may be fresh, frozen, canned or bottled, but should be drained of any syrup or liquid. Mix the plums and castor sugar and put into a buttered ovenware dish. Warm together the butter, treacle and syrup, then add the milk and beaten egg and leave to cool. Mix the sieved flour, granulated sugar, spices and soda, and mix into the cooled treacle mixture. Blend well and pour over the fruit. Bake at 325°F/170°C/Gas Mark 3 for 1¼ hours. Serve hot with custard or cream.

Serves 4

Rhubarb hotcake

8 oz (225 g) self-raising flour
Pinch of salt
¼ teaspoon ground nutmeg
1 oz (25 g) butter
1 oz (25 g) sugar
1 egg
¼ pint (150 ml) milk
A little icing sugar

Filling:
8 oz (225 g) rhubarb
2 oz (50 g) sugar
½ oz (15 g) butter

Sieve together the flour, salt and nutmeg and rub in the butter until the mixture is like fine breadcrumbs. Add the sugar, egg and milk to form a soft dough. Divide into two pieces and roll each out into a 7 in (17.5 cm) round. Put one round on a baking sheet, cover with chopped rhubarb mixed with sugar and butter. Divide the second round into eight triangles with a sharp knife and put these wedges on top of the rhubarb. Bake at 375°F/190°C/Gas Mark 5 for forty minutes. Dust with icing sugar and serve hot with custard or cream.

Serves 4

Gooseberry marmalade charlotte

3 slices white bread
Butter
Marmalade
8 oz (225 g) gooseberries
½ pint (250 ml) milk
1 egg

Serves 4

Spread the bread thickly with butter and marmalade. Simmer the gooseberries in a little water until just soft; frozen fruit should be cooked, but bottled or canned fruit will be tender enough and only needs draining. Cut the bread into fingers and line the base and sides of a piedish. Put in the gooseberries and pour over the milk and egg mixed together. Leave to stand for thirty minutes. Bake at 350°F/180°C/Gas Mark 4 for one hour.

Apple crisps

3 large eating apples
3 thick slices white bread
Butter
Sugar

Serves 4

Peel and cut the apples into thick slices. Take the crusts from the bread, and cut it into cubes. Fry the apples in butter until cooked and put them into a dish, sprinkling with sugar. Fry the bread cubes in butter, drain and mix with the apples. Serve with cream or custard.

Apple amber

1 lb (450 g) apples
2 oz (50 g) sugar
1 oz (25 g) butter
Rind and juice of ½ lemon
2 small eggs, separated
2 oz (50 g) caster sugar

Serves 4

Peel and core apples and cook gently with sugar, butter and lemon until tender, then beat with a fork, adding egg yolks and beating well. Put into greased oven dish, put in cold oven, and cook while oven heats to 325°F/170°C/Gas Mark 3. Whisk egg whites very stiff, fold in castor sugar, and pile meringue on top of apples. Cook until meringue is set and just tipped with brown. If liked the apples can be put into a lightly cooked pastry case.

Blackberry pie

1½ lb (700 g) blackberries
2 tablespoons butter
8 oz (225 g) sugar
4 tablespoons cornflour
8 oz (225 g) shortcrust
    pastry

Serves 4

Butter a deep piedish and put in 1 lb (450 g) blackberries. Dot with butter and stir in 6 oz (175 g) sugar. Cook remaining blackberries with the rest of the sugar and very little water until soft, and put through a sieve. Thicken with cornflour blended with six tablespoons water. Pour over the raw berries and cover with pastry. Bake at 400°F/200°C/Gas Mark 6 until lightly brown, then reduce heat to 350°F/180°C/Gas Mark 4 and cook for thirty minutes. Serve cool with cream.

Blackberry and apple pudding

1 lb (450 g) blackberries
2 large apples
4 oz (100 g) sugar
White bread

Serves 4

Simmer blackberries with peeled and sliced apples, sugar and ½ pint (300 ml) water until soft. Strain, keeping the juice, and rub the fruit through a sieve. Add half the juice to the fruit pulp and sweeten with more sugar to taste. In the bottom of a soufflé dish or straight-sided casserole, put a layer of thinly sliced white bread without crusts. Cover with a layer of blackberry purée, then another layer of bread and purée, and so on until the dish is filled, making sure each layer of bread is well soaked with the fruit, and finishing with a layer of bread. Put a plate on top with a heavy weight, and leave overnight. Turn out to serve, with the rest of the blackberry juice thickened with cornflour to make a sauce and with cream if liked.

Cinnamon plum tart

4 oz (100 g) butter
6 oz (175 g) plain flour
10 oz (275 g) caster sugar
1 egg yolk
Iced water
3 teaspoons lemon juice
1½ lb (700 g) plums
1 teaspoon cinnamon

Serves 4

Rub 3 oz (75 g) butter into flour and stir in 3 oz (75 g) sugar. Mix to a dough with egg yolk, one teaspoon lemon juice and three tablespoons iced water. Chill pastry well, then roll out to fit a 9 in (22.5 cm) pie plate or sandwich tin, fluting the edges. Halve and stone plums and arrange in a pattern, cut side up, all over the pastry. Mix together remaining sugar and cinnamon and sprinkle half on plums. Pour over remaining lemon juice and dot with remaining butter. Bake at 350°F/180°C/Gas Mark 4 for forty minutes, then sprinkle with remaining cinnamon sugar. Serve warm or cold.

Baked apple dumplings

These are also very good served with heated sieved apricot jam, and make a pleasant variation on the apple pie theme.

8 oz (225 g) shortcrust
    pastry
4 small cooking apples
1 oz (25 g) seeded raisins
¾ oz (20 g) brown sugar
¾ oz (20 g) butter
¼ teaspoon cinnamon

Serves 4

Make shortcrust pastry and roll out, cutting four circles round a saucer. Peel and core apples and put one in the centre of each piece of pastry. Fill centre of apples with mixture of raisins, sugar, butter and cinnamon. Enclose apples completely in pastry and invert on baking sheet. Brush pastry with egg or milk and bake at 425°F/220°C/Gas Mark 7 for twenty-five minutes. Sprinkle with castor sugar as they come out of the oven and serve hot or cold with cream.

Upside-down apple tart

A little cinnamon or a dash of rum may be sprinkled on the apples before the pastry is added.

5 oz (150 g) self-raising flour
5 oz (150 g) butter
4 oz (100 g) sugar plus 2 teaspoons sugar
2 lb (1 kg) apples

Serves 4

Rub 3 oz (75 g) butter into flour with the two teaspoons sugar, and water to mix. Use a deep 7 in (17.5 cm) round cake tin or ovenproof dish for this pudding. Butter the dish well and sprinkle with 2 oz (50 g) caster sugar. Peel, core and cut apples into slices (crisp eating apples are nicest for this). Put a layer of apples in dish then sprinkle with remaining sugar and melted butter. Put on another layer of apples, then cover with the pastry rolled out $\frac{1}{8}$ in (35 mm) thick, allowing the edges of the pastry to fall inside. Bake at 400°F/200°C/Gas Mark 6 for ten minutes, then continue cooking for thirty minutes at 375°F/190°C/Gas Mark 5. Turn out on a hot serving dish, and serve with cream.

Dutch apple squares

8 oz (225 g) plain flour
4 oz (100 g) butter or margarine
Pinch of salt
1½ lb (700 g) cooking apples
2 tablespoons black treacle
1 oz (25 g) brown sugar
1 teaspoon cinnamon

Serves 4

To make handling easier, put long strips of greased, greaseproof paper along the length of the bottom of a 7 × 11 in (17.5 × 27.5 cm) swiss roll tin. Let paper come well over the shorter sides of the tin.

Make pastry with the flour, fat and salt, and enough cold water to mix. Divide pastry into two pieces and roll to fit the tin. Line tin with one piece of pastry, and prick lightly with a fork. Peel, core and slice apples, and mix slices with treacle, sugar and cinnamon. Put on to pastry and top with lid, moistening and sealing edges. Bake at 425°F/220°C/Gas Mark 7 for fifteen minutes, then at 350°F/180°C/Gas Mark 4 for thirty minutes. Cool slightly and lift pie from the tin, cutting into squares. Sift a little icing sugar on top. Serve with brown sugar and thick cream.

Mincemeat apples

Delicious when hot, but can be carried cold for a packed lunch.

4 large cooking apples
4 tablespoons golden syrup
4 tablespoons mincemeat
1 oz (25 g) butter

Core the apples and place each one on a piece of foil. Fill centres with syrup and mincemeat and top with a flake of butter. Wrap tightly in foil. Bake at 400°F/200°C/Gas Mark 6 for forty-five minutes.

Serves 4

Victoria plum sponge

1 lb (450 g) Victoria
   plums
3 oz (75 g) sugar
2 tablespoons water
1 oz (25 g) roasted
   hazelnuts
4 oz (100 g) self-raising
   flour
1 level teaspoon baking
   powder
4 oz (100 g) soft margarine
2 eggs

Topping:
2 oz (50 g) plain flour
1 level teaspoon mixed
   spice
1 oz (25 g) margarine or
   butter
2 oz (50 g) demerara
   sugar
1 oz (25 g) roasted
   hazelnuts
2 tablespoons plum jam

Serves 4

If no fresh plums are available, use frozen, canned or bottled fruit, adjusting liquid and sugar accordingly. Put plums, sugar, water and hazelnuts into a greased 2½ pint (1.5 l) oven-proof dish. Sift flour and baking powder together, and add margarine and eggs. Beat for two minutes and spoon over plums, spreading evenly. Bake at 375°F/190°C/Gas Mark 5 for thirty minutes until risen and golden.

To prepare topping, sift flour and spice together. Rub in margarine or butter and mix in sugar and nuts, which have been roughly chopped. Remove pudding from the oven and quickly spread top of sponge with warm jam. Sprinkle on topping evenly. Bake pudding for further fifteen minutes until topping is lightly browned. Serve hot with cream, custard or ice-cream.

Spiced apple and raisin pudding

8 oz (225 g) cooking
   apples
2 tablespoons water
12 oz (350 g) self-raising
   flour
1 level teaspoon cinnamon
½ level teaspoon mixed
   spice
3 oz (75 g) butter
1 oz (25 g) walnuts
3 oz (75 g) stoned raisins
4 oz (100 g) soft brown
   sugar
2 eggs
4 tablespoons milk

Serves 4

Lightly grease a 1½ pint (1 l) pudding mould or basin. Peel, core and slice apples and stew in water. Cool and sieve. Sieve flour, cinnamon and spice, rub in butter, and add chopped walnuts, raisins and sugar. Lightly beat eggs and fold into dry ingredients, together with apple purée. Blend well, adding enough milk to make a soft dropping consistency. Put into the mould and cover with greased greaseproof paper and foil. Steam for 2½ hours. Serve with a jam or honey sauce.

Apple cobbler

1 lb (450 g) cooking apples
6 oz (175 g) sugar
1 tablespoon plain flour
½ teaspoon cinnamon
Pinch of salt
1 tablespoon soft butter

Batter:
2 oz (50 g) plain flour
2 oz (50 g) sugar
½ teaspoon baking powder
Pinch of salt
2 tablespoons soft butter
1 egg

Serves 4

Peel and slice apples and mix in a bowl with sugar, flour, salt, cinnamon and 2 tablespoons water. Turn into a baking tin about 9 in (22.5 cm) square and dot with butter. Make batter by combining all ingredients and drop batter in nine portions on apples, spacing evenly (mixture will spread in cooking). Bake forty minutes at 375°F/190°C/Gas Mark 5 until crust is golden brown. Serve warm with cream.

Special apple charlotte

3 oz (75 g) fine fresh
   breadcrumbs
3 oz (75 g) finely grated
   Cheddar cheese
2 oz (50 g) seedless raisins
12 oz (350 g) cooking
   apples
Juice and rind of ½ lemon
½ oz (15 g) brown sugar

Serves 4

Mix cheese and breadcrumbs and line bottom and sides of a greased 1 pint (600 ml) piedish with three-quarters of the mixture, pressing it well down. Fill the piedish with layers of raisins, thinly sliced apples, sugar, lemon juice and rind, then sprinkle the remaining cheese and breadcrumbs on top, pressing down firmly. Cover with buttered paper and bake at 350°F/180°C/Gas Mark 4 for forty-five minutes. Serve hot or cold with cream.

Rum and apple flan

7 in (17.5 cm) baked flan
   case or sponge flan
1 oz (25 g) butter
1½ lb (700 g) peeled,
   cored and diced
   cooking apples
2 tablespoons apricot jam
4 oz (100 g) brown sugar
¼ pint (150 ml) double
   cream
1 tablespoon rum
Toasted almonds

Serves 4

Melt butter, and put in apples, jam and sugar. Cover and cook gently until apples are tender, stirring once. Cool and fill flan case. Beat cream until it starts to thicken, then add rum and continue beating until thick but not buttery. Spread evenly over apple filling, and spike all over with toasted split almonds. Serve very cold. The apples set so that the flan will slice into neat pieces.

Fruit batters

4 oz (100 g) self-raising
 flour
Pinch of salt
1 egg
½ pint (300 ml) milk

Serves 4

Make a batter of flour, salt, egg and milk. Heat ½ oz (15 g) cooking fat in a tin 12 × 8 in (30 × 20 cm), until hot, pour in batter and cook in centre of oven set at 425°F/220°C/Gas Mark 7 for thirty-five minutes. Add fruit according to directions:

Rhubarb batter: put 8 oz (225 g) cut rhubarb into fat in the tin, sprinkle with 4 oz (100 g) sugar and pour in batter.

Apricot and almond batter: soak 3 oz (75 g) cut-up dried apricots in ¼ pint (150 ml) boiling water for thirty minutes. Drain and put into fat with 1 oz (25 g) chopped almonds and 2 oz (50 g) sugar. Pour in batter.

Date and orange batter: put 2 oz (50 g) chopped dates and two thinly sliced oranges into fat in tin and spoon over three level tablespoons honey or golden syrup. Pour in batter.

Apple batter: put 1 lb (450 g) thinly sliced, peeled cooking apples into fat in tin, and pour over batter.

Sweet Puddings

There is nothing nicer than a good steamed pudding to finish a meal during the gloomy 'backend' days. You need not make it with suet. Breadcrumbs are a good basis for many steamed puddings – and make them lighter.

The pudding can be made in an ordinary basin, or can be steamed in a cake tin or jelly mould – particularly attractive if there is a good sauce to pour over it. Be sure the mould is well greased before filling, and that the water in the saucepan is boiling before the pudding goes in. Water should come about halfway up the basin and boil evenly and steadily. Fresh boiling water should be added from time to time.

Sauces play a useful part in improving plain suet and sponge puddings. I like to use melted thin honey with a little lemon juice over a light sponge pudding, and also add chopped walnuts to a traditional chocolate sauce. A hot butterscotch sauce is good, made from equal weights of butter, brown sugar and marshmallows with a little milk.

Autumn pudding

4 oz (100 g) butter
2 oz (50 g) Barbados sugar
2 eggs
2 tablespoons
   blackcurrant jam
4 oz (100 g) plain flour
1 teaspoon baking powder

Serves 4

Cream the butter and sugar and work in the eggs separately. Add the jam and mix in the flour sifted with the baking powder. Add a little milk if required. Mix lightly and put into a buttered mould. Cover and steam for 1½ hours. Serve with melted blackcurrant jam or custard.

Old-fashioned bread pudding

To eat as a cake, leave to cool in tin, sprinkle with icing sugar, and cut in squares. For a pudding, serve hot with real egg custard.

8 slices bread (toast
   thickness) from a large
   loaf
½ pint (300 ml) milk
12 oz (350 g) mixed dried
   fruit
2 oz (50 g) chopped peel
1 apple
3 tablespoons brown
   sugar
2 tablespoons marmalade
3 tablespoons self-raising
   flour

2 eggs
Squeeze of lemon juice
1 teaspoon ground
   cinnamon
4 oz (100 g) butter

Soak bread in milk for twenty minutes. Add fruit, chopped peel, grated peeled apple, sugar, marmalade, flour, eggs, lemon juice and cinnamon, and beat very well together. Melt butter and add half of it to the mixture. Put mixture into a greased meat tin and pour remaining butter on top. Bake for 1½ hours at 300°F/150°C/Gas Mark 2, then thirty minutes at 350°F/180°C/Gas Mark 4.

Bread and butter pudding

1 oz (25 g) butter
4 slices white bread
6 oz (175 g) raisins
2 oz (50 g) sugar
2 eggs
1 pint (600 ml) milk
1 tablespoon granulated
   sugar

Serves 4

Butter a pudding dish. Take the crusts off the bread, butter the slices and cut into 1 in (2.5 cm) wide fingers. Put half the bread, butter side up, in the bottom of the dish and cover with raisins and 2 oz (50 g) sugar. Top with the remainder of the bread. Beat the eggs with the milk and pour over the pudding. Leave to stand for fifteen minutes. Sprinkle with the tablespoon of sugar and bake at 300°F/150°C/Gas Mark 2 for 1½ hours.

Brown bread pudding

The Victorians loved using brown breadcrumbs for puddings and ices. Here is one version of a pudding which may be served hot or cold with jam, fruit syrup or custard.

6 oz (175 g) brown
  breadcrumbs
½ pint (300 ml) milk,
  heated
3 oz (75 g) butter
4 oz (100 g) sugar
3 eggs
2 oz (50 g) raisins (or
  chopped candied peel)
Grating of nutmeg
1 teaspoon cinnamon
Pinch of salt

Put breadcrumbs in a bowl and pour on hot milk. Add the spices, raisins, salt. Cream butter and sugar and add the eggs one at a time. Gradually work in the breadcrumb mixture. Put into a well-buttered mould, cover with foil or buttered paper and steam for two hours.

Serves 4

Upstairs pudding

12 oz (350 g) self-raising
  flour
6 oz (175 g) suet
Salt
12 oz (350 g) jam

Serves 4

Grease a pudding basin. Mix flour and suet and add enough water and a pinch of salt to produce a stiff paste. Divide paste into two pieces. Roll one out about 1½ times the size of the top of the basin, and line the basin with this. Halve remaining paste, and roll one piece to fit the top of the basin. Roll out the remaining piece and cut into four squares. Put in alternative layers of jam and pastry until the basin is full. Damp the top edge of the pudding and cover with the top circle. Cover and steam for three hours.

Alexandra pudding

This is good with a lightly flavoured lemon sauce.

6 oz (175 g) breadcrumbs
¾ pint (400 ml) milk
2 eggs
2 oz (50 g) sultanas
2 oz (50 g) currants
2 oz (50 g) candied peel
3 oz (75 g) sugar
Grated rind of 1 lemon

Put the crumbs into a mixture of milk beaten with eggs, and stir lightly so the liquid is absorbed. Stir in dried fruit, peel, sugar and lemon rind. Put into a greased basin, cover and steam for 1½ hours.

Serves 4

Steamed raisin batter

8 oz (225 g) plain flour
2 eggs
¾ pint (450 ml) milk
3 oz (75 g) raisins (use the large sticky ones and remove the stones)
3 oz (75 g) granulated sugar
1 teaspoon baking powder

Serves 4

Put the flour into a mixing bowl and gradually work in the eggs and milk to make a batter about the consistency of thick custard. Beat hard for ten minutes and leave the batter to stand for an hour. Grease the pudding basin and decorate the bottom and sides with raisins, saving some to go into the batter. Just before cooking add the sugar and remaining raisins to the batter and mix in the baking powder. Put into the basin, cover and steam for two hours. Good with melted golden syrup or custard.

Spice box pudding

9 oz (250 g) plain flour
¼ teaspoon ground mace
½ teaspoon ground cloves
1 teaspoon ground ginger
1 teaspoon ground cinnamon
6 oz (175 g) black treacle
6 oz (175 g) golden syrup
4 oz (100 g) butter
1 egg
¾ teaspoon bicarbonate of soda
A little milk

Sift the flour and spices. Put treacle, syrup and butter into a saucepan, and warm them enough to melt. Whisk up the egg, and gradually add syrup mixture. Turn into the flour and mix thoroughly, beating well. Stir the soda into a little milk and add to mixture. Fill a buttered mould two-thirds full, cover and steam for 1½ hours. Serve with custard.

Serves 4

Ginger fruit pudding

8 oz (225 g) self-raising flour
½ level teaspoon salt
2 rounded teaspoons ginger
4 oz (100 g) butter or margarine
3 oz (75 g) soft brown sugar
4 oz (100 g) mixed dried fruit
2 large eggs (beaten)
About 6 tablespoons milk to mix

Sift together dry ingredients, rub in fat, add sugar and fruit. Stirring briskly, mix to a soft dropping consistency with the beaten eggs and milk. Cover with greaseproof paper or aluminium foil, and steam steadily for 1½ hours. Turn out on a warm dish and serve with a sauce made by blending four tablespoons marmalade with two tablespoons water and heating gently until boiling.

Serves 4

Toffee pudding

8 oz (225 g) plain flour
4 oz (100 g) butter
4 oz (100 g) golden syrup
1 tablespoon coffee essence
4 oz (100 g) soft brown sugar
1 egg
¼ teaspoon bicarbonate of soda
A little milk
A few blanched almonds

Grease the basin and scatter it with a few almonds. Sieve the flour into a mixing bowl. Put the butter, syrup, coffee essence and sugar into a saucepan, and melt them without boiling. Cool a little and whisk in the egg. Pour the toffee mixture into the flour and beat well. Add soda mixed with a little milk, and put into the basin. Cover and steam for two hours. Serve with custard.

Serves 4

Chocolate fudge pudding

This recipe makes a spiced chocolate pudding with its own sauce in one dish.

2 oz (50 g) caster sugar
1 oz (25 g) cocoa
¼ teaspoon ground cinnamon
2 oz (50 g) fine semolina
1 teaspoon baking powder
1 oz (25 g) butter
½ teaspoon vanilla essence
2 eggs
1 tablespoon walnuts
½ pint (300 ml) hot water
3 oz (75 g) brown sugar
½ oz (15 g) extra cocoa

Sift sugar, cocoa, cinnamon, semolina and baking powder. Melt butter and blend with vanilla essence and beaten eggs, and stir into dry mixture. Add chopped walnuts, and put into well-greased 1½ pint (900 ml) piedish. Blend hot water, brown sugar, and extra cocoa, and pour gently in circular movement over top. Bake at 375°F/190°C/Gas Mark 5 for thirty minutes. Serve warm.

Serves 4

Syrup sponge

4 oz (100 g) butter or margarine
4 oz (100 g) sugar
4 level tablespoons golden syrup
2 standard eggs
6 tablespoons milk
8 oz (225 g) self-raising flour
Pinch of salt

Serves 4

Cream fat, sugar and two tablespoons syrup till light and fluffy. Beat in eggs, one at a time, then fold in sifted dry ingredients alternately with the milk, to make a fairly slack mixture. Well grease a 2 pint (1 l) pudding basin and pour in remaining syrup. Top with pudding mixture, spread evenly, then hollow out centre slightly. Cover with aluminium foil or with two sheets of greased greaseproof paper, and steam for two hours. Turn out on to a warm dish.

Chocolate raisin puddings

3 oz (75 g) seedless raisins
3 slices white bread
1 egg
½ oz (15 g) sugar
½ pint (300 ml) milk
½ oz (15 g) grated plain
  chocolate

Serves 4

Cover raisins with cold water and bring to the boil, then cover and leave to stand for five minutes before draining. Remove crusts from bread and cut into small cubes, then mix bread and raisins together and divide between four individual dishes. Make a custard by lightly beating egg and sugar together, warming milk to blood heat and pouring on to egg. Strain into a double saucepan, add chocolate, and stir until custard begins to thicken. Pour over bread and raisins, making sure bread is well soaked. Chill until set and decorate with a little cream and some raisins or walnuts.

Caramel pudding and coffee sauce

1½ oz (40 g) cube sugar
¼ pint (150 ml) milk
4 oz (100 g) butter or
  margarine
4 oz (100 g) caster sugar
2 eggs, separated
6 oz (175 g) plain flour
½ teaspoon baking powder

Serves 4

Dissolve sugar over gentle heat in one table-spoon water, and boil until it turns caramel colour, then add hot milk carefully to dissolve caramel, and leave to cool. Cream butter or margarine and caster sugar and add egg yolks. Stir in flour sifted with baking powder and the caramel milk alternately. Fold in stiffly whipped egg whites, put into a greased basin, cover and steam for two hours. Turn out and serve with custard made with half milk and half strong coffee.

Orange meringue

4 oranges
3 oz (75 g) caster sugar
1 pint (600 ml) milk
3 eggs
1 tablespoon cornflour
2 tablespoons icing sugar

Serves 4

Peel the oranges, remove pith and cut them into thin slices. Put into an ovenware dish and scatter the sugar on the fruit. In a double saucepan, or a bowl over a pan of hot water, bring the milk to the boil. Separate the eggs, and pour a little of the milk on to the yolks and mix well. Return to the remaining milk and add the cornflour mixed with a little water. Stir constantly until it thickens and then pour over the fruit. Whisk the egg whites to stiff peaks. Fold in the icing sugar and spread the mixture lightly over the top of the pudding. Bake at 325°F/170°C/Gas Mark 3 for fifteen minutes.

Orange roly poly

8 oz (225 g) self-raising
    flour
Pinch of salt
4 oz (100 g) shredded suet
2 large oranges
2 oz (50 g) fine white
    breadcrumbs
2 oz (50 g) brown sugar

Serves 4

Mix together the flour, salt and suet and mix to a firm paste with cold water. Roll out into a thin rectangle. Peel the oranges and remove the pith. Cut into slices and take out pips. Arrange the slices on the suet pastry and sprinkle with breadcrumbs and sugar. Roll up firmly and put into a floured cloth. Boil gently for three hours and serve with some hot marmalade.

Pies

If you prefer pies, make up pastry specially, or use the remains from a baking day to make an extra tart for teatime or the next day's main meal. Frozen pastry may of course be used. It is also useful to bake some extra flan cases and store them in the freezer so that a flan may be quickly assembled when needed.

If jam tarts are your standby, try that old favourite 'Thame Tart' which delighted thousands of Oxford undergraduates before the war. If you like to bake flan cases in advance, this is the ideal way to transform them into party food. Just spread a thick layer of raspberry jam in a baked flan case, top with a thick layer of lemon curd, and finish off with a thick layer of whipped cream.

Fruit and almond tart

This is particularly good with early rhubarb or cooked dried apricots.

8 oz (225 g) plain flour
Salt
1 teaspoon ground
    cinnamon
2 oz (50 g) caster sugar
4 oz (100 g) lard
1 egg yolk
2 tablespoons cold water
4 egg whites
6 oz (175 g) caster sugar
4 oz (100 g) ground
    almonds
1½ lb (700 g) cooked fruit
    (plums, gooseberries,
    rhubarb)

Sift flour with a pinch of salt, cinnamon and 2 oz (50 g) caster sugar, and rub in lard until mixture is like fine breadcrumbs. Beat egg yolk with water and use to make a stiff dough; leave in cold place for fifteen minutes. Whisk egg whites until stiff and fold in sugar and ground almonds. Roll out pastry and line a 9 in (22.5 cm) flan ring. Spread egg mixture in pastry case and arrange well-drained fruit over filling. Bake at 400°F/200°C/Gas Mark 4 for thirty-five minutes.

Serves 4

Syrup and sultana tart

5 oz (150 g) plain flour
Pinch of salt
1½ oz (40 g) butter
1 oz (25 g) lard

Filling:
8 oz (225 g) golden syrup
3 oz (75 g) butter
5 oz (150 g) fresh white
  breadcrumbs
1 egg
3 teaspoons lemon juice
3 oz (75 g) sultanas

Make pastry with flour, salt, butter, lard and cold water to mix, and line an 8 in (20 cm) flan ring or a deep pie plate. Put golden syrup into a pan with butter and melt them together. Remove from heat and stir in breadcrumbs and lemon juice, beaten egg and sultanas. Pour into pastry case. Bake at 375°F/190°C/Gas Mark 5 for thirty minutes.

Serves 4

Butterscotch pie

1 baked pie case
¾ pint (450 ml) water
8 oz (225 g) dark brown
  sugar
6 oz (175 g) butter
1 oz (25 g) cornflour
¾ pint (450 ml) milk
3 egg yolks

Serves 4

Put water into top of double saucepan, add sugar and butter, and heat, stirring all the time, until sugar and butter have melted. Mix cornflour with a little of the milk, then add to sugar mixture, together with milk and egg yolks. Cook, stirring constantly, until thickened. Cool slightly, then pour into baked pastry case and chill before serving. Serve with whipped cream.

  If liked, the remaining egg whites may be made into a meringue with six tablespoons caster sugar spooned on top of filling and baked at 350°F/180°C/Gas Mark 4 for twelve minutes.

Walnut raisin pie

Excellent topped with
ice-cream.

8 oz (225 g) shortcrust
  pastry
3 eggs, separated
8 oz (225 g) caster sugar
1 saltspoon salt
¼ teaspoon ground
  cinnamon
¼ teaspoon ground nutmeg
1 tablespoon lemon juice
2 oz (50 g) melted butter
3 oz (75 g) walnuts
3 oz (75 g) seedless raisins

Line a deep pie plate with pastry, reserving trimmings for decoration. Beat egg whites until stiff and lightly beat in yolks, then sugar, salt, spices, lemon juice, butter, broken walnuts and raisins. Prick pastry case with a fork and pour in mixture. Form trimmings of pastry into a lattice and bake at 375°F/190°C/Gas Mark 5 for thirty-five minutes. Serve hot or cold.

Serves 4

Raisin meringue pie

7 in (17.5 cm) shortcrust
    pastry flan case
2 oz (50 g) plain flour
½ pint (300 ml) water
8 oz (225 g) seedless
    raisins
4 oz (100 g) sugar
2 oz (50 g) butter
2 eggs, separated
Rind and juice of 1 lemon

Serves 4

Blend flour with small amount of the water. Cover raisins with rest of water and bring to boil, add sugar and simmer until raisins are soft. Add butter and stir until it has melted, then gradually add liquid to blended flour, return to pan and bring to boil, cooking for two minutes and stirring all the time. Remove from heat and beat in egg yolks, lemon rind and juice, and pour into lightly baked flan case. Whisk egg whites and fold in 2 oz (50 g) castor sugar for each white. Put on top of the raisin mixture, and bake at 300°F/150°C/Gas Mark 2 for thirty minutes.

Dundee orange tart

6 oz (175 g) shortcrust
    pastry
3 tablespoons black
    treacle
3 oz (75 g) butter or
    margarine
3 oz (75 g) caster sugar
2 teaspoons finely
    grated orange rind
1 egg
1 oz (25 g) ground
    almonds
4 oz (100 g) self-raising
    flour
2 tablespoons orange juice
1½ oz (40 g) blanched
    half almonds

Line a 7 in (17.5 cm) ovenproof pie plate with pastry, and spread with black treacle. Cream fat and sugar with orange rind until light and fluffy. Beat in eggs, stir in ground almonds, then fold in sifted flour alternately with the orange juice. Put mixture into the lined pie plate, spread evenly with a knife, then decorate with blanched almonds. Bake at 425°F/220°C/Gas Mark 7 for twenty minutes, then at 325°F/170°C/Gas Mark 3 for twenty minutes. Serve hot or cold.

Serves 4

Honey and date tart

1 baked flan case
8 oz (225 g) stoned dates
3 oz (75 g) hazelnuts
2 oz (50 g) butter
Grated rind and juice of
    1 lemon
1 tablespoon honey

Chop the dates. Chop the nuts coarsely and brown them in the oven. Cream the butter, and add the dates, lemon rind and juice, honey and nuts. Work together until light and creamy and fill the pastry case. Decorate with more chopped nuts and cream.

Serves 4

Party Puddings

The proof of the pudding is undoubtedly in its disappearance. However easy and healthy it may be to serve fresh fruit and cheese after a meal, I find I can't get away with it for long, before somebody asks for a nice sweet, sticky pudding – and men love them for parties.

Puddings don't have to be expensive because the ingredients are usually household basics anyway, and it's the combination of these ordinary materials with a touch of genius which make the perfect pud and encourages clean plates.

Toffee soufflés

1 oz (25 g) almonds
3 oz (75 g) butter
4 oz (100 g) Barbados
  sugar
1 tablespoon hot water
½ oz (15 g) plain flour
½ pint (300 ml) milk
1 egg, separated, and
  1 egg white
¼ oz (8 g) gelatine

Serves 6

Skin the almonds, chop them and bake gently until golden. Melt 2 oz (50 g) butter and add the sugar and hot water. Dissolve slowly and boil the syrup for three minutes, and then leave to cool. Melt the remaining butter in another saucepan, stir in the flour, and when it is well blended, stir in the milk and bring to the boil. Simmer for a few minutes until the sauce is thick. Stir in the beaten egg yolk, and heat gently, without letting the mixture boil, until the sauce is creamy. Take off the heat and gradually stir in the toffee mixture. Dissolve the gelatine in one tablespoon water and let it stand in a saucepan of hot water until the gelatine is syrup. Stir it into the toffee sauce and add half the almonds. When the mixture is beginning to set, fold in stiffly whisked egg whites. Put into six individual dishes and leave until cold. Sprinkle with the remaining nuts.

Chocolate almond pudding

Very rich and very luscious indeed.

4 oz (100 g) butter
4 oz (100 g) icing sugar
4 oz (100 g) plain
  chocolate, grated
4 oz (100 g) ground
  almonds
6 eggs, separated

Cream butter, icing sugar, grated chocolate and ground almonds until light and fluffy and beat in the egg yolks. Fold in the stiffly whipped egg whites, turn into a well-buttered pudding basin dusted with granulated sugar, cover and steam for one hour. Serve hot with whipped cream.

Serves 6

Liqueur soufflé

This is probably my family's favourite ending to a meal. The method is simple and the ingredients easily to hand except for the liqueur, although many people have some left over from Christmas or a duty-free trip. Make sure everybody is ready at the table for this one, as it should be served straight from the oven.

5 tablespoons butter
2 tablespoons plain flour
Pinch of salt
2 tablespoons sugar
4 fl oz (100 ml) milk
2 eggs, separated, and 1
  egg white
5 tablespoons Cointreau
  or Grand Marnier

Melt together the butter, flour and salt. Add the sugar and boiling milk and cook until smooth and thick (I often prepare the recipe this far earlier in the day, and finish it off just before the meal starts). Leave until cool. Add the egg yolks one at a time and beat well, and stir in the liqueur. Fold in stiffly beaten egg whites and put into a buttered 6 in (15 cm) soufflé dish. Bake at 350°F/180°C/Gas Mark 4 for twenty minutes and then at 400°F/200°C/Gas Mark 6 for ten minutes. Eat hot, with some extra liqueur and cream if you're really gluttonous, but it is delicious on its own.

Serves 4

Pavlova

This is an easy party piece, which is particularly good with strawberries, raspberries, peaches or apricots. The base can be made in advance and stored in an airtight tin.

4 egg whites
10 oz (275 g) caster sugar
1 teaspoon vinegar
1 teaspoon cornflour
Fresh, canned or frozen
  fruit
½ pint (300 ml) double
  cream

Serves 6

To make the base, beat the egg whites until stiff and gradually add the sugar, beating all the time. Add the vinegar and cornflour and continue beating until the mixture is stiff enough to stand in peaks. Put a piece of buttered paper on a flat baking tray and spoon on the mixture in a round about 8 in (20 cm) diameter, piling it up in the centre. Bake at 250°F/125°C/Gas Mark ½ for 1¼ hours. The meringue should be like a marshmallow in the centre, but if you like it crisp, turn it over and continue cooking until it is the way you like it. Put on to a flat serving dish and cover with whipped cream, and then with the fruit. Serve at once.

Chocolate rum cream

8 oz (225 g) plain
  chocolate
3 teaspoons instant coffee
  powder
2 tablespoons rum
¾ pint (450 ml) double
  cream
4 tablespoons honey

Melt chocolate over a pan of hot but not
boiling water, and add the coffee dissolved in
rum. Add cream beaten with honey, and blend
thoroughly. Pour into bowl to chill and serve
very cold with more cream.

Serves 6

Coffee gâteau

3 large eggs
3 oz (75 g) caster sugar
4 oz (100 g) self-raising
  flour
6 oz (175 g) butter
12 oz (350 g) icing sugar
3 tablespoons coffee
  essence
4 oz (100 g) chopped nuts

Serves 6

Whisk eggs and sugar till thick and creamy, and
fold in sifted flour. Bake in a swiss roll tin
lined with greased greaseproof paper at 400°F/
200°C/Gas Mark 6 for fifteen minutes. Take
out, remove paper and cool.

Cream butter well, gradually beat in sifted
icing sugar and coffee essence. Cut the cake in
three slices and sandwich together with two
layers of icing. Cover sides with icing, and lift
cake by top and bottom and roll on greaseproof paper covered with chopped nuts, so
that sides are coated. Cover top with icing and
sprinkle on remaining nuts.

Orange cools

This is a delicious pudding
which is pretty enough
for a party if the
meringue is decorated
after cooking with a slice
of angelica, a sprinkling
of flaked almonds, or
mint leaves.

4 large oranges
1 large pear
4 tablespoons clear honey
1 oz (25 g) desiccated
  coconut
1 egg, separated
2 oz (50 g) caster sugar

Slice tops off oranges, scoop out flesh and
chop. Put into basin with peeled and chopped
pear, honey, lightly toasted coconut and egg
yolk and mix thoroughly. Fill each orange with
the mixture. Whisk egg white until thick, add
half the sugar, and continue whisking until
stiff enough to form peaks. Stir in remaining
sugar and pile on top of oranges. Stand them
in shallow ovenproof dish and bake at 325°F/
170°C/Gas Mark 3 for thirty minutes, until
meringue has set and is golden brown. Serve
hot or cold.

Serves 4

Cherry dumplings

¾ pint (400 ml) water
12 oz (350 g) sugar
1 tablespoon rum
2 oz (50 g) butter
¼ pint (150 ml) sour cream
8 oz (225 g) plain flour
½ teaspoon salt
½ teaspoon baking powder
½ teaspoon bicarbonate of
soda
3 tablespoons softened
butter
3 tablespoons sugar
2 lb (1 kg) pitted black
cherries

Mix water and sugar, simmer for five minutes, and add rum. Pour into a cake tin measuring about 8 × 12 × 2 in (20 × 30 × 5 cm). Blend together butter and sour cream and work in flour, salt, baking powder and soda. Knead gently and roll about ¼ in (65 mm) thick in a rectangle 9 × 18 in (22.5 × 45 cm). Spread with softened butter and sugar and add cherries. Roll up like a swiss roll, cut in 1½ in (3.75 cm) slices and put in hot syrup in cake tin. Bake at 450°F/230°C/Gas Mark 8 for twenty minutes, basting with syrup. Serve with cream.

Serves 6

Cherry pudding

2 lb (1 kg) cherries
Sugar
3 tablespoons water
3 fl oz (75 ml) red wine
8 thin slices bread
Butter

Serves 6

Stone cherries and put in a fireproof dish. Sprinkle lavishly with sugar, pour over water and wine and cook at 350°F/180°C/Gas Mark 4 until cherries are soft (about thirty minutes). Cut crusts off bread and fry in butter until golden. Put bread on a serving dish, and pour over cherries and liquid. Leave to stand for a few minutes for the bread to absorb the syrup. Serve with pouring cream.

Rhubarb summer charlotte

1 lb (450 g) young
rhubarb
4 oz (100 g) sugar
2 oz (50 g) butter
6 oz (175 g) fresh white
breadcrumbs
2 oz (50 g) soft brown
sugar
¼ pint (150 ml) double
cream

Serves 4

Cut the rhubarb into short lengths and cook in two tablespoons water and the sugar until tender, then cool. Melt the butter, remove from the heat and stir in the breadcrumbs and brown sugar. Put a layer of the crumb mixture into a serving bowl. Add a layer of rhubarb and continue with alternate layers of crumbs and rhubarb. Top with a layer of softly whipped cream.

For additional flavour, add a little grated lemon or orange rind to the rhubarb, or a pinch of ginger. For a stronger flavour and colour, cook the rhubarb in 4 oz (100 g) raspberry jam instead of water and sugar.

Soft fruit shortcake

4 oz (100 g) butter
4 oz (100 g) caster sugar
2 eggs
Grated rind of 1 orange
4 oz (100 g) self-raising
flour
Pinch of salt
1 lb (450 g) strawberries,
raspberries or currants
½ pint (300 ml) double
cream

Serves 6

Cream the butter and sugar. Beat the eggs with the orange rind and add to the fat alternately with the flour sifted with the salt. Mix thoroughly and spread in two greased sandwich tins. Bake at 375°F/190°C/Gas Mark 5 for twenty-five minutes. Cool on a rack and sandwich together with lightly crushed fruit and whipped cream.

This shortcake may also be topped with cream and whole fruit for decoration; it can be made with drained canned fruit or frozen fruit.

Lemon flummery

¾ oz (20 g) butter
Grated rind and juice of
1 lemon
1 oz (25 g) plain flour
4 oz (100 g) caster sugar
1 egg, separated

Serves 4

Boil ½ pint (300 ml) water with butter and the grated rind of the lemon. Mix flour and sugar, make a well in the centre, and pour in the hot liquid, whisking to avoid lumps. Blend egg yolk with a little of the hot liquid, then return all the liquid to the pan. Bring slowly to the boil and cook gently for ten minutes. Whisk egg white until stiff, add the juice of the lemon to the saucepan, pour into a bowl and fold in the egg white. Cool and scatter top with crushed macaroons or digestive biscuits. Serve cold with cream.

Summer flummery

5 tablespoons white wine,
cider or lemon juice
6 level tablespoons fine
semolina
4 level tablespoons caster
sugar
2 egg whites

Serves 4

Put white wine, cider or lemon juice in a pan with ½ pint (300 ml) water. Heat gently and scatter semolina on warm but not boiling liquid. Bring just to the boil and reduce heat. Stir and cook for three minutes, then add castor sugar. Continue stirring for five minutes, cool, beat egg whites stiffly and fold in mixture. Pour into well-oiled 1 pint (600 ml) mould and chill to set firmly. Turn out and decorate with strawberries or raspberries. Serve with a sauce made from sieved and sweetened strawberries or raspberries.

Gooseberry tansy

1 lb (450 g) gooseberries
4 oz (100 g) butter
2 egg yolks
¼ pint (150 ml) double
  cream
4 oz (100 g) sugar
1 lemon

Simmer gooseberries in butter until cooked and add the beaten egg yolks and slightly whipped cream. Add sugar and heat gently until dissolved. Turn into dish and sprinkle with juice of a lemon and more sugar, and serve hot or cold.

Serves 4

Blackberry fool

All fools look and taste nicer if served in small dishes, with little crisp sweet biscuits.

1 lb (450 g) blackberries
Caster sugar
1 pint (600 ml) double
  cream

Stew blackberries in just enough water to cover them, and sweeten to taste. Put through a fine sieve and mix with cream.

Serves 6

Pineapple fritters

2 oz (50 g) plain flour
Pinch of salt
2 teaspoons caster sugar
1 egg, separated
½ oz (15 g) cool melted
  butter
¼ pint (150 ml) milk
16 oz (450 g) can
  pineapple rings

Serves 6

Sieve flour and salt and add sugar. Beat egg yolk with melted butter and milk. Make a well in centre of flour and pour in egg mixture, beat until smooth, cover and leave in a cool place for an hour. Whisk egg white until stiff and fold into batter. Heat deep fat or oil, dip drained pineapple rings in batter, and fry in hot fat until golden brown. Drain on crumpled kitchen paper, toss in caster sugar and serve hot.

Strawberry cake

5 eggs, separated
6 oz (175 g) caster sugar
1½ lb (700 g) strawberries
3 oz (75 g) fine white
  breadcrumbs
1 teaspoon vanilla essence

Serves 4

Beat egg yolks and sugar until light and fluffy, and stir in crushed strawberries. Fold in breadcrumbs and vanilla and mix thoroughly. Finally fold in egg whites beaten until stiff but not dry. Butter an oven dish and sprinkle with sugar. Pour in mixture and bake at 375°F/190°C/Gas Mark 5 for thirty-five minutes. Serve cold with whipped cream (a few sliced strawberries may be folded into the whipped cream).

Strawberry parfait

Raspberries may also be used for this recipe. If a fancy mould is not available, a cake tin may be used.

8 oz (225 g) sugar
¼ pint (150 ml) water
4 egg yolks
2 lb (1 kg) strawberries
1 pint (600 ml) double
  cream

Cook together sugar and water for five minutes until syrupy. Beat egg yolks in top of double boiler and pour on syrup slowly, stirring all the time. Cook until thick, then remove from heat and stir until cold. Add crushed strawberries and fold in whipped cream. Pour into mould and freeze at normal ice-making temperature for three to five hours. Dip mould in hot water and unmould on cold dish. Serve garnished with fresh fruit and with small sweet biscuits.

Serves 6

Orange compôte

This is just the pudding to finish a heavy meal and refresh the palate.

6 large oranges
¼ pint (150 ml) water
4 oz (100 g) sugar
8 oz (225 g) redcurrant
  jelly

Serves 6

Using large juicy oranges and a sharp knife, skin the oranges thinly and cut the peel in very fine strips. Cook the peel for thirty minutes, changing the water three times to take away bitterness. Remove all white pith from the oranges, and cut them in crosswise slices. (If you have the patience they can be divided into segments instead, and each segment skinned.) Boil the water, sugar and jelly, for ten minutes, then add the cooked peel and boil for fifteen minutes. Pour over oranges and chill.

Orange puff

3 tablespoons butter
1 oz (25 g) plain flour
7 fl oz (200 ml) milk
4 eggs
8 tablespoons sugar
1 tablespoon orange juice
1 teaspoon grated orange
  rind

Serves 4

Melt butter and stir in flour, then gradually blend in milk. Bring to boiling point, stirring well, and remove from heat. Separate eggs and beat whites stiff then fold in half the sugar, and set aside. Beat yolks until thick with remaining sugar and orange juice. Add yolk mixture to hot milk mixture, and fold in whites. Steam for thirty-five minutes. Serve with hard sauce flavoured with orange juice and grated orange rind, or with a little melted marmalade laced with orange liqueur.

Cakes
and
Biscuits

Time for Tea

Everyone is so busy these days that tea often gets missed out and a hot meal later saves time, but what's more comforting than a cup of tea and a little something to ruin our figure?

Anyone for toast?

Then try making that old favourite, *Anchovy toast*, spreading the toast with a mixture of two raw egg yolks, 2 oz (50 g) melted butter, two teaspoons anchovy essence and plenty of pepper. Or why not *Cinnamon toast*, using bread browned on one side only, then spreading the untoasted side thickly with butter and sprinkling with a mixture of sugar and cinnamon, toasting until the butter has melted. *Dripping toast*, of course, but the best results are made by keeping the different-flavoured drippings separately in bowls, and spreading the dripping thickly with a mixture of fat and richly flavoured deposit from the bottom of the bowl, seasoning well with salt and pepper and serving very hot. Hungry children? Give them toast spread with peanut butter and sprinkled with crisply grilled bacon. A sweet-tooth in the family? Try spreading the untoasted side of the bread with a mixture of 2 oz (50 g) butter, 2 oz (50 g) sugar, the grated rind of two oranges, and two tablespoons orange juice, then toasting until the mixture bubbles.

Anyone for sandwiches?

Try toasted sandwiches, making the sandwiches a little thicker than normal, using generous filling but not butter, then brushing the outside with melted butter and toasting on both sides? Or what about fried sandwiches (a useful way of using up leftovers), dipping sandwiches in a mixture of an egg beaten with a breakfastcup of milk, frying them in deep fat or in butter. For a hungry family who may miss the evening meal, make club sandwiches which are triple deckers made with toast or bread, using meat or poultry as one filling, and a salad with mayonnaise for the other filling. For just plain sandwiches, try some new fillings such as chopped ham, lettuce and horseradish sauce; or shrimps, hard-boiled egg and onion; or cheese with shredded raw cabbage, sliced apple and mayonnaise; or crisp bacon with liver sausage and tomato.

Easy breads and biscuits are other teatime favourites.

California raisin bread

This is an old favourite, delicious as a tea bread spread thickly with butter, and also very good for those who like a sweet bread at breakfast time.

6 oz (175 g) seedless
  raisins
8 oz (225 g) plain flour
2 teaspoons baking
  powder
¾ teaspoon bicarbonate of
  soda
1 teaspoon salt
3 oz (75 g) rolled oats
2 oz (50 g) butter
2 oz (50 g) sugar
1 egg
½ pint (300 ml) sour milk

Plump raisins by covering with cold water, bring to boiling and leave to stand for five minutes before draining. Sieve dry ingredients and add rolled oats and raisins. Cream butter and sugar until light and fluffy and beat in egg gradually. Add dry ingredients alternately with the milk to make a soft dough. Put in a greased and floured loaf tin and bake at 350°F/180°C/ Gas Mark 4 for one hour.

Potato wholemeal bread

Potatoes give a good flavour and texture to bread, and help to keep it fresh and moist.

8 oz (225 g) freshly boiled
  and sieved potatoes
½ pint (300 ml) hot potato
  water
½ tablespoon sugar
1 oz (25 g) butter
½ oz (15 g) yeast
1½ lb (750 g) 100%
  wholemeal flour
3 teaspoons salt

Mix the potatoes, hot water, sugar and butter in a bowl, stirring until well blended. Allow to cool to lukewarm. Crumble in the yeast, mix and leave in a warm place for ten minutes. Add the flour and salt gradually to make a soft dough that does not stick to the bowl or hands. Knead until smooth and elastic. Put in a large bowl, cover with a clean cloth and put in a warm place to rise until double its size. Knead again and shape into two loaves. Place in greased tins, cover and leave to rise until double the bulk. Bake at 450°F/230°C/Gas Mark 8 for fifteen minutes, reduce heat to 375°F/170°C/Gas Mark 5 and bake for 30–45 minutes until the bread gives a hollow sound when tapped on the bottom.

Baking-powder bread

1 lb (450 g) plain flour
2 oz (50 g) lard
2 teaspoons baking
  powder
1 teaspoon salt
½ pint (300 ml) milk

Rub the lard into the flour. Add the baking powder and salt, and mix well. Add enough milk to make a light dough. Shape into one large round and put on a greased baking sheet. Bake at 400°F/200°C/Gas Mark 6 for thirty minutes.

Soda bread

8 oz (225 g) wholemeal
   flour
8 oz (225 g) plain white
   flour
2 teaspoons sugar
1 teaspoon bicarbonate of
   soda
1 teaspoon salt
2 teaspoons dripping
Milk

Mix together flours, and add sugar, soda and salt. Rub in dripping and mix to a batter with milk, to make a dough which is stiff, but will roll easily. Roll out in a round 1 in (2.5 cm) thick, and cut into four sections. Cook on a hot griddle ten minutes each side.

Potato scones

1 lb (450 g) freshly
   boiled potatoes
4 oz (100 g) plain flour
Pinch of salt
1 oz (25 g) butter

Mash the potatoes well, add flour and salt and softened butter, and mix well. Roll out thinly on a floured board. Cut in rounds or triangles, and prick with a fork. Cook quickly on a lightly greased heavy frying pan or griddle, about three minutes each side. Serve hot with lots of butter. Left-overs can be fried in bacon fat for breakfast.

Ginger shortbread

8 oz (225 g) butter or
margarine
9 oz (250 g) light brown
   sugar
1 lb (450 g) plain flour
4 teaspoons ground ginger
3 oz (75 g) chopped mixed
   peel

Cream the fat and sugar and mix in the flour, ginger and peel. Press into a large greased swiss roll tin. Bake at 300°F/150°C/Gas Mark 2 for thirty minutes. Mark into squares and cut into pieces when cold. Leave in the tin until completely cold and crisp.

Mocha cookies

8 oz (225 g) butter
4 oz (100 g) caster sugar
8 oz (225 g) self-raising
   flour
2 oz (50 g) cocoa

Filling:
2 oz (50 g) cocoa
¼ pint (150 ml) strong
   coffee
2 oz (50 g) butter
Sugar to taste

Cream butter and sugar, and work in flour and cocoa to make a stiff mixture. With the hands, form balls the size of a walnut, put out on buttered tins and flatten with a fork dipped in water. Bake at 350°F/180°C/Gas Mark 4 for twelve minutes. Lift carefully on to rack, and when cool sandwich together with filling. Make this by cooking cocoa in coffee until the mixture is a thick cream. Beat in butter off the fire, add sugar to taste. Leave till cold before using.

Nutty flapjacks

12 oz (350 g) margarine
6 oz (175 g) granulated
  sugar
12 oz (350 g) golden syrup
1 lb (450 g) porridge oats
Pinch of salt
4 oz (100 g) chopped
  peanuts

Melt the margarine over low heat and stir in the sugar and syrup until the sugar has dissolved. Remove from heat and stir in the oats, salt and nuts. Press into a large greased swiss roll tin. Bake at 325°F/170°C/Gas Mark 3 for thirty minutes. Leave in the tin and mark into pieces while hot. Cut into pieces and remove from the tin when cold.

Chocolate walnut cookies

6 oz (175 g) self-raising
  flour
Pinch of salt
3 oz (75 g) butter
3 oz (75 g) soft brown
  sugar
3 oz (75 g) granulated
  sugar
½ teaspoon vanilla essence
½ teaspoon water
1 egg
2 oz (50 g) chopped
  walnuts
4 oz (100 g) chocolate
  chips

Sift flour and salt together. Combine butter, sugars, vanilla essence and water, and blend well. Beat in the egg, and stir in the flour and salt. Add chopped nuts and chocolate chips. Drop by teaspoonfuls on to greased baking sheets. Bake at 350°F/180°C/Gas Mark 4 for ten minutes.

Coconut crisps

These are crisp and sweet biscuits which store very well.

4 oz (100 g) butter
3 oz (75 g) soft brown
  sugar
4 oz (100 g) granulated
  sugar
1 egg
1 teaspoon vanilla
  essence
5 oz (150 g) plain flour
½ teaspoon baking powder
½ teaspoon bicarbonate of
  soda
½ teaspoon salt
4 oz (100 g) desiccated
  coconut
1 oz (25 g) cornflakes

Cream butter, add brown and granulated sugar, egg and vanilla essence, and cream the mixture until light and fluffy. Sift together flour, baking powder, soda and salt and stir into the creamed mixture. Stir in coconut and cornflakes. Chill slightly, then shape into small balls, about 1 in (2.5 cm) diameter. Put about 2½ in (6.25 cm) apart on an ungreased baking sheet, and flatten with a damp fork. Bake at 350°F/180°C/Gas Mark 4 for ten minutes. Cool slightly before removing from baking sheet.

Toffee bars

4 oz (100 g) butter
3 oz (75 g) brown sugar
1 egg yolk
2 oz (50 g) plain flour
2 oz (50 g) porridge oats

Topping:
3 oz (75 g) plain chocolate
1 tablespoon butter
Walnuts

Beat together butter, sugar and egg yolk until smooth. Add flour and oats and stir well until smooth. Press mixture in a rectangular tin and bake at 375°F/190°C/Gas Mark 5 for fifteen minutes. Cool slightly. Melt chocolate and butter over hot water, spread over warm biscuit mixture, and decorate with whole or chopped walnuts. Cut into bars while warm, but leave to cool completely in tin before removing.

Butterscotch brownies

6 oz (175 g) brown sugar
3 oz (75 g) melted butter
1 egg
5 oz (150 g) self-raising flour
½ teaspoon salt
½ teaspoon vanilla essence
2 oz (50 g) shelled walnuts

Mix together sugar and melted butter. Stir in egg, flour, salt and vanilla essence and add roughly chopped walnuts. Spread in a greased swiss roll tin and bake for twenty minutes at 350°F/180°C/Gas Mark 4. Cool in the pan and cut in 2 in (5 cm) squares.

Cut-and-Come-Again Cakes

Cut-and-come-again cakes! What a lovely old-fashioned phrase. Unfortunately there's too much truth in it, because most families come again not once, but two or three times when home-made cake is on the table. As a tight-pursed acquaintance of mine once remarked: 'The trouble with home-made cakes is that they get eaten.' Still, even though psychologists tell us we bake cakes to compensate for other failings in family life, at least we can all enjoy this weakness while cheerfully ruining our figures.

One of the disadvantages of cakes which are made for cutting-and-coming is that any icing gets rather messy. But sweet-tooth toppings can be easily spread on rich butter or sultana cakes before baking, and don't make too much mess in storage tins. Try 2 oz (50 g) butter creamed with 3 oz (75 g) brown sugar and 3 oz (75 g) desiccated coconut; or 1 oz (75 g) each of butter and brown sugar; or 1½ oz (40 g) plain flour, and ½ teaspoon cinnamon sprinkled through a sieve over the cake mixture; or try a mixture of one tablespoon each of coconut, chopped walnuts and glacé cherries pressed lightly on to the surface of the cake mixture.

Dundee cake

An old favourite, but this is a special recipe which gives marvellous results.

8 oz (225 g) butter
8 oz (225 g) sugar
5 eggs
8 oz (225 g) self-raising flour
½ teaspoon ground nutmeg
12 oz (350 g) mixed currants and sultanas
3 oz (75 g) ground almonds
3 oz (75 g) chopped glacé cherries
2 oz (50 g) chopped candied peel
2 oz (50 g) split blanched almonds

Cream butter and sugar and add eggs one at a time, each with a sprinkling of flour to avoid curdling. Beat well after each addition. Stir in most of the flour and lastly the fruit lightly coated with the rest of the flour. Turn into a 9 in (22.5 cm) cake tin lined with greased paper, smooth the top and arrange almonds on surface. Bake at 325°F/170°C/Gas Mark 3 for 2–2½ hours.

Lemon Scotch cake

4 oz (100 g) butter
4 oz (100 g) caster sugar
2 tablespoons lemon curd
2 eggs
6 oz (175 g) seedless raisins
6 tablespoons whisky
6 oz (175 g) self-raising flour

Grease a 7 in (17.5 cm) square cake tin and line the bottom with greaseproof paper. Cream butter, sugar and lemon curd until light and fluffy. Separate eggs and beat yolks into creamed mixture one at a time with a little flour. Add raisins and whisky with a little more flour. Whisk egg whites until stiff and fold into mixture, then fold in remaining flour. Put mixture into tin and bake at 350°F/180°C/Gas Mark 4 for 1¼ hours. Turn out and cool on a wire rack.

Marmalade cake

The marmalade gives a nice tangy flavour to a plain cake.

4 oz (100 g) butter
4 oz (100 g) sugar
2 eggs
2 rounded tablespoons marmalade
8 oz (225 g) self-raising flour
4 tablespoons milk

Cream butter and sugar and beat in eggs. Mix in marmalade, then add flour and enough milk to give a soft dropping consistency. Put in a greased 7 in (17.5 cm) cake tin and bake at 350°F/180°C/Gas Mark 4 for an hour. For immediate use, this is good topped with whipped cream or orange butter icing, decorated with strips of candied peel.

Honey walnut cake

8 oz (225 g) plain flour
3 teaspoons baking
  powder
Pinch of salt
4 oz (100 g) butter
4 oz (100 g) caster sugar
4 oz (100 g) sliced stoned
  dates
1 oz (25 g) chopped
  walnuts
2 lightly beaten eggs
4 tablespoons milk
2 tablespoons clear honey

Sieve flour, baking powder and salt into a bowl and rub in the butter. Add sugar, dates and walnuts and mix to a soft consistency with the eggs, milk and honey. Pour into a greased 7 in (17.5 cm) square tin and bake at 350°F/180°C/Gas Mark 4 for 1¼ hours.

Sultana orange cake

This is a good lunch cake with a delicate orange flavour.

8 oz (225 g) self-raising
  flour
Pinch of salt
4 oz (100 g) margarine
4 oz (100 g) caster sugar
2 large eggs
7 oz (200 g) sultanas
Grated rind of 1 small
  orange
1 tablespoon strained
  orange juice

Sift flour and salt. Cream margarine and sugar until light and fluffy, then add eggs one by one, beating well. Fold in half the flour, then the sultanas and grated rind. Fold in the rest of the flour, and add enough orange juice to give a stiff dropping consistency. Turn into a 6 in (15 cm) cake tin lined with greased paper and bake at 350°F/180°C/Gas Mark 4 for one hour.

Raisin parkin

12 oz (350 g) medium
  oatmeal
6 oz (175 g) plain flour
1 oz (25 g) sugar
1 teaspoon ground ginger
¼ teaspoon salt
4 oz (100 g) seedless raisins
4 oz (100 g) margarine
1 lb (450 g) black treacle
2½ fl oz (65 ml) milk
1 teaspoon bicarbonate of
  soda

Grease a Yorkshire pudding tin about 8 × 10 in (20 × 25 cm) and line bottom with greaseproof paper. Put oatmeal, flour, sugar, ginger, salt and raisins into a bowl and mix well together. Warm treacle and margarine together, but do not allow to get too hot. Warm milk to blood heat, add soda and mix into dry ingredients with treacle. Pour into tin and bake at 350°F/180°C/Gas Mark 4 for forty-five minutes until firm to the touch. Cool a little before turning out, and keep in a tin for a few days before eating.

Boiled fruit cake

This is a moist, fruity cake which keeps well and is excellent for packed meals.

5 oz (150 g) butter
6 tablespoons golden
 syrup
¼ pint (150 ml) milk
4 oz (100 g) chopped dates
8 oz (225 g) currants
4 oz (100 g) sultanas
8 oz (225 g) stoned or
 seedless raisins
4 oz (100 g) chopped
 mixed peel
8 oz (225 g) self-raising
 flour
1 teaspoon mixed spice
1 teaspoon nutmeg
Pinch of salt
2 eggs
½ teaspoon bicarbonate
 of soda

Put butter, syrup, milk, fruit and peel into a saucepan and heat gently until the butter has melted. Simmer gently for five minutes, stirring once or twice. Remove from heat and cool. (Do this in the evening, so that the fruit is cool and ready to use early on a baking morning.) Sieve the flour, spices and salt together, make a well in the centre, add eggs, but do not stir. Add soda to the fruit mixture and add to the dry ingredients, mixing thoroughly and beating well. Pour into a greased and lined 10 in. (25 cm) round tin and bake at 325°F/160°C/ Gas Mark 3 for 1¾ hours.

Fruit spice cake

1½ lb (750 g) seedless
 raisins
4 oz (100 g) mixed
 chopped candied peel
4 oz (100 g) walnuts
10 oz (300 g) plain flour
1 teaspoon bicarbonate
 of soda
¾ teaspoon ground
 cinnamon
¾ teaspoon ground
 nutmeg
¼ teaspoon ground cloves
¼ teaspoon ground ginger
8 oz (225 g) butter
7 oz (200 g) caster sugar
4 eggs
6 tablespoons golden
 syrup or black treacle
6 tablespoons cold black
 coffee

Mix the dried fruit, peel and nuts together. Sieve flour, soda and spices together. Cream the butter and sugar together until light and fluffy. Add the eggs, syrup or treacle and coffee and beat well. The batter may curdle slightly, but it does not matter. Stir in the nuts and fruit, and add the flour and spices. Mix thoroughly and put into a greased round 9 in (22.5 cm) tin lined with paper. Smooth the top with a knife. Bake at 300°F/150°C/Gas Mark 2 for 2½ hours. Leave in the tin to cool before turning out. Store in the paper lining, in a tin, and remove paper when ready to eat.

Caraway seed cake

6 oz (175 g) butter
6 oz (175 g) sugar
3 eggs
8 oz (225 g) plain flour
¼ teaspoon baking powder
½ oz (15 g) caraway seeds

Cream butter and sugar until very soft, and gradually add beaten eggs. Gradually add flour and baking powder, and then the caraway seeds. Turn into a greased 7 in (17.5 cm) cake tin and bake at 350°F/180°C/Gas Mark 4 for 1¼–1½ hours.

Shilling cake

8 oz (225 g) plain flour
¼ teaspoon bicarbonate
  of soda
Grated rind of ½ lemon
4 oz (100 g) butter
6 oz (175 g) seedless raisins
4 oz (100 g) sugar
1 egg
Milk

Sieve the flour and bicarbonate of soda. Stir in the lemon rind, and rub in the butter. Add the raisins and sugar. Beat the egg lightly and beat into the mixture with enough milk to make a soft dropping consistency. Put into a greased 6 in/15 cm cake tin and bake at 325°F/170°C/Gas Mark 3 for 1¼ hours.

Date and seed cake

12 oz (350 g) self-raising
  flour
6 oz (175 g) caster sugar
5 oz (150 g) dripping
4 oz (100 g) stoned dates
1 teaspoon vinegar
1 egg, beaten
1 teaspoon caraway
  seeds
Milk

Beat the sugar and dripping to a creamy consistency. Gradually add the flour, chopped dates and caraway seeds to the creamed mixture, alternately with the beaten egg. Add a little milk to make a soft dropping consistency, and then the vinegar. Beat well and put into a greased 7 in (17.5 cm) round cake tin. Bake at 325°F/170°C/Gas Mark 3 for 1¼ hours.

Prune cake

5 oz (150 g) butter
5 oz (150 g) caster sugar
Grated rind of 1 lemon
2 eggs
6 oz (175 g) prunes, stoned
8 oz (225 g) plain flour
1 teaspoon baking powder
Milk

Cream the butter and sugar until light and soft. Add the lemon rind and beat in the eggs. Chop the prunes finely and add to the mixture with sieved flour and baking powder. Add a little milk if needed to give a soft consistency. Put into a greased and lined 7 in (17.5 cm) round cake tin and bake at 325°F/170°C/Gas Mark 3 for 1½ hours.

The Gingerbread Men

Ginger must be one of our favourite British spices. For centuries, we've used it lavishly in cakes, biscuits and puddings, drinks and preserves, and in such childish delights as gingerbread men and Hansel-and-Gretel houses.

Gingerbread can take many different forms. Some of us prefer light spongecakes, others like rich heavy sticky ones, and still others prefer the chewy biscuits which are so good for lunchboxes. Gingerbread need not be used only as a cake; a wedge with a chunk of cheese is a traditional northern snack. Gingerbread with whipped cream flavoured with a grating of orange peel is a delicious pudding; so is gingerbread with smooth apple sauce, or baked over fresh or tinned fruit. Most gingerbreads incorporate golden syrup or black treacle, but care must be taken in baking since these mixtures tend to 'catch' quickly if the oven is hot. The flavour of gingerbread is improved by a little powdered cloves, nutmeg and cinnamon added to the ginger in the recipe.

Coventry gingerbread

6 oz (175 g) wholemeal
    flour
3 oz (75 g) caster sugar
1 teaspoon ground
    ginger
4 oz (100 g) butter
2 oz (50 g) crystallized
    ginger

Shift together flour, sugar and ginger. Rub in butter lightly, then add chopped crystallized ginger. Press the mixture very lightly into a 7 in (17.5 cm) sponge tin and bake at 325°F/170°C/ Gas Mark 4 for thirty minutes. Remove from tin to cool and break into pieces to serve.

Gingerbread men

This same mixture may be used for a variety of biscuit shapes, such as animals or stars, which can be decorated with icing, silver balls, cherries.

6 oz (175 g) plain flour
¼ teaspoon salt
1 tablespoon ground
    ginger
1 teaspoon ground mixed
    spice
2 oz (50 g) butter

Sift together flour, salt and spices. Cream butter and sugar, and mix in flour and enough syrup to form a stiff dough. Roll out to ½ in (1.25 cm) thickness and cut out men with a biscuit cutter (or a cardboard template). Put on greased baking sheet and bake at 375°F/190°C/ Gas Mark 5 for fifteen minutes. Remove and cool, and use small pieces of cherry for buttons and eyes.

4 oz (100 g) demerara
    sugar
4 tablespoons warm
    golden syrup
Glacé cherries

Ginger and walnut teabread

8 oz (225 g) self-raising
  flour
¼ level teaspoon salt
2 teaspoons ground ginger
1 teaspoon baking powder
2 oz (50 g) butter
2 oz (50 g) sugar
3 oz (75 g) chopped
  walnuts
1 oz (25 g) chopped
  crystallized ginger
1 beaten egg
¼ pint (150 ml) milk
1 teaspoon demerara
  sugar

Sift together flour, salt, ginger and baking powder. Rub in butter until mixture resembles fine breadcrumbs. Stir in sugar, walnuts and crystallized ginger. Mix most of the beaten egg with the milk and add to flour and butter. Beat thoroughly (this is a very sticky dough), and put into greased 1 lb (450 g) loaf tin. Brush top with remaining beaten egg and sprinkle with demerara sugar. Bake at 350°F/180°C/Gas Mark 4 for 1 hour 5 minutes, until golden brown. Turn out on wire rack; the loaf will sound hollow when tapped underneath. Serve sliced and spread with butter.

Gingerbread meringue house

This is an excellent cake for those who have neither time nor skill to fiddle with cutting out pieces to make the traditional 'house' for a children's party. A serving board can be decorated with more meringue or royal icing 'snow' and finished with pine trees, snowmen, coloured sweets or whatever is appropriate.

12 oz (350 g) plain flour
1 teaspoon bicarbonate
  of soda
2 teaspoons ground
  ginger
2 oz (50 g) sultanas
3 oz (75 g) butter
3 oz (75 g) golden syrup
3 oz (75 g) black treacle
4 oz (100 g) soft brown
  sugar
1 egg and 3 egg yolks
2 teaspoons milk

Sift flour, soda and ginger, mix in sultanas. Melt butter, add syrup, treacle and brown sugar and heat gently until sugar dissolves. Add flour mixtures and beaten eggs, and beat thoroughly, adding milk to give a dropping consistency. Put into greased 2 lb (1 kg) loaf tin and bake at 350°F/190°C/Gas Mark 4 for five minutes. Leave to cool slightly.

Meanwhile reduce temperature to 325°F/170°C/Gas Mark 3. Whisk egg whites until stiff and dry and whisk in the sugar gradually, until the meringue becomes thick and shiny. Put some of the meringue into a piping bag fitted with a fine plain writing nozzle and pipe the outline of doors and windows on the sides of the cake. Using a palette knife and the remaining meringue, shape the roof and chimney-pot of the house. Bake at 325°F/170°C/Gas Mark 3 for fifteen minutes when the meringue will be crisp and dry.

Meringue:
3 egg whites
3 oz (75 g) caster sugar

Cornish gingerbreads

1½ lb (750 g) plain flour
8 oz (225 g) soft brown
   sugar
2 oz (50 g) ground ginger
2 oz (50 g) mixed candied
   peel
Pinch of ground mixed
   spice
8 oz (225 g) butter
1 lb (450 g) black treacle
1 oz (25 g) bicarbonate of
   soda
2 tablespoons milk

Stir together flour, sugar, ginger, peel and spice, and stir in butter melted with the treacle. Dissolve soda in the milk and stir into the mixture. Blend thoroughly together. Form long sausage shapes with the hand, cut into small pieces, and roll each piece in the hands into walnut-sized balls. Put on greased baking sheets, allowing room to spread, and bake at 400°F/200°C/Gas Mark 6 for ten minutes. Cool on a wire rack and store in an airtight tin.

Sticky gingerbread

8 oz (225 g) butter
8 oz (225 g) soft brown
   sugar
8 oz (225 g) black treacle
1 lb (450 g) plain flour
1 teaspoon bicarbonate of
   soda
1 large teaspoon ground
   ginger
12 oz (350 g) medium
   oatmeal
3 large eggs

Melt butter, sugar and treacle slowly. Sift together flour, soda and ginger, and mix in oatmeal. Stir in treacle mixture, then add well-beaten eggs. Bake at 350°F/180°C/Gas Mark 4 for forty-five minutes.

Fruit gingerbread

This makes a ginger fruit cake which is delicious and filling, and keeps very well. It is an excellent picnic cake.

1 lb (450 g) plain flour
2 teaspoons bicarbonate
   of soda
8 oz (225 g) mixed fats
4 oz (100 g) caster sugar
4 oz (100 g) sultanas
4 oz (100 g) currants
3 oz (75 g) mixed peel
3 oz (75 g) ground
   almonds
2 teaspoons ground
   mixed spice

4 teaspoons ground
   ginger
2 teaspoons ground
   cinnamon
1 teaspoon ground cloves
8 oz (225 g) golden syrup
2 eggs
½ pint (300 ml) beer or ale

Mix the fruit together. Sieve flour and spices. Cream fats and sugar and add melted syrup which has cooled but not stiffened, then the eggs one at a time. Work in flour, almonds and fruit. Dissolve soda in beer and stir into mixture. Put into prepared 8 in (20 cm) tin. Bake in the centre of the oven set at 300°F/150°C/Gas Mark 2 for 2½ hours.

Harvest Cider Cakes

Harvest has been a traditional time for cakes which fed the workers and celebrated the gathering of the corn. Cider in the recipe adds a special flavour.

Cider crumble cake

1 lb 2 oz (500 g)
  self-raising flour
Pinch of salt
4 oz (100 g) soft brown
  sugar
2 oz (50 g) chopped dates
3 tablespoons black
  treacle
½ pint (300 ml) dry cider
2 beaten eggs

Topping:
1½ oz (40 g) butter
1½ oz (40 g) plain flour
1½ oz (40 g) chopped
  walnuts
½ level teaspoon
  cinnamon
3 tablespoons plum jam

Sieve flour and salt into a basin and stir in the sugar and dates. Heat the treacle and cider together gently, until the treacle has dissolved. Stir the cider mixture and eggs into the flour and blend well. Put into a greased and base-lined 9 in (22.5 cm) square tin. Bake at 325°F/180°C/Gas Mark 3 for thirty minutes.

Rub together the topping butter, flour and sugar, and mix in the walnuts and cinnamon. Remove the cake from the oven and spread the jam on top. Sprinkle the topping mixture over the jam. Return cake to oven for twenty minutes. Cool on a rack. Keep the cake wrapped in foil for two days.

Date and cider cake

8 oz (225 g) block dates
  (chopped)
¼ pint (150 ml) dry cider
6 oz (175 g) caster sugar
8 oz (225 g) butter
4 beaten eggs
10 oz (300 g) plain flour
1 teaspoon bicarbonate of
  soda
2 teaspoons baking
  powder
Few drops of vanilla
  essence

Put the dates, cider and sugar into a saucepan and bring to the boil. Cook gently, stirring occasionally, until the dates are soft, which will take about ten minutes. Add the butter and stir until melted; allow mixture to cool slightly. Gradually beat in the beaten eggs, then fold in the flour, bicarbonate of soda and baking powder. Stir in the vanilla essence. Turn the mixture into a greased and lined 7 in (17.5 cm) square cake tin, and spread level. Bake in the centre of the oven at 350°F/180°C/Gas Mark 4 for one hour until the cake is firm to the touch. Leave to cool in the tin, and then wrap the cake in aluminium foil and keep for at least a day before eating.

Somerset tea ring

4 fl oz (100 ml) dry cider
8 oz (225 g) plain flour
½ teaspoon caster sugar
1 teaspoon dried yeast
½ teaspoon salt
2 oz (50 g) butter
½ egg, beaten
2 oz (50 g) demerara
    sugar
2 oz (50 g) chopped
    mixed peel
1 teaspoon ground
    cinnamon

Icing:
¼ pint (150 ml) dry cider
4 oz (100 g) icing sugar

Put the cider into a saucepan and heat gently to blood heat. Put 2½ oz (45 g) flour into a bowl, and blend in the warm cider, caster sugar and yeast. Leave in a warm place for about twenty minutes, until frothy. Mix the remaining flour with the salt and rub in 1 oz (25 g) butter. Add the beaten egg and the flour mixture to the yeast batter and beat well to give a fairly soft dough. Turn on to a lightly floured board and knead lightly. Roll out to a rectangle approximately 12 × 9 in (30 × 22.5 cm). Melt the remaining butter and brush over the dough. Mix together the demerara sugar, mixed peel and cinnamon, and sprinkle evenly over the dough. Roll up tightly from the long edge, then bring ends round and seal together to form a ring. Place on a greased baking tray.

Using scissors, cut slashes at an angle about 1 in (2.5 cm) apart, to within ½ in (1.25 cm) of the centre. Turn each section slightly to one side so that a pinwheel pattern shows. Cover with a greased polythene bag and leave to rise in a warm place for about thirty minutes. Bake at 375°F/170°C/Gas Mark 5 for twenty-five minutes until golden brown. Cool on a rack.

To make the icing, put the cider in a saucepan, bring to the boil, and boil steadily until reduced to two tablespoons. Add icing sugar to make a coating consistency. Trickle the icing over the tea ring, and decorate with glacé cherries or chopped nuts.

Devonshire fruit loaf

12 oz (350 g) mixed
    dried fruit
½ pint (300 ml) medium
    sweet cider
10 oz (300 g) self-raising
    flour
2 oz (50 g) chopped
    walnuts
6 oz (175 g) soft brown
    sugar
2 beaten eggs

Put the dried fruit and cider in a basin, cover and leave overnight in a cool place. Put the fruit and cider into a saucepan and bring to the boil. Remove from heat and leave to cool. Mix together the flour, walnuts and sugar, and add the beaten eggs and fruit mixture. Mix well. Turn into a greased and base-lined 2 lb (1 kg) loaf tin. Bake at 350°F/180°C/Gas Mark 4 for thirty minutes, then reduce heat to 325°F/170°C/Gas Mark 3 for forty-five minutes until loaf is golden brown and firm. Turn out on a rack and leave to cool. Eat alone, or with butter on the slices.

Christmas

Countdown to Christmas

Our traditional Christmas feasting has changed little down the centuries. A few years ago the twelve days of Yuletide cheer were a longed-for respite from the horror of everyday poverty. Our ancestors, returning to today's kitchens, would find no difficulty in cooking or eating familiar festive food. We still tuck away mounds of rich meats, embellished with seasonal vegetables; we munch winter nuts with our wine; we enjoy the occasional extravagance of spirits and liqueurs; we use imported spices, dried fruits and citrus fruits which all used to be rare treats for recipes we treasure from year to year.

It is fun for the cook and the family if our festive food is a mixture of old favourites and new ideas, but the secret of success is to start preparations early.

Christmas cake

A rich fruit Christmas cake will mature in the tin, so it is a good idea to get this chore out of the way early. The almond paste and royal icing must remain tasks for the last week of preparation.

8 oz (225 g) butter
8 oz (225 g) soft brown sugar or caster sugar
1 tablespoon black treacle
4 large eggs
4 tablespoons strong cold tea, or sherry or brandy
Grated rind of 1 lemon
½ teaspoon vanilla essence
4 oz (100 g) self-raising flour
6 oz (175 g) plain flour
¼ teaspoon salt
1 teaspoon ground mixed spice
Pinch of ground cinnamon
Pinch of ground nutmeg
12 oz (350 g) currants
12 oz (350 g) sultanas
8 oz (225 g) stoned raisins
2 oz (50 g) chopped almonds
2 oz (50 g) halved glacé cherries
2 oz (50 g) chopped peel

Cream the butter and sugar until light and fluffy. Beat together black treacle, eggs, tea or other liquid, lemon rind and vanilla essence – enough to break up the eggs. Sift together flours, salt and spices. Add treacle mixture and flour mixture alternately to the creamed mixture but do not beat. Add all the remaining ingredients and mix. Put into a greased 10 in (25 cm) round tin lined with two thicknesses of paper, leave for an hour to stand, then bake at 300°F/150°C/Gas Mark 2 for four hours. The cake is done when it stops 'singing'. Cool for an hour in tin before turning on to a rack. When cold, wrap and store in a tin. If this is too large a cake for your family, halve the mixture, using a 7 in (17.5 cm) round tin, and bake for 3-3½ hours.

Almond paste

12 oz (350 g) ground
  almonds
6 oz (175 g) caster sugar
6 oz (175 g) icing sugar
½ teaspoonful lemon juice
3 drops vanilla essence
6 drops almond essence
3 egg yolks

Mix the almonds and caster sugar, and stir well with the sieved icing sugar until the mixture is evenly coloured. Add lemon juice, vanilla and almond essences, and mix to a stiff paste with enough yolk to bind the mixture.

Be sure to brush all crumbs from the cake before beginning to put on the almond paste. Brush the top and sides of the cake with warm, sieved apricot jam or redcurrant jelly. Divide, allowing one-third for the top of the cake. Roll this smaller piece into a circle to fit the cake. Measure the depth and circumference of the cake and roll out remaining paste into a rectangle. Press well on to the cake. Leave to dry for two days before applying royal icing.

Royal icing

This is best put on in two coats, allowing the first coat to dry for two days before putting on the top layer.

First coat:
1 lb (450 g) icing sugar
2 large egg whites
½ teaspoon glycerine

Second coat:
12 oz (350 g) icing sugar
2 small egg whites
½ teaspoon glycerine

Make the first coat by sifting the icing sugar, add the egg whites to the glycerine and gradually work in about two-thirds of the icing sugar. Beat well and add remaining sugar. The icing should be thick enough to stand in peaks. Apply the icing and leave for two days.

Make the second coat of icing in the same way. It will be thick enough to coat the back of a wooden spoon, but thinner than the first coat. Ice and leave to harden before putting on cake frill or ribbon.

Mincemeat and mince pies

Mince pies are always popular at Christmas, the old tradition of 'a happy month for every pie' keeping consumption high. Mincemeat is quick and easy to prepare, and can be stored for many months.

Rich mincemeat

1 lb (450 g) currants
1 lb (450 g) seeded raisins
1 lb (450 g) sultanas
1½ lb (750 g) beef suet
1 lb (450 g) dark soft
brown sugar
1 oz (25 g) mixed spice
1 lb (450 g) apples
(weighed after peeling
and coring)
Grated rind 2 lemons
Grated rind 2 oranges
4 fl oz (100 ml) brandy
4 fl oz (100 ml) rum

Chop raisins, grate suet, and mince apples, saving all the juice which runs from them. Mix all ingredients together very well. Put into clean dry jars and cover well, and store in a cool place. Stir well before using.

Mince pies

Pies may be made with short or flaky pastry. Small pies are traditional, but for informal meals large open or covered pies seem more generous. They can be made in spongecake tins or in ovenglass flan dishes.

Do not overcook pies, as they are usually reheated, though they are at their best served freshly cooked. Reheating is best done slowly, using a low oven. Sifted icing sugar can be scattered on pies, or they can be brushed with water or milk and scattered lightly with caster sugar before baking, to give a glazed finish; but the sugar should be sparing or the pastry will be tough and fail to rise.

Freezing mince pies: highly spiced mincemeat can lose flavour in the freezer, so pies should not be stored longer than one month. They may be baked and packed in cartons for freezing, or left unbaked in their baking tins. Unbaked pies will have a better flavour and scent, and be crisper and flakier.

Accompaniments: brandy, rum butter or thick cream go well with mince pies. Some people like to lift the lids and pop the 'butter' or cream directly on to the hot mincemeat. With large open mince pies, try vanilla ice-cream spiked with a little liqueur.

Christmas pudding

Puddings made for year-long storage can be eaten at various celebration meals during the year. Those for storage should be covered with clean dry cloths and kept in a cool dry place. This mixture makes four medium-sized puddings.

8 oz (225 g) self-raising flour
8 oz (225 g) breadcrumbs
8 oz (225 g) shredded suet
8 oz (225 g) currants
8 oz (225 g) soft brown sugar
12 oz (350 g) sultanas
12 oz (350 g) stoned raisins
Grated rind and juice of 1 orange and 1 lemon
6 well-beaten eggs
1 teaspoon salt
1 teaspoon mixed spice
½ pint (300 ml) ale (or large wineglass brandy)
4 oz (100 g) finely chopped candied peel
4 oz (100 g) finely chopped glacé cherries
1 small grated carrot
1 small grated apple
6 oz (175 g) blanched almonds (cut finely).

Fruit should be fresh and plump; stoned raisins are best and some of the sultanas should be cut in half. Ale, stout or brandy gives a good colour to the mixture and helps it keep. Breadcrumbs give lightness and should be rubbed fine. Mix all ingredients to a stiff, but not dry mixture – a little milk may be added – and put into basins, leaving a 2 in (5 cm) space below the top of each bowl. A cover of foil or cloth should be tied on tightly, and the puddings put into a saucepan of boiling water. Don't allow the saucepan to boil dry: it should be topped up periodically with boiling water. Puddings are best boiled gently for eight hours, then for a further three hours before serving.

A lighter pudding

For people who do not enjoy the heavy type of pudding mix together 8 oz (225 g) each of breadcrumbs, sultanas, currants, raisins, mixed peel, suet, brown sugar and four eggs with the grated rind of two lemons. Steam for four hours and serve with brandy butter or orange butter (butter, icing sugar, orange juice and grated rind).

Accompaniments : serve a delicious sauce with the pudding and thick cream, or custard for the children.

Hard sauce

2 oz (50 g) butter
4 oz (100 g) icing or caster sugar
1 tablespoon brandy or rum

Cream butter and sugar and slowly add rum or brandy. Keep cold until serving.

Brandy butter

3 oz (75 g) butter
3 oz (75 g) caster sugar
3 tablespoons brandy

Cream butter and work in sugar and brandy. Keep in a cold place (but not the refrigerator).

Rum butter

3 oz (75 g) unsalted butter
3 oz (75 g) soft brown sugar
3 tablespoons rum
½ teaspoon grated lemon rind
Squeeze of lemon juice

Cream the butter until white and beat in the sugar a little at a time with the grated rind and lemon juice. Beat in the rum gradually until completely absorbed. Pile in a glass dish and chill.

Fluffy rum cream sauce

3 oz (75 g) butter
3 oz (75 g) icing sugar
3 tablespoons rum
2 beaten eggs
¼ pint (150 ml) thick whipped cream

Cream the butter and sugar and work in the eggs. Slowly add rum and finally fold in whipped cream.

The Christmas Bird

Choosing the Christmas bird doesn't begin and end with a visit to the butcher or a quiet word with a friend about the contents of field or farmyard. Today's choice has to be made after considering a whole series of problems. How many are you catering for? Shall the bird be fresh or frozen? How will you stuff and accompany the main part of the most-looked-forward-to meal of the year? Will you cook the bird slowly or quickly, in foil or without? How can you carve to get the best from your choice? How, oh how, are you going to use up the carcass?

Stuffings for poultry

Stuffing poultry helps to improve the flavour of its flesh, stretches the helpings and counteracts greasiness. Stuffing can be prepared in advance and stored in a covered dish in a cold place; it can also be frozen for up to one month. Poultry should not be frozen with stuffing inside; in any case a bird should not be stuffed until just before cooking.

Making the stuffing: use two-day-old bread, as new bread makes stuffing heavy. Crumbs or cubes lightly toasted will improve the stuffing. Sausages, giblets and other meat must be cooked before adding to stuffing. Allow one breakfastcup of stuffing to each lb (450 g) ready-to-cook weight of bird.

Filling the bird: do not pack stuffing too tightly. Use enough in the neck end to make the bird look plump when served, but allow for swelling so that the skin does not burst. It is easy to stuff the bird by using an icing bag without a nozzle. Extra stuffing can be cooked in a casserole if covered with bacon or salt pork and a little meat stock, and baked slowly for at least an hour.

Left-over stuffing: do not leave stuffing in cold carcass, but remove and keep in a covered dish in the refrigerator for up to three days. Reheat just enough for one meal at a time. Stuffing can be crumbled thickly on top of a poultry casserole, dotted with dripping and browned until crisp. It may also be used in meat sandwiches with a little redcurrant jelly or cranberry sauce. Toasted sandwiches can be filled with turkey and hot stuffing, topped with hot gravy and a spoonful of cranberry sauce.

Turkey

How to choose: take the measurements of your oven first. Your turkey may have to go on the bottom of the oven instead of a runner. A 10-13 lb (5-7 kg) turkey will serve 10-12 people for one hot meal. Larger birds have a higher proportion of flesh to bone. Hen birds are preferable to cock birds; and a good bird should have a broad breast. Avoid fresh birds which look dark and scrawny; on a frozen bird watch for browning areas of 'freezer burn' which can indicate long and improper storage, or dehydration. Allow frozen turkeys to defrost completely before cooking (about thirty-six hours for a 9 lb (4.5 kg) bird).

Stuffing for turkey:
4 oz (100 g) melted butter
1 lb (450 g) breadcrumbs
½ teaspoon salt
¼ teaspoon pepper
½ teaspoon thyme
4 oz (100 g) chopped walnuts
3 oz (75 g) raisins, *or* sultanas
1½ lb (750 g) cooked chestnuts
6 oz (175 g) chopped prunes
8 oz (225 g) crisp apples
8 oz (225 g) sausagemeat
Pinch each of salt, pepper and cinnamon
1 tablespoon Calvados
1 oz (25 g) melted butter

How to cook: many people like to cook the turkey in foil, which speeds up cooking time and gives a moist tender bird. This is not true roasting, however, and sometimes results in a stewed taste, particularly with a frozen bird which may contain a lot of excess moisture. The advantages of slow over quick roasting are debatable. Quick cooking seals the bird and gives better flavour, while the slower and more carefree method reduces shrinkage. The best compromise is to put the bird into a hot oven, 425°F/220°C/Gas Mark 7 for twenty minutes, then reduce heat to 375°F/190°C/Gas Mark 5 for remaining cooking time. The breast should be covered with bacon, and the turkey basted at intervals. For a bird under 14 lb (7 kg) allow fifteen minutes a lb (450 kg) and fifteen minutes over. For a larger bird allow ten minutes a lb (450 kg) and ten minutes over.

Cook the turkey on a rack in a shallow tin and brush the bird with melted butter. Cut the string around the drumsticks after an hour when they should be set, so that the heat circulates. Test with a skewer in the thickest part of the drumstick to see if cooking is finished; this can be judged when the skewer goes in easily but no liquid runs out. To prevent the breast drying out before the legs are cooked, cover the breast after the first hour of cooking with a cloth dipped in melted butter. Allow 20-30 minutes for dishing up and making gravy.

How to carve: be sure the dish is large and the knife sharp. Put fork firmly into 'knee' joint, and slice thigh flesh away from body until ball-and-socket hip joint is exposed. Cut joint between thigh and drumstick. Repeat with other leg. Take off wings and divide at major joint if bird is large. Slice the breast beginning at the neck area, and slice thinly across the grain the entire length of the breast. If the bird is large, use only one side, so the rest remains moist for cold serving.

Accompaniments: stuffing is important for turkey. Melted fat or cold water used to bind the bread will give a light loose texture. For a crumbly stuffing with a delicious flavour, fry the breadcrumbs in a little butter. For sausage-meat stuffing, add a little chopped parsley or onion. For chestnut stuffing, mix cooked chestnuts with a little fried bacon and minced onion, and put through a sieve or vegetable mill for fine texture. For easy cranberry sauce, cook cranberries in a little boiling water until they pop, and add plenty of sugar.

Leftovers: for packed meals, make *Turkey Roll* by mincing 12 oz (350 g) cold turkey, 8 oz (225 g) ham and one small onion, with a pinch of mace, $\frac{1}{2}$ teaspoon thyme, salt and pepper and 2 oz (100 g) breadcrumbs, bound with one large egg, then steamed in a greased tin for an hour, finally rolling in brown breadcrumbs while still warm.

Goose

How to choose: make sure the bird is a young one, as there's nothing tougher than an old goose. This is a wasteful bird, and loses about half its weight in cooking. A 10 lb (5 kg) goose should feed eight people. A young bird has supple yellow legs with traces of down, and a soft underbill.

How to cook: rub the bird all over with flour to give a crisp skin. Cook the goose on a rack in a large tin, and twenty minutes after cooking starts, prick the skin with a fork to allow the fat to run out; drain off some of the fat during cooking, and baste two or three times. Start the bird at a high temperature (450°F/230°C/Gas Mark 8) for thirty minutes then reduce the oven to 400°F/200°C/Gas Mark 6 for the rest of the cooking time, allowing fifteen minutes a lb (450 g) and fifteen minutes over.

Stuffing for goose:
8 oz (225 g) small bread
    cubes
¼ pint (150 ml) cold
    water
1 chopped onion
2 oz (50 g) chopped
    celery
1 tablespoon chopped
    parsley
2 oz (50 g) melted butter
1 teaspoon salt
¼ teaspoon pepper
½ teaspoon thyme
8 oz (225 g) mashed
    potatoes
1 beaten egg

How to carve: proceed as for turkey.

Accompaniments: all fruit goes well with goose, and apple sauce, fried apples, or pineapple rings are excellent. A sour apple cooked in the pan with the goose improves the flavour of the gravy. The bird may be stuffed with sage and onion, prune and apple, or an oatmeal stuffing, or merely rubbed over with a lemon and a peeled lemon placed inside. Red cabbage is good to serve with goose, and some rosy baked apples make an attractive garnish.

Leftovers: serve cold with a crisp salad of celery, apple and walnut, and a baked potato.

Goose 'extras' are particularly useful in the kitchen. The liver can be turned into a rich pâté, or can be soaked in milk, then sprinkled with seasoned flour and cooked in butter until lightly brown, before being simmered with sliced apples and onions until tender. A wineglass of Madeira added at the last minute makes this a very special dish.

The giblets can be turned into an old dish called *Gallimaufry*. Simmer all the giblets except the liver with a little water, seasoning, bay leaf, parsley and thyme until tender. Cut the giblets into walnut-sized pieces and mix with 1 lb (450 g) steak and the liver cut into cubes. Brown all the meat in a little dripping and sprinkle lightly with flour. Simmer in the giblet stock for another hour, adding a wineglass of port halfway through cooking. Serve hot with forcemeat balls and small triangles of toast.

Duck

How to choose: look for a broad-breasted bird weighing about 5 lb (2.5 kg) which should serve six people with careful carving. A young bird up to eight months makes the best eating, with soft webbing between feet, and soft underbill.

How to cook: rub salt into the breast and roast with ½ in (1.25 cm) water in the pan and no extra fat, turning the bird halfway through cooking to brown the breast. Put bird into a hot oven (450°F/230°C/Gas Mark 8) for ten minutes then reduce heat to 350°F/180°C/Gas Mark 4 and continue cooking, allowing fifteen minutes a lb (450 g).

Stuffing for duck:
8 oz (225 g) chopped
   prunes soaked in 1
   miniature cherry
   brandy
8 oz (225 g) mashed
   liver sausage
1 finely chopped shallot
1 crushed bay leaf
Pinch of mace
Pinch of salt and pepper
Squeeze of lemon juice
Grating of lemon rind

How to carve: cut off right leg portion by inserting knife point into right leg between tail end of breast, bringing knife forward round thigh to middle of back; then turn bird on its side and bring knife down the centre of the back to the parson's nose and back between leg and tail end of the breast. Repeat on opposite side for left leg portion. Take off right wing portion by cutting along the breast in a straight line, placing the knife on the centre of the tapered part of the breast back, then turning the bird over and continuing the cut along the back to the end of the meat. The left wing portion is tackled the same way. The two final portions are achieved by bringing the knife to the centre back as near the breast bone as possible, cutting right along the breast bone and into the carcass.

Accompaniments: duck is good left unstuffed. Garnish with baked apples stuffed with sausagemeat, or with tiny onions simmered in stock and glazed in butter. Apple sauce is popular, or a salad of sliced orange.

Leftovers: slice the cooked flesh and heat in a sauce made from ½ pint (300 ml) brown sauce with the juice of four oranges and the shredded peel of two oranges and one small tin of tomato purée, and garnish with orange segments. Or try reheating the duck flesh with a sauce made from ¼ pint (150 ml) white stock, a wineglass Madeira or sherry, two teaspoons cherry brandy, salt and pepper, and drained canned Morello cherries.

Chicken

How to choose: a chicken weighing about 5 lb (2.5 kg) will feed a small family over the Christmas period, or a capon up to 8 lb (4 kg) will feed a larger party.

How to cook: some people like to roast a joint of pork to serve with the chicken, and the combination of flavours is delicious. Roast the bird at 400°F/200°C/Gas Mark 6, allowing fifteen minutes a lb (450 g). The bird may have fat bacon tied on the breast, or be basted with butter. If the bird is not stuffed, a bunch of herbs or some tarragon can be tucked inside.
   Another good stuffing can be made from a

Stuffing for chicken:
1 chopped onion
2 oz (50 g) chopped
    celery
4 oz (100 g) melted
    butter
8 oz (225 g) small bread
    cubes
1 chopped green pepper
2 rashers crumbled fried
    bacon
1 teaspoon salt
½ teaspoon pepper
Cold water to moisten

mixture of breadcrumbs and suet, flavoured with chopped ham or bacon, parsley, thyme and lemon rind, lightly bound with beaten egg. This can be used to stuff under the breast, and a sausagemeat stuffing used for the body cavity.

Accompaniments: small bacon rolls and chipolata sausages are popular accompaniments, and bread sauce well flavoured with cloves and onion, with thick cream stirred in at the last minute.

How to carve: proceed as for turkey.

Leftovers: use minced chicken on toast, or in sandwiches. Use the livers for pâté.

Favourite Sauces

Bread sauce
(for turkey, chicken, pheasant)

1 onion
1 pint (600 ml) milk
Salt, pepper and nutmeg
3 oz (75 g) day-old bread
    made into crumbs
Cream

Chop onion coarsely and simmer in some of the milk until quite soft, adding salt, pepper and nutmeg. Gradually add breadcrumbs and more milk and cook for ten minutes. Add a generous dollop of cream before serving. Some people like to stick the onion with a few cloves while it is cooking.

Cranberry sauce
(for turkey)

8 oz (225 g) cranberries
4 oz (100 g) sugar
½ pint (300 ml) water

Cook cranberries in water until they begin to pop. When they are tender, put through a sieve, add sugar and stir until dissolved. Pour into a mould and leave to set for twelve hours, so the sauce can be turned out. For a hot sauce, serve berries whole, or purée like an apple sauce.

Apple sauce
(for goose, duck or pork)

1 lb (450 g) apples
2 oz (50 g) sugar

Peel and slice apples, and cook with just enough water to prevent burning. Put through a sieve, add sugar and reheat.

Cumberland sauce
(for ham)

1 shallot
1 orange
1 lemon
8 oz (225 g) redcurrant jelly
1 wineglass port
½ teaspoon mustard powder
½ teaspoon powdered ginger
Pinch of cayenne

Chop shallot finely, plunge it into boiling water, and drain. Take off the zest from one-quarter each of the orange and lemon and cut zest in very thin strips. Melt the redcurrant jelly, and add the shallot, zest of orange and lemon, juice of orange and lemon, port and seasonings. Stir well and serve cold.

The Cold Collation

One of my favourite words has always been 'collation' – a light repast. It conjures up a picture of Victorian plenty, a sideboard laden with delectable morsels, a well-sharpened carving knife and a rank of assorted pickle jars and salad bowls. At Christmas, the cold collation comes into its own. Palates ruined by too much drinking and smoking, and by a surfeit of sweet things, welcome the savoury pies and cooked meats. Busy families can be catered for whatever time they may condescend to drop into meals; casual guests need not go hungry; wavering dieters can be persuaded that a savoury snack isn't quite so fattening as another glacé fruit.

Of course, these dishes are also marvellous for buffet parties as they may be prepared in advance, and are easy to slice thinly when cold.

Spiced beef

Serve cold with baked
jacket potatoes and salad.

4 lb (2 kg) boned
   brisket
10 oz (300 g) block salt
2 shallots
3 bay leaves
1 teaspoon ground cloves
1 teaspoon ground mace
1 teaspoon ground
   allspice
3 oz (75 g) soft brown
   sugar
½ teaspoon black pepper
½ teaspoon chopped
   thyme

Do not roll the beef. Rub it all over with
three-quarters of the salt. Put into a bowl and
cover with a clean teacloth. Leave for twenty-
four hours in a cool place – I use the bottom
of the refrigerator. Mix the remaining salt with
all the other ingredients and each day, for
seven days, rub a little of this mixture into the
meat, pouring off any liquid. Roll the spiced
meat and tie with string. Put into a saucepan,
cover with water, cover and bring to the boil.
Skim and then simmer for five hours. Leave
to cool in the liquid.

Baked salt beef

Very good with tomato
salad, chutney and
potatoes in their jackets.

5 lb (2.5 kg) silverside
   beef
Carrots
Onions
1 garlic clove
2 bay leaves
6 peppercorns
½ pint (300 ml) cider

Soak beef in water for two hours. Drain and
put in deep oven dish. Put in two or three
large sliced carrots and onions, crushed garlic
clove, bay leaves, peppercorns and cider, and
fill pot with water. Cover tightly and cook at
325°F/170°C/Gas Mark 3 for four hours. Drain
(saving stock for soup), wrap meat in greaseproof paper and put in deep bowl. Put on
heavy weights and leave until next day.

Rolled ox tongue

1 pickled ox tongue
3 cloves
1 carrot
1 onion
½ oz (15 g) soft brown
   sugar

Soak the tongue overnight. Put in a pan with
cloves, sliced onion and carrot, sugar and cold
water to cover. Bring to the boil and skim,
then simmer until nearly cooked. Take out the
tongue and put into a bowl of cold water.
Remove the skin and any small bones from the
root of the tongue. Return to the pan and
continue simmering until tender. Drain and
put into a round cake tin or straight-sided
circular dish. Put a plate on top and some
scale weights or cans of food so that the tongue
is lightly pressed. Leave in a cold place until
set and then turn out.

Jellied beef

The meat should be soft enough to cut with a spoon when hot, but will be firmed when cold and will cut in slices. A dish which is a little trouble, but delicious, and particularly good for a buffet lunch.

4 lb (2 kg) lean beef
   joint
4 bacon rashers
4 garlic cloves
Salt and pepper
2 onions
Dripping
3 fl oz (75 ml) brandy
½ pint (300 ml) red wine
Thyme and bay leaf
2 calves' feet (or pigs'
   trotters)
Beef stock
2 lb (1 kg) carrots

Cut bacon and garlic into small pieces and insert these in the beef with a larding needle or sharp knife. Rub meat with a little salt and black pepper. Brown sliced onions in a little dripping, then brown the meat in the fat. Pour over warmed brandy and set light to it. When it stops burning, pour in wine and leave to bubble for two minutes. Add herbs and split feet, cover with stock or water, put on lid and simmer on stove or in oven for four hours. Add sliced carrots one hour before cooking time is finished. Drain beef and put into serving dish, arrange carrots round, and strain on stock. The next day, when the jelly has set, remove any fat with a spoon dipped in hot water.

Farmer's pâté

3 rashers streaky bacon
4 oz (100 g) small
   mushrooms
1 oz (25 g) butter
1 tablespoon oil
1 medium onion
3 oz (75 g) chicken livers
1 lb (450 g) pork
   sausagemeat
Salt and pepper
½ teaspoon mixed herbs
4 oz (100 g) fresh
   breadcrumbs
2 eggs
2 bay leaves

Remove the rind from the bacon and stretch the rashers with a broad-bladed knife until very thin. Grease a 1 lb (450 g) loaf tin and put the rashers across the narrow way of the tin with one in the centre and one at each end. Slice eight of the mushrooms and arrange between the rashers. Melt the butter and oil together and fry the chopped onion until soft and golden. Remove the onion and keep it on one side. Fry the chicken livers very lightly and chop roughly. Chop the remaining mushrooms and fry for three minutes. Add the liver and mushrooms to the onions with the remaining ingredients, except the bay leaves, to give a soft mixture. Put into the prepared tin and fold over the bacon. Press bay leaves on top. Stand the loaf tin in a roasting tin of hot water and bake at 325°F/170°C/Gas Mark 3 for 1½ hours. Take off bay leaves. Chill and turn out when cold. Serve with toast or salad.

Make a Different Christmas Cake

Most of us stick to our Christmas traditions all our lives, particularly where food is concerned, and an awful lot of people don't like to confess they are not very fond of plum pudding or rich fruit cake. The cake in particular is usually the finishing touch for over-strained digestions, teatime is only nominal when there are hefty lunches and party suppers to eat, and the result is that the heavily iced rich fruit cake languishes in its tin. These cakes will tempt the casual caller for a cup of tea or coffee and will delight the children, while still retaining a festive air.

Christmas Eve wigs

Very good with mulled elderberry wine, or dipped in ale.

3 oz (75 g) butter
8 oz (225 g) self-raising flour
1 oz (25 g) caster sugar
1 oz (25 g) chopped mixed peel
2 teaspoons caraway seeds
1 egg
A little milk

Rub butter into flour, add sugar, peel and caraway seeds. Mix to a soft dough, with egg and a little milk. Put into greased patty tins, and bake at 425°F/220°C/Gas Mark 7 for twenty minutes.

Snowman cake

Bake a sponge mixture in 1 pint (600 ml) pudding bowl and in two ¼ pint (150 ml) bowls. Invert larger cake on board or plate. Put two smaller cakes together with butter cream and trim to a neat sphere. Fix head on body with butter icing, running a cocktail stick through the two pieces for extra security. Ice with white butter icing. Make a black paper hat and use a ribbon for a scarf. Use blackcurrant fruit jellies for eyes, nose, mouth and buttons, a liquorice stick for a broom, and a sprinkling of coconut on cake and board to represent snow.

Christmas log

4 oz (100 g) caster sugar
2 large eggs
2½ oz (65 g) plain flour

Icing:
7 oz (200 g) butter
5 oz (150 g) caster
  sugar
2 egg yolks
2 tablespoons strong
  black coffee
3 oz (75 g) melted plain
  chocolate

Heat oven to 450°F/230°C/Gas Mark 8 and warm sugar in some foil in the oven for exactly six minutes. Put eggs into a bowl and beat in hot sugar until light, fluffy and white. Fold in flour and smooth the mixture into a swiss roll tin lined with greaseproof paper. Bake for six minutes. Turn out on a rack, leave until cool, and remove the paper.

Meanwhile, make the icing by creaming butter and sugar until light and fluffy, beating in egg yolks, coffee and chocolate until quite smooth. Spread one-third of the filling on the sponge, roll up firmly and cover with the remainder of the icing. Mark with a fork to resemble a log, scatter thinly with icing sugar to resemble snow, and decorate with holly leaves and robins.

Twelfth Night cake

This is a very good cake to eat with hot punch. Traditionally a haricot bean is hidden in the centre of the cake, and the person who gets the bean is king of the Twelfth Night revels.

12 oz (350 g) butter
8 oz (225 g) caster sugar
4 eggs
1¼ lb (675 g) plain flour
Pinch of mixed spice
1¼ lb (675 g) currants
8 oz (225 g) chopped
  mixed candied peel
4 oz (100 g) split
  blanched almonds
2 fl oz (50 ml) brandy
2 fl oz (50 ml) sherry

Beat butter and sugar to a cream, then add eggs one by one, alternately with a little of the flour sifted with the spice. Beat very thoroughly, then add currants, peel, almonds, brandy and sherry. Pour into a well-buttered and lined 10 in (25 cm) cake tin and bake at 325°F/170°C/Gas Mark 3 for 2½ hours.

Log cabin cake

Bake sponge cake in $7\frac{1}{2}$ in (19 cm) square cake tin. Cut off strip $2\frac{1}{2}$ in (6. 25 cm) wide from the cake. Cut this strip through diagonally from top right-hand edge to bottom left-hand edge. Put these two triangles together to form a large triangular 'roof' and fix to the top of the larger cake to form a house. Make a chimney with marzipan or with a small individual sponge cake, cutting out an upturned V so that it can be easily fixed to the roof. Make windows and door from marzipan. Coat the cake with chocolate icing, or if liked spread on icing and fix chocolate finger biscuits all over like logs. If the cake is set on a board with white icing for snow, icing can also be used on roof and window sills to simulate snow, and small fir trees used as a background.

Uncooked Christmas cake

8 oz (225 g)
   marshmallows
$1\frac{1}{2}$ lb (750 g) digestive
   biscuits
1 oz (25 g) angelica
3 tablespoons orange
   juice
10 tablespoons
   evaporated milk
$\frac{1}{2}$ teaspoon ground
   cinnamon
$\frac{1}{2}$ teaspoon ground
   nutmeg
$\frac{1}{4}$ teaspoon ground cloves
12 oz (350 g) mixed
   sultanas and seedless
   raisins
8 oz (225 g) chopped
   mixed peel
4 oz (100 g) glacé
   cherries
4 oz (100 g) chopped
   dates
4 oz (100 g) walnuts

Chop marshmallows with a pair of wet scissors. Crush biscuits with a rolling pin. Chop angelica finely. Leave marshmallows to stand in orange juice and milk for twenty minutes. Mix spices, angelica, chopped fruit and nuts. Stir in marshmallows and liquid and finally biscuit crumbs. Press very firmly into a lined 9 in (22.5 cm) round cake tin, cover with foil, and leave for two days before turning out and cutting. Store in refrigerator. This cake can be topped with a little glacé icing, and decorated with glacé fruit and nuts.

Or try a new icing

Fruity finish: brush the top of your fruit cake with melted sieved apricot or raspberry jam, or redcurrant jelly. Arrange a pattern of glacé fruit (pineapple and apricots) on top and fill in the gaps with glacé cherries and walnut halves. Brush thickly with more melted jam or jelly and leave in a cool place until firm.

Almond addiction: if you like almond icing, you can finish the cake with it. Cover the top and sides (or top only) with a layer of almond icing. Use trimmings for fruit or leaves. Take small pieces, colour them delicately with vegetable colourings and roll out. Cut or stamp out holly leaves, roll tiny balls for holly berries, or shape and colour oranges and apples. Roll the balls over a nutmeg grater for a rough 'orange' finish. You can form a holly wreath of leaves and berries round the edge of the cake, or make a simple central decoration. Put a paper frill round the edge of the cake.

American-style: this icing does not need icing sugar, but is made with granulated sugar and it can be 'peaked up' to look like a snow scene. Use a double boiler, or a bowl over a saucepan of hot water. Put in one egg white, 6 oz (175 g) sugar, two tablespoons cold water, $\frac{1}{4}$ teaspoon cream of tartar and a pinch of salt. Stir until the sugar has dissolved and put over fast boiling water. Beat with an egg beater until stiff enough to stand in peaks, which should take about seven minutes. Keep the sides of the bowl clean with a spatula as you work. Flavour to taste, and use quickly when the peaks form.

Drinks

Old-Fashioned Thirst Quenchers

Hot weather and hard work in the fields produce raging thirsts, and there is nothing like the old-fashioned harvest drinks to quench them. They are cheap to make, far nicer and less cloying than bought, synthetic squashes, and most of them can be enjoyed within a week of bottling.

The ginger beer plant

We always keep a batch of ginger beer going, and divide the 'plant' to give to friends. Had they all kept making plants and dividing them, the sea would be made of ginger beer by now.

To start the plant, mix ½ oz (15 g) fresh yeast, two teaspoons ground ginger and two teaspoons sugar with ¾ pint (450 ml) water. Leave for twenty-four hours, then feed daily with one teaspoon ground ginger and one teaspoon sugar. After seven days strain through a cloth. The remaining solid is the 'plant': Mix it with ¾ pint (450 ml) water and repeat the process for more ginger beer. The plant should be halved about every two weeks.

To finish the ginger beer, mix the strained liquid with 5 pints (2.75 l) cold water, the juice of two lemons, and 1½ lb (700 g) sugar dissolved in 2 pints (1 l) hot water. Mix well, pour into screwtop beer or cider bottles, and leave for a week before using.

Lemon barley water

4 oz (100 g) pearl barley
2 lemons
2 oz (50 g) loaf sugar
2 pints (1 l) boiling water

Wash the barley and put it in a saucepan. Just cover with cold water and bring to the boil. Boil for four minutes and strain off the water. Put the barley into a large jug. Rub off the yellow part of the lemon rind on to the sugar and add to the barley. Pour over 1 quart (1 l) boiling water. Stir to dissolve the sugar and leave until cold. Stir in the juice of the lemons. Strain into a jug.

Fresh lemonade

4 lemons
2 lb (1 kg) sugar
1 teaspoon tartaric acid
2 pints (1 l) boiling water

Squeeze the lemons over sugar in a basin. Add the tartaric acid. Pour on boiling water. Stir well to dissolve sugar and leave until cold. Pour into bottles and cork firmly. Store in a cool place, and dilute with water to taste.

Elderflower champagne

Ready to drink in a few
days.

4 heads of elderflowers
1½ lb (700 g) sugar
2 tablespoons white wine
    vinegar
8 pints (4.5 l) cold water
2 lemons

Put elderflowers, sugar, vinegar and water into
a bowl. Squeeze in the lemon juice. Cut the
lemons in quarters and add to the liquid.
Leave to stand for twenty-four hours, stirring
occasionally. Strain and bottle into screwtop
bottles.

Raspberry vinegar

8 lb (4 kg) raspberries
2 pints (1 l) white wine
Distilled white vinegar

Pick over the raspberries, cover them with
vinegar and leave to stand for twenty-four
hours. Strain this liquid through a sieve without
pressing the fruit, and pour it on the remaining
raspberries. Leave again for twenty-four hours,
then strain. Measure the juice and allow 1½ lb
(700 g) sugar to each pint of liquid. Put in a
deep jar and place this in a pan of hot water
until the sugar has been dissolved. Remove all
scum and boil until no more scum rises. Leave
until the next day then pour into bottles.
Cork tightly and keep in a cold place. Dilute
to taste.

Treacle ale

1 lb (450 g) golden syrup
8 oz (225 g) black treacle
8 pints (4.5 l) water
1 oz (25 g) yeast
½ oz (15 g) ground
    ginger (optional)
Rind of 1 lemon
    (optional)

Melt the syrup and treacle in the boiling
water. Cool and add yeast. Cover the bowl
with a thick cloth and keep in a warm room
for three days. Syphon off the liquid without
disturbing the yeast deposit, bottle and cork.
Keep several days before drinking. When
ginger and lemon rind are used, add with the
boiling water.

Mulls, Punches and Cockle-Warmers

*There's nothing like a mug of steaming punch to
greet guests. Quite apart from its festive connotations,
punch has a double advantage: a bottle of wine
or spirit can be stretched to satisfy many guests
and the alcoholic kick need not be too strong, since a
hot drink is somewhat self-limiting and few people
can drink large quantities.*

*Punch needs a strong wine or spirit base (a cup is a
milder concoction using light wine). Punches should be*

served very hot, while cups must be chilled. There's often a problem about serving punch, but thick pottery mugs are the most practical container. Thick glasses can be used, but only with handles, and a metal spoon should stand in each container as the hot drink is poured in, to avoid accidents.

If you don't care for mixed drinks, mulled wine is delicious, and if you're feeling the financial squeeze, an old-fashioned hot beer drink is nourishing and seasonal. Whatever you choose, be sure the strength of the drink suits the time of the day and the mood of your guests.

Use inexpensive wine and kitchen-cupboard spices. Be sure to serve your drink hot, but don't keep it on the boil or it will lose its 'kick'; the best way to keep wines hot is to pour the mixture into bottles after making, and then stand the bottles in a basin or jug of hot water. Alternatively, keep the mixture in a saucepan and warm it with a red hot poker – which seems to make the drink smoother.

Mulled Beer and Cider

Spiced cider

In a saucepan heat together 1¾ pints (1 l) cider, two whole allspice berries, two whole cloves and 3 in (7.5 cm) cinnamon stick. Simmer five minutes, add 2 oz (50 g) brown sugar and simmer five minutes more.

6 glasses

Eighteenth-century spiced ale

Heat 2 pints (1 l) brown ale, grated rind of ½ lemon, one teaspoon ground ginger, one teaspoon ground nutmeg and one stick cinnamon in a large saucepan. Plunge in a red hot poker until the bubbling subsides. Whip three eggs and 3 oz (75 g) soft brown sugar together until frothy, warm ¼ pint (150 ml) brandy and ¼ pint (150 ml) rum in a small pan. Pour the spirits into the ale and whisk in the egg mixture until smooth and creamy. Serve at once.

8 glasses

Mulled ale

In a saucepan mix 1¾ pints (1 l) brown ale, ¼ pint (150 ml) brandy, one tablespoon sugar, four cloves and ¼ teaspoon each of nutmeg and ginger. Bring almost to the boil, add a nut of fresh butter, and serve very hot.

6 glasses

Lambs wool

Slit four large apples round the skin in the centre, and bake in the oven until the flesh mashes easily. Heat together 1¾ pints (1 l) brown ale, 1 pint (600 ml) sweet white wine and one stick cinnamon with ½ teaspoon each nutmeg and ginger. Mash the apples and stir into the ale mixture. Remove cinnamon stick, and press mixture through a sieve. Reheat, adding sugar to taste.

8 glasses

Wassail

Slit three small red apples through their skins and bake in the oven with three tablespoons soft brown sugar and 3 fl oz (75 ml) brown ale, until flesh is soft. Heat 1¾ pints (1 l) brown ale with ½ pint (300 ml) sherry, ¼ teaspoon each of cinnamon, nutmeg and ginger and a thin curl of lemon peel. Simmer for five minutes, then add apples to ale, together with brown sugar to taste, and serve very hot.

6 glasses

Punches and Mulled Wines

Bishop

Stick a lemon with cloves and roast it until golden brown. Bring 1¾ pints (1 l) port nearly to boiling point, then add 1 pint (500 ml) hot water, a good pinch of mixed spice and the roasted lemon. Rub 2 oz (50 g) lump sugar on the rind of another lemon, and put sugar into bowl, together with the juice of ½ lemon. Add wine and serve very hot.

20 glasses

Mulled wine

Squeeze the juice from two large oranges and two large lemons and strain into a pan with four cloves, 2 in (5 cm) stick cinnamon, one level teaspoon ground nutmeg and 4 oz (100 g) sugar. Heat gently until the juice begins to boil. Cool and add to one bottle dry red wine. Heat the mixture but do not boil, and pour in ¼ pint (150 ml) brandy. Strain into a warm bowl and add one thinly sliced orange and one thinly sliced apple.

8 glasses

Churchwarden

Stick twelve cloves into a lemon, put on a heat-resistant plate to heat in the lowest possible oven until the lemon starts to turn brown. Heat one bottle red wine without boiling. Put in the lemon and 1 pint (600 ml) weak China tea, scalding hot. Stir in 4 oz (100 g) lump sugar and a sliced apple.

8 glasses

Buttered rum

Put about 2 in (5 cm) rum into a tumbler and stir in 1½ teaspoons soft brown sugar and ½ oz (15 g) unsalted butter. Fill with boiling water, stir and sip slowly. Excellent after a walk on a cold day and quick to make for any number of people.

Cardinal's mull

Make this like Bishop, but using claret or burgundy instead of port, flavouring with cinnamon and nutmeg and substituting an orange for the roasted lemon.

Dr Johnson's choice

Heat one bottle red wine in a saucepan with twelve lumps sugar and six cloves. Just before boiling point, add 1 pint (600 ml) boiling water, one wineglass orange Curaçao and one wineglass brandy. Serve with grated nutmeg on top.

10 glasses

Sir Roger de Coverley

Heat together one bottle light red wine, one glass port and two tablespoons orange Curaçao, with one small teaspoon cinnamon, one small teaspoon mixed spice, a dash of nutmeg, six cloves and sugar to taste. Bring slowly to boiling point, simmer two minutes while stirring, strain and serve in warm glasses.

10 glasses

Madison mull

Stud an apple with cloves and bake in a moderate oven for thirty minutes. Heat to boiling point 1 pint (600 ml) dry vintage cider with the apple, and one bottle claret. Heat without boiling, strain into a bowl and add two tablespoons Calvados.

16 glasses

Malmsey mull

Stud one large sweet orange with cloves and bake in a moderate oven for one hour. Heat one bottle Malmsey Madeira and four table-spoons apricot brandy and a pinch of ground ginger with the orange floating on top, to boiling point. Just before serving, add ½ pint (300 ml) boiling water.

15 glasses

Rum punch

Boil six cloves and 1 in (2.5 cm) cinnamon stick in 1½ pints (1 l) water for five minutes. Wash an orange and rub twelve lumps of sugar over the rind until they are yellow and full of zest. Add them to the water and boil for five minutes. Strain on to 1 pint (600 ml) dark old rum and serve hot.

20 glasses

Apple posset

In each glass, put two tablespoons Calvados and fill up with hot apple juice, stirring with a cinnamon stick.

Flaming punch

Stick an orange with cloves and bake in a moderate oven for one hour. In a saucepan, combine two bottles claret, one sliced lemon, 1½ in (3.75 cm) cinnamon stick, 2 oz (50 g) blanched whole almonds, 2 oz (50 g) raisins and 2 oz (50 g) sugar. Add the orange and simmer uncovered for fifteen minutes. Remove cinnamon stick and pour punch into serving bowl. In a saucepan, put 2 oz (50 g) sugar and ¼ pint (150 ml) brandy. Heat very gently, ignite with a match, and while flaming pour into punch bowl.

Cambridge milk punch

This is a delicious, and apparently innocuous, drink, which is just the thing for maiden aunts.

Put the thin rind of ½ small lemon into 1 pint (600 ml) new milk with twelve lumps sugar. Simmer very slowly to extract the flavour of the lemon, take off the fire and remove the lemon rind. Stir in the yolk of an egg mixed with one tablespoon cold milk, two tablespoons brandy and four tablespoons rum. Whisk very thoroughly, and serve when frothy.

4 glasses

Prince Regent's punch

This punch has the advantage that it can be started a week in advance for the flavour to mature. It is very potent and may be diluted with soda water.

Mix a bottle of brandy and a bottle of rum, add the lightly grated peel of two oranges and two lemons, 2 in (5 cm) cinnamon stick, and a small piece of vanilla pod. Leave for two days at least, but preferably a week. Some hours before serving, boil 4 pints (2.25 l) water, add 1 oz (25 g) China tea and leave to draw. Then add the juice of seven lemons and two oranges and 1½ lb (700 g) sugar. Stir over heat until the sugar has dissolved, then strain and cool. Strain the spices from the spirits, and mix the spirits with the syrup. Chill thoroughly. A few Maraschino cherries will make the punch bowl attractive.

For the Children

Mulled pineapple juice

In a saucepan, put 1 pint (600 ml) pineapple juice, 1 in (2.5 cm) stick cinnamon, and a dash each of nutmeg, allspice and cloves. Bring to boiling point, cover and simmer gently for thirty minutes. Serve warm.

6 glasses

Spiced cocoa

Make up drinking chocolate with hot milk, then reheat carefully with ½ teaspoon cinnamon and ¼ teaspoon nutmeg to 2 pints (1 l) milk. Serve hot, topped with marshmallows in each mug.

Negus

Mrs Beeton said this drink was more usually drunk at children's parties than any other, so the wine need not be old or expensive. This quantity was supposed to be enough for nine or ten children. Traditionally made with port, it may also be made with sherry or sweet white wine.

Put 1 pint (600 ml) port into a jug and into it rub 4 oz (100 g) lump sugar over the yellow part of the rind of a lemon. Add the juice of the lemon, 2 pints (1 l) boiling water and grated nutmeg to taste. (For parental tastes, 1 pint (600 ml) is probably enough.)

Snapdragon

Another children's treat of Victorian days which has always been one of my favourites too. Use a punch-bowl, a heat resistant glass mixing bowl, or an old meat dish that you don't care too much about. Cover it liberally with big fat sticky raisins from which the stones have been extracted. Heat some brandy gently, pour over the raisins, and set light to it. Turn out all the lights, and everyone grabs for hot raisins. There is no danger – addicts lick their grabbing fingers first – and everyone becomes excited. For a really fine flavour, soak the raisins in the brandy in a screwtop jar for a couple of hours before you plan the snapdragon.

Old-Fashioned Sweetmeats

There's nothing like sweet-tooth fudge, slightly sticky toffee, and gooey Turkish Delight to bring back memories of our lost youth and cold rainy afternoons shut out by the cosy warmth of a busy kitchen.

Equipment can be just as simple as in those far-off nursery days, and results just as tempting. While a sugar-boiling thermometer is useful to any cook, it is not necessary for simple sweets. For fudge-making, the soft-ball stage must be reached, when a little dropped into cold water can be moulded into a soft ball with the hands. For toffee-making, the 'crack' must be reached, when a little toffee dropped in cold water will break with a snap.

Large quantities of sweets may be made very cheaply, the yield roughly equalling the weight of ingredients. The finished products are best stored in airtight tins, wrapped in waxed paper or in kitchen foil. Special paper sweet cases make the most homely sweet look attractive.

Cracker toffee

1 lb (450 g) demerara sugar
¼ pint (150 ml) water plus 2 tablespoons
2 teaspoons golden syrup
1 large pinch cream of tartar
2 oz (50 g) unsalted butter

Dissolve sugar in water over low heat, then add golden syrup, cream of tartar and butter. Boil hard until a little toffee dropped in cold water will break with a snap. Pour into greased tin and leave until completely cold. Break into pieces and store in airtight tin.

Granny's old-fashioned fudge

1 tablespoon golden syrup
1 lb (450 g) sugar
¼ pint (150 ml) milk
4 oz (100 g) plain chocolate
2 oz (50 g) butter
½ teaspoon vanilla essence
1 teaspoon rum

Grease a heavy saucepan. Heat the sugar, milk and syrup, stirring gently until sugar has dissolved. Add chocolate and stir until melted and mixture is boiling. Cook to 238°F (or until mixture forms a soft ball when a little is dropped into cold water). Take off heat, add butter and cool without stirring. Add vanilla and rum and beat until fudge is thick and loses its shine. Put into a shallow buttered tin and cut into squares while warm.

Bonfire toffee

12 oz (350 g) soft brown
   sugar
2 oz (50 g) butter
1 tablespoon vinegar
2 tablespoons boiling
   water
Pinch of salt

Bring all ingredients to boil and cook to 290°F (when a little of the syrup separates into threads when poured into cold water, and a ball of the toffee is brittle when tapped against the side of the pan). Pour into buttered tin, about 8 × 14 in (20 × 35 cm), cool slightly and mark in squares.

Chocolate raisin fudge

1 lb (450 g) sugar
8 oz (225 g) plain
   chocolate
½ pint (300 ml) single
   cream
½ pint (300 ml) milk
2 oz (50 g) butter
3 tablespoons water
6 oz (175 g) stoned
   raisins

Put all ingredients except chocolate and raisins into a heavy saucepan and stir over very gentle heat until the sugar dissolves. Add chocolate and stir until melted. Boil until the mixture reaches soft ball stage (238°F or until a little dropped in cold water forms a soft ball). Stir in raisins and beat until the fudge loses its shine. Pour into well-buttered tin, set and cut in squares.

Fruit and nut fudge

2 lb (1 kg) sugar
½ pint (300 ml) milk
4 oz (100 g) margarine
½ teaspoon vanilla
   essence
2 oz (50 g) raisins or
   sultanas
2 oz (50 g) chopped
   walnuts or almonds

Soak sugar in milk for an hour, then cook very slowly until sugar dissolves. Add margarine, and when melted, bring mixture to boil. Cook steadily until a temperature of 238°F is reached (soft ball stage). Remove from heat, cool slightly, then beat until fudge is thick and creamy. Add essence, fruit and nuts, and pour quickly into a well-greased shallow tin. Smooth with a knife, mark into squares and cut when cool and set.

Quick chocolate fudge

2 tablespoons seedless
   raisins
2 tablespoons sherry
4 oz (100 g) plain
   chocolate
2 oz (50 g) butter
4 tablespoons evaporated
   milk
12 oz (350 g) icing sugar

Soak raisins in sherry overnight. Put chocolate and butter in a bowl over hot, but not boiling, water, and stir until melted and smooth. Remove from heat and stir in evaporated milk and drained raisins. Gradually stir in sieved icing sugar until fudge is smooth and thick. Turn into a tin which has been greased with butter and lined with waxed paper. Leave until cold, then cut fudge into squares.

Rum raisin fudge

1 lb (450 g) sugar
2 oz (50 g) butter
¼ pint (150 ml)
  evaporated milk
¼ pint (150 ml) water
1 teaspoon rum
4 oz (100 g) seedless
  raisins

Put the sugar, butter, milk and water into a large saucepan. Heat gently till the sugar has dissolved and the fat has melted, then bring to the boil. Boil rapidly, stirring until a temperature of 238°F is reached (or until a little of the mixture forms a soft ball when dropped into cold water). Remove from heat, add rum and raisins, and beat well until the mixture becomes thick and creamy. Pour into a greased tin about 6×8 in (15×20 cm). When nearly set, mark into squares with a sharp knife.

Biscuit fudge

12 oz (350 g) crushed
  sweet biscuits
6 oz (175 g) sultanas
4 oz (100 g) stoned
  raisins
2 oz (50 g) halved
  cherries
2 oz (50 g) chopped
  walnuts
1 egg
4 oz (100 g) butter
4 oz (100 g) soft brown
  sugar
1 teaspoon clear honey
1 teaspoon vanilla
  essence

Break the biscuits into tiny pieces or crush them with a rolling pin, and add fruit and nuts. Beat egg, add butter and sugar, and heat gently until sugar has melted. Add honey and essence and combine with biscuit mixture until the crumbs are damp. Line 8 in (20 cm) square tin with greaseproof paper. Tip in mixture and press evenly into a firm cake. Chill thoroughly until firm, lift out of tin and cut into pieces.

Freezer fudge

This will keep up to three months in the freezer, and takes about fifteen minutes to thaw.

4 oz (100 g) plain
  chocolate
4 oz (100 g) butter
1 egg
1 lb (450 g) sifted icing
  sugar
2 tablespoons sweetened
  condensed milk

Melt the chocolate and butter in a double saucepan or in a bowl over hot water. Beat the egg lightly, mix with sugar and milk, and stir into the melted chocolate. Pour into a greased rectangular tin. Cover with foil and freeze for six hours, mark into squares, and return to freezer.

Creamy cherry fudge

2 oz (50 g) butter
4 tablespoons evaporated
  milk
1 lb (450 g) sifted icing
  sugar
2 oz (50 g) glacé cherries

Melt the butter in a basin over hot water, and stir in evaporated milk. Gradually add icing sugar, beating well. Take off the heat and stir in chopped cherries. Pour into a greased rectangular tin and cool. Cover with foil and put in the ice compartment of the fridge.

Sugar balls

4 oz (100 g) plain
  chocolate
3 tablespoons single
  cream
2 oz (50 g) caster sugar
16 sponge finger biscuits
2 tablespoons sherry

Put chocolate in a basin over hot but not boiling water. Stir until smooth and take off heat. Stir in cream and sugar, and add finely crushed biscuit crumbs and sherry. Blend well and leave in a cool place overnight to stiffen. Roll heaped teaspoons of the mixture into balls and roll in castor sugar. Store in screw-topped jars.

Adelaide chews

8 oz (225 g) plain
  chocolate
8 oz (225 g) stale cake
  crumbs
Juice of 1 orange
3 oz (75 g) stoned raisins
  (chopped)
2 oz (50 g) sultanas
1½ oz (40 g) glacé
  cherries and candied
  peel (chopped)
1 teaspoon vanilla
  essence

Melt the chocolate slowly over water. Combine all ingredients, mix thoroughly with chocolate and press into a buttered swiss roll tin and chill until firm. Cut into small squares.

Chocolate truffles

8 oz (225 g) plain
  chocolate
1 heaped tablespoon
  caster sugar
2 oz (50 g) butter
2 tablespoons rum or
  cream
1 egg yolk
Cocoa or chocolate
  vermicelli

Melt the chocolate over hot water. Remove from heat and stir in sugar, butter, rum or cream and egg yolk. Beat until thick and cool. Shape in small balls and leave to dry, and then roll in cocoa or chocolate vermicelli.

No-cook fondants

4 tablespoons evaporated
  milk
1 lb (450 g) icing sugar
Flavouring and colouring

Put the milk into a bowl, sieve icing sugar and gradually work into the milk. Knead until smooth and shiny, and add flavouring and colouring to make a variety of sweets.

To make *peppermint creams*, add a few drops of oil of peppermint, and a little green colouring if liked. For *orange creams* add orange-flower water and orange colouring. For *rose creams* add rosewater and cochineal. (Oil of peppermint, orange-flower water and rose-water are all obtainable at any chemist.) For *fruit rolls*, knead in 4 oz (100 g) chopped mixed peel and 1 oz (25 g) chopped glacé cherries with a little more icing sugar if necessary. Shape into 6 in (15 cm) logs about 1 in (2.5 cm) diameter and chill until firm before cutting each roll into twelve pieces. All the fondants may be shaped by this easy method, or else rolled out and cut with canapé cutters. Tops of the sweets may be decorated with nuts, coloured balls, crystallized petals or angelica.

Peppermint creams

1½ oz (40 g) full fat soft
  cheese
½ teaspoon peppermint
  essence
7 oz (200 g) sifted icing
  sugar
Green colouring

Blend the cheese and essence until smooth and gradually mix in icing sugar. Knead in a few drops of colouring. Turn out on a board dusted with icing sugar, and roll out ¼ in (½ cm) thick. Cut into 1 in (2.5 cm) rounds, put on greaseproof paper and leave to dry overnight. This makes about thirty sweets which stay creamy and soft in the centre.

If liked, dip the peppermint creams in melted plain chocolate, covering either half or the whole surface. For a change, omit peppermint essence and green colouring, and use two teaspoons coffee essence and an extra 1 oz (25 g) of icing sugar.

Chocolate walnuts

4 oz (100 g) walnut
  halves
4 oz (100 g) plain
  chocolate

Melt chocolate over hot water. Sandwich walnut halves together with melted chocolate. When set, dip the whole walnuts into the softened chocolate and set in sweet-paper cases to set.

Index

255